Anonymous

Rump

Or, An exact Collection of the Choycest Poems and Songs relating to the late Times

Anonymous

Rump
Or, An exact Collection of the Choycest Poems and Songs relating to the late Times

ISBN/EAN: 9783337181673

Printed in Europe, USA, Canada, Australia, Japan

Cover: Foto ©Thomas Meinert / pixelio.de

More available books at **www.hansebooks.com**

RUMP:

OR AN
EXACT COLLECTION
Of the Choycest
POEMS
AND
SONGS
RELATING TO THE
Late Times.

By the most Eminent Wits, from *Anno* 1639. to *Anno* 1661

LONDON,
Printed for *Henry Brome* at the *Gun* in *Ivy-lane*, and *Henry Marsh* at the *Princes Armes* in *Chancery-lane*. 1662.

TO THE READER.

THou hast here a Bundle of Rodds; not like those of the Roman Consulls, *for these are signes of a* No-Government. *If thou read* these Ballads (and not sing them) *the poor Ballads are undone. They came not hither all from one Author; (thou wilt soon perceive the same hand held not the Pen) yet none but shew either Wit or Affection (and that's better) or Both, which is best of all. The truth is, this* **Rump,** *and indeed the whole Carcase was so odious and*

To the Reader.

bloody a Monster, that every man has a stone or rotten Egge to cast at it. Now if you ask who nam'd it Rump, *know 'twas so stil'd in an honest Sheet of Paper (call'd* The Bloody Rump) *written before the Tryal of our late* Soveraign *of Glorious Memory: but the Word* obtain'd *not universal notice till it flew from the mouth of Major General* Brown *at a Publick Assembly in the daies of* Richard Cromwell. *You have many Songs here, which were never before in Print: We need not tell you whose they are; but we have not subjoyned any Authors Names; heretofore it was unsafe, and now the Gentlemen conceive it not so proper. 'Tis hoped they did His Majesty some Service, 'twas for that end they were scribbled. Now (thanks be to God) we have liv'd to that day, that there is no* Cavalier, *because there is nothing else, and 'tis wondrous happy to see how many are his Majesties Faithfull Sub-*

To the Reader.

jects, who were ready to hang the Authors *of these* Ballads. *But he that does not blot out all that's past, and frankly embrace their New Allegiance, or remembers ought but what shall preserve Universal Peace and Charity, let him be* Anathema; *For he were a strange man that should now be unsatisfied, when those that writ against the* King *do now write for Him, and those who wrote for Him, need now write no more. Let Heaven now continue these Blessings on His Majesty, that no one Enemy live unreconciled, nor any false Friend be undiscovered, that so there be no strife, but who shall shew most Duty to so Excellent a KING.*

Farewell.

The Stationers to the Reader.

Gentlemen,

You are invited here to a Feast, and if Variety cloy you not, we are satisfied. It has been our Care to please you; and it is our Hope you will retribute an Acknowledgement. These are select Things, a work of Time, which for your sake we Publish, assuring you that your Welcome will Crown the Entertainment.

            Farewell.

Yours,

           H. B. H. M.

RUMP-SONGS.

The First Part.

The ZEALOUS PURITAN.
1639.

MY Brethren all attend,
And list to my relation:
This is the day, mark what I say,
Tends to your renovation;
Stay not among the Wicked,
Lest that with them you perish,
But let us to *New-England* go,
And the Pagan People cherish;
   Then for the truths sake come along, come along,
   Leave this place of Superstition:
   Were it not for we, that the Brethren be,
   You would sink into Perdition.

There you may teach our hymns,
Without the Laws controulment:
We need not fear, the Bishops there,
Nor Spiritual-Courts inroulment;

Nay, the Surplice shall not fright us,
Nor superstitious blindness;
Nor scandals rise, when we disguise,
And our Sisters kiss in kindness;
  Then for the truths sake, &c.

For Company I fear not,
There goes my Cosin *Hannah*,
And *Ruben*, so perswades to go
My Cosin *Joyce, Susanna*.
With *Abigal* and *Faith*,
And *Ruth*, no doubt, comes after;
And *Sarah* kind, will not stay behind;
My Cosin *Constance* Daughter;
  Then for the truth, &c.

Tom Tyler is prepared,
And th' Smith as black as a coal;
Ralph Cobler too with us will go,
For he regards his soul;
The Weaver, honest *Simon*,
With *Prudence, Jacobs* Daughter,
And *Sarah*, she, and *Barbary*,
Professeth to come after;
  Then for the truth, &c.

When we, that are elected,
Arrive in that fair Country,
Even by our faith, as the Brethren saith,
We will not fear our entry;
The Psalms shall be our Musick,
Our time spent in expounding,
Which in our zeal we will reveal
To the Brethrens joy abounding;
  Then for the truths sake, &c.

Part I. *Rump Songs.*

Pyms *Juncto.* 1640.

TRuth I could chide you Friends, why, how so late?
My Watch speaks Eight and not one pin o' th
State
This day undone, can such remisnesse fit
Your Active spirits, or my more Hellish wit?
The Sun each step he mounts to Heavens Crown,
Whilst *Pym* commands, should see a Kingdome down;
Y'ave spurs enough I'me sure to make you run.
HOPES guilty, FORTUNES crackt, and th' ILLS y'ave
done.
Thus Whilome seated was Great *James* his Heir,
Just, as you see me now, ith' Kingdoms Chair:
There the Great Seal, there *Richmond, Hertford* sate,
There *Marshall, Dorset, Bristoll's* temperate pate,
But there sate *Pembroke*, life of Loyalty,
There *Holland*, flower of Fidelity.
We are no lesse then *Charles* in power and state,
You are our Junctoes, who were his of late;
Here sits *K———* Holy *Say*, and *Seal*,
With *Wharton, Warwick, Brookes* inspired zeal:
Stroud, Hampden, H——— *Haslerigge*, bold spirits,
Bold *Martin, Ludlow, Vain*, unmatched wights,
But their Church-Elder, *Whites* Religious beard,
There sits Abomination Statists: *Perd:*
Charles wear at *York* thy Crown that pretty thing
We must most humbly be at *London* King.
But what's the businesse of the House this day,
How speaks my note, Commissioners of Array,

1—2

The nineteen Propositions to be scand
A second time, M—— Train-band,
Letters from *Tristram Whitcombe*, and from *Hull*,
From *Amsterdam*, the Admirall ; how full
Of high concernments are we Sirs, advise
How we most warily may weigh our prise :
I do conceive it must be our first play,
Be't right or wrong, by Vote to damn th' Array,
If ever that take footing and advance,
Farewell Militia, and our Ordinance,
But what will the appearance be? yet stay,
Who dares our leading Votes and Wills gainsay?
Should any haughty spirit presume so far,
What serves the Tower for then, or the Bar?
But if we fear the businesse will not bend
As may be most conducing to our end :
By some feigned wile it must be our next Plot
To put it off, and a new time alot,
And just Jumpe for our turn : these Letters shall
From *Whitcombe, Hotham,* or our Admirall,
(Though forg'd untruths) be interpos'd and read,
To spend the time, and maze the Peoples head ;
If the next day we yet suspect to find
Such whose just Conscience cannot be inclin'd
To be made Vassals to our desperate sence,
'Tis easie to procure a Conferrence,
Which shall out-spin the leisure of the morn,
Then we'le resume the House, and so adjourn
Till five at night, the moderate wearied thus,
Will quit their seats and leave us, none but us ;
There's President for this, this was the feat
That pluckt the Bishops from the Barons seat,
This wrought good Orders, manag'd many a Vote,
This Art must my Disciples learn by Rote.

Part I. *Rump Songs.*

But if the Accommodation chance to spring
Into debate, then your Artillery bring,
And lay that flat, that cold: my Genius starts
With fear to find ith' House two Loyal hearts;
Seem though we must teeth outwards to comply,
And humbly kisse the feet of Majesty,
Yet live we cannot, but obedience dead,
Nor stand elsewhere but on the Kingdoms head;
Calmes proper are for guiltlesse sons of Peace,
Our Vessels bear our best in storming Seas;
Charles must not reign secure whilst reigns a *Pym*,
The Sun if it rise with us must set with him;
You have one pleasure which must be exprest
To *Leicester*, *Pembroke*, *St.* ———— and your rest,
Bid *Essex*, *Percy*, and your Quondam Grom
O'th stool, to wait us in the Princes Room:
Some of your subtilly may in *Cottons* walk,
Sit and allure Affections by your talk,
'Twill be a work worthy your nimble wit,
To gain the Devil and us a Proselyte.
So, to your businesse, yet ere you be gone
Take my advice, then blessing light upon
Your nimble Votes, and first be sure you shroud
Your dark designs in a Religious Cloud,
Gods Glory, Churches Good, Kings head Supreme,
A Preaching Minister must be your Theame;
Next structure of your *Babel* to be built,
Must speciously be varnisht o're, and gilt
With Liberty, Propriety of lives
And fortunes, 'gainst th' high stretcht Prerogatives.
And then a Speech or two most neatly spent,
For Rights and Privilege of Parliament;
These two well mixt, you'le need no other lures
To gain the People, and to make them yours.

If *Charles* displeased, with some witty, tart
Message (and justly too) shall make you start,
Saying ye have put him to his Guard, be sure
Ye then be loud enough, and first cry Whore,
War rais'd against the Parliament, a great
Hinderance of the *Irish* Ayde, and strong Abet
Unto the Rebels: then if any thing
You have may blast the Honour of the King,
Be it bad enough, no matter from what hand,
Wee'l Vote it true, and then to believe command;
But on your memories if I impose no more,
You cannot misse your way when I'me before:
Rise *Synna, Sylla, Marius, Gracchus* Ghost,
With the rest of the whole Mechanick Host,
Romes greatest Earth-quakes, and this little trunck
Make with your desperate Spirits deeply drunk,
Up from your drousie urnes, the Ghost of those
My Ancestors that *Richard* did depose,
Drop fresh into my breast, my soul inspire,
And strongly actuate me with your fire,
That theirs thus mixt with my Malitious Gall,
Mine may with theirs fully possesse you all.
Go and exceed their Villanies as much more
As theirs did all attempts that was before;
Act past example, that it may be known
You copied no example but your own.
And if in after times, when silently
We sleep, another firebrand chance to be,
'Twill be chief Crown and Glory unto him,
To say he playd his Prancks like you and *Pym*.

Upon Mr. Pyms *Picture.*

Reader, behold the Counterfeit of him
Who now controuls the land ; *Almighty Pym* !
A man whom even the Devil to fear begins,
And dares not trust him with succesless sins ;
A man who now is wading through the Floud
Of Reverend *Lauds,* and Noble *Straffords* Bloud,
To strike so high as to put Bishops down,
And in the *Miter* to controul the *Crown;*
The Wretch hath mighty thoughts, and entertains
Some Glorious Mischief in his Active Brains,
Where now he's plotting to make *England* such
As may out-vye the villany of the *Dutch ;*
He dares not go to Heaven, 'cause he doth fear
To meet (and not pull down) the Bishops there :
Is it not strange, that in that Shuttle-head
Three Kingdoms ruines should be buried ?
Is it not strange there should be hatch't a Plot
Which should out-doe the Treason of the *Scot,*
And even the Malice of a *Puritan ?*
Reader behold, and hate the poysonous man ;
The Picture's like him ; yet 'tis very fit
To adde one likeness more, that's hang like it.

A Song.

To the Tune of *Blue Cappe for me.*

LEt *Scots* now return at *Lesleys* demand,
How all the Affairs in the North-part do stand,
And tell him the Parliament is fully agreed
To send him good stores of Money with speed,
   To serve their occasions: thus say, they shall find
   For to come to passe, when the Devil is blind.

Let all their Brethren be new circumcis'd,
And *Burton* and —— for Saints canonis'd;
And at the Sacrament sit for their ease,
And pray unto God, even just when they please;
   The *Scots* in despite shall please their own mind,
   And do what they please, when the Devil is blind.

Next they will have in each City and Town
All painted Glasse-windows to be pull'd down;
One Bell in a Church to call them away,
It's enough when the Spirit doth move them to pray,
   Without any Surplice or Tippet behind
   The Priest shall say Service, when the Devil is blind.

Lastly, the Parliament in any case
Will down with all Organs, for Piping is base;

No cringing below the Altar shall be,
For that is a Trick of Idolatry :
  Now tell me good *Scots*, are not *English-men* kind,
  But when this comes to passe, say the Devil is blind.

Mr. Hampdens *Speech against* Peace *at the close Committee.*

To the Tune of *I went from England.*

Ut will you now to Peace incline,
And languish in the Main design,
      And leave us in the lurch?
I would not Monarchy destroy,
But only as a way t' enjoy,
      The ruine of the Church.

Is not the Bishops Bill deny'd,
And we still threatned to be try'd?
      You see the King embraces
Those Councellours he approv'd before ;
Nor doth he promise, which is more,
      That we shall have their Places.

Did I for this bring in the *Scot*,
(For 'tis no Secret new) the Plot
      Was *Sayes* and mine together :
Did I for this return again,
And spend a Winter there in vain,
      I went more to invite them hither.

Though more our Mony than our Cause
Their Brotherly assistance draws,
      My labour was not lost.
At my Return I brought you thence,
Necessity, their strong Pretence,
      And these shall quit the Cost.

Did I for this my County bring
To help their Knight against their King,
      And raise the first Sedition?
Though I the Business did decline,
Yet I contriv'd the whole Design,
      And sent them their Petition.

So many nights spent in the City
In that Invisible Committee;
      The Wheele that governs all;
From thence the Change in Church and State,
And all the Mischiefs bear the date
      From *Haberdashers* Hall.

Did we force *Ireland* to despair,
Upon the King to cast the War,
      To make the World abhor him:
Because the Rebells us'd his Name,
Though we our selves can do the same,
      While both alike were for him.

Then the same Fire we kindled here
With that, was given to quench it there,
      And wisely lost that Nation:
To do as crafty Beggars use,
To maim themselves thereby to abuse
      The simple mans compassion.

Have I so often past between
Windsor and *Westminster* unseen,
   And did my self divide:
To keep his Excellence in awe,
And give the Parliament the Law,
   For they knew none beside?

Did I for these take pains to teach
Our zealous Ignorants to preach,
   And did their Lungs inspire,
Read them their Text, shew'd them their Parts,
And taught them all their little Arts,
   To fling abroad the Fire?

Sometimes to begg, sometimes to threaten,
And say the Cavaliers are beaten,
   And stroke the Peoples ears;
Then streight when Victory grows cheap,
And will no more advance the heap,
   To raise the price of Fears.

And now the Book, and now the Bells,
And now the Act the Preachers tells
   To edifie the People;
All our Divinity is News,
And we have made of equal use
   The Pulpit and the Steeple.

And shall we kindle all this Flame,
Onely to put it out again,
   And must we now give o're,
And only end where we begun
In vain this Mischief we have done,
   If we can do no more?

If men in Peace can have their right,
Where's the Necessity to fight,
   That breaks both Law, the Oath;
They'le say they fight not for the Cause,
Nor to defend the King and Laws,
   But as against them both.

Either the Cause at first was ill,
Or being good it was so still;
   And thence they will infer,
That either now, or at the first
They were deceiv'd, or which is worse,
   That we our selves may erre.

But Plague and Famine will come in,
For they and we are near of kin,
   And cannot go asunder:
But while the wicked starve, indeed
The Saints have ready at their need
   Gods Providence and Plunder.

Princes we are if we prevail,
And Gallant Villains if we fail,
   When to our fame 'tis told;
It will not be our last of prayse,
Sin' a New State we could not raise
   To have destroy'd the old,

Then let us stay and fight, and vote
Till *London* is not worth a Groat;
   Oh 'tis a patient Beast:
When we have gall'd and tyr'd the Mule,
And can no longer have the rule,
   We'le have the Spoyle at least.

A Song.
To the Tune of *The Queens old Souldier.*

TO make *Charles* a great King, and give him no Power,
To Honour him much, and not obey him an Hower;
To provide for his Safety, and take away his Tower,
And to prove all is sweet, be it never so sower.
The new Order of the Land, & the Lands new Order.

To secure men their Lives, Liberties and Estates
By arbitrary Power, as it pleaseth the Fates
To take away Taxes, by imposing great Rates,
And to make us a Playster by breaking our Pates.
The new Order of the Land, & the Lands new Order.

To sit and consult for ever and a day,
To counterfeit Treason by a Parliamentary way,
To quiet the land by a tumultuous sway,
New Plots to devise, then them to betray.
The new Order, &c.

To leave all Votes free by using of Force.
That one make Petitions for Counties by course,
To make *Pym* as great as his Mothers great Horse,
Which *William* left *Agnus*, though his meaning was worse.
The new Order, &c.

To encourage good Souldiers by cashiering the Band,
To hearten brave Spirits by expelling the Land,

To quit *Digby* and *Deering*, whom they can't understand.
To frame not new Laws, but new Words, if well scan'd.
  The new Order, &c.

To put by brave Doctors, because th'are not taught,
To set for Preachers men, very well wrought,
Who all the day fish, but nothing ere caught;
This, Bretheren, were good, if not very naught.
  The new Order, &c.

To send men their Zealots to Heaven in a string,
Who else to Confusion Religion will bring,
Who say the Lords Prayer is a Popish thing,
Who pray for themselves, but leave out their King.
  The new Order of the Land, and the Lands new Order.

A Song.

To the Tune of *Cuckolds all a-row.*

Know this my Brethren Heaven is clear,
  And all the clowds are gone,
The righteous men shall flourish now
  Good dayes are comming on;
Come then my Brethren and be glad,
  And eke rejoyce with me,
Lawn sleeves and Rochets shall go down,
  And hey then up go we.

Wee'l break the Windows which the Whore
   Of *Babylon* hath painted,
And when the Popish Saints are down,
   Then *Burges* shall be Sainted;
There's neither Crosse nor Crucifix
   shall stand for men to see,
Romes trash and trumpery shall go down,
   And hey then up go we.

What ere the Popish hands have built,
   Our Hammers shall undoe,
Wee'l break their Pipes, and burn their Copes,
   And pull down *Churches* too;
Wee'l exercise within the Groves,
   And teach beneath a Tree,
Wee'l make a *Pulpit* of a *Cask*,
   And hey then up go we.

Wee'l down with all the *Versities*,
   Where Learning is profest,
Because they practice and maintain
   The language of the Beast;
Wee'l drive the *Doctors* out of doors,
   And parts what ere they be;
Wee'l cry all *Arts* and *Learning* down,
   And hey then up go we.

Wee'l down with *Deans* and *Prebends* too,
   And I rejoyce to tell ye
How that we will eat *Pigs* our fill,
   And *Capon* by the belly;
Wee'l burn the *Fathers* Learned Books,
   And make the School-men flee;
Wee'l down with all that smells of wit,
   And hey then up go we.

If once the *Antichristian* crew
    Be crush'd and overthrown,
Wee'l teach the Nobles how to stoop,
    And keep the Gentry down ;
Good manners have an ill report,
    And turns to pride we see,
Wee'l therefore cry good manners down,
    And hey then up go we.

The name of *Lords* shall be abhorr'd,
    for every man's a Brother,
No reason why in *Church* and *State*
    One man should rule another.
But when the Change of Government
    Shall set our fingers free,
Wee'l make the wanton *Sisters* stoop,
    And hey then up go we.

What though the *King* and *Parliament*
    Do not accord together,
We have more cause to be content,
    This is our Sun-shine weather ;
For if that reason should take place,
    And they should once agree,
Who would be in a *Round-heads* case?
    And hey then up go we.

What should we do then in this case,
    Let's put it to a venture,
If that we hold out seven years space,
    Wee'l sue out our indenture,
A time may come to make us rue,
    And time may set us free,
Except the *Gallows* claim his due,
    And hey then up go we.

The Humble Petition of the House of Commons.

IF *Charles* thou wilt but be so kind
To give us leave to take our mind,
      Of all thy store.
When we thy Loyal Subjects, find
Th'ast nothing left to give behind,
      Wee'l ask no more.

First, for Religion, it is meet
We make it go upon new feet,
      'Twas lame before:
One from *Geneva* would be sweet,
Let *Warwick* fetch't home with his Fleet,
      Wee'll ask no more.

Let us a Consultation call
Of Honest men, but Round-heads all,
      God knows wherefore;
Allow them but a place to baul
'Gainst Bishops Courts Canonical,
      Wee'll ask no more.

Let him be hang'd a Surplice wears,
And Tippet on his shoulders bears,
      Raggs of the Whore;
Secure us from our needlesse fears,
Let —— and *Burton* have their ears,
      Wee'll ask no more.

Reform each University,
And in them let no Learning be,
   A great Eye-sore;
From hence make *Romes Arminians* flee,
That none may have free-will but wee,
   Wee'll ask no more.

Lest the Elect should go astray,
Let Coblers teach you the right way
   To Heavens door;
And lest their soles should wear away,
Let them their Sisters underlay,
   Wee'll ask no more.

Next from the Bishops Hierarchy,
Oh the word sounds but scurvily,
   Let's hear't no more;
It ne're was taught the Apostles by,
Lay-Elders may the place supply,
   Wee'll ask no more.

Next, for the State, we think it fit
That Mr. *Pym* should govern it,
   He's very poor:
The money that's for *Ireland* writ,
Faith let them have the Devil a bit,
   Wee'll ask no more.

For ordering the Militia,
Let us ordain a new new way,
   Ne're heard before;
Let the Great Council bear the sway,
If you will give us leave you may,
   Wee'll ask no more.

In this we will not be deny'd,
Because in you wee'll not confide,
   We know wherefore
The Citizens their Plate provide,
Do you but send in yours beside,
   Wee'll ask no more.

Now if that you'll make *Hull* your own,
There's one thing more we must set down
   Forgot before;
Sir *John* shall then give up the Town,
If you will but resign your Crown,
   Wee'll ask no more.

The Answer to the Petition, &c.

I*F Charles* the King will be so kind,
To give you leave to take your mind,
   Of all my store,
When I you Loyal Subjects find,
And you those Members have resign'd,
   I askt before.

And when Religion's all your cares,
Or *London* have such heed of theirs,
   They had before:
When *Warwick* from *Geneva* dares,
Now Printed, bring the Common-Prayers,
   And read them o're.

When all your Consultations tend,
To pay what you have made men lend,
   None knows wherefore ;
When you no more shall say you'll send,
And bring me fairly to mine end,
   You'll ask no more.

When your Smectymnuus Surplice wears,
Or Tippet on his shoulders bears,
   Raggs of the Whore ;
When *Burton*, —— and *Bastwick* dares,
With your good leaves, but show their Eares,
   They'll ask no more.

When what I borrowed I shall see,
Y'have paid each Universitie,
   Of th' City store :
And Doctors, Chaplains, Fellows, be
Free-willers of pluralitie,
   They'll ask no more.

When the elect shall make such hast,
By th' Bretheren to be embrac't
   In Tubs on floore ;
When Coblers they shall preach their last
At Conventicles on a Fast,
   They'll ask no more.

When Bishops all the House adorns,
And Round-heads for their absence mourns,
   A great Eye-sore ;
When ev'ry Citizen lesse scorns
Lord *Wentworth's* head, then *Essex* horns,
   You'll ask no more.

When you no more shall dare hereafter,
A needlesse thing which gains much laughter,
      Granted before;
When *Pym* is sent to *Ireland* slaughter,
And ne're more hopes to marry my Daughter,
      You'll ask no more.

When you have found a clearer way
For ordering the Militia,
      Then heard before;
When *Atkins* on the Training day,
Sha'nt dare his Office to bewray,
      Hee'll ask no more.

When naught to me shall be deny'd,
And you shall all in me confide,
      Good cause therefore!
When *Denmark* shall for me provide,
And now Lord *Digby's* on my side,
      Ask me no more.

Last, when I shall make *Hull* my own,
This one thing more I must set down,
      Forgot before,
When I have got into the Town,
I'le make ten more besides that Clown,
      Kneele and implore.

To the five Principal Members of the Honourable House of Commons.
The Humble Petition of the POETS.

After so many Concurring Petitions
From all Ages and Sexes, and all conditions,
We come in the Rear to present our Follies
To *Pym, Stroude, Haslerig, Hampden,* and ——
And we hope for our labour we shall not be shent,
For this comes from *Christendom,* & not from *Kent;*
Though set form of *Prayers* be an *Abomination,*
Set forms of *Petitions* find great Approbation :
Therefore, as others from th' bottom of their souls,
So wee from the depth and bottom of our *Bowles,*
According unto the blessed form taught us,
We thank you first for the *Ills* you have brought us,
For the *Good* we receive we thank him that gave it,
And you for the Confidence only to crave it.
Next in course, we Complain of the great *violation*
Of *Privilege* (like the rest of our Nation)
But 'tis none of yours of which we have spoken
Which never had being, untill they were broken :
But our is a *Privilege* Antient and Native,
Hangs not on *Ordinance,* or power *Legislative.*
And first, 'tis to speak whatever we please
Without fear of a *Prison,* or *Pursuivants* fees.
Next, that we only may *lye* by Authority,
But in that also you have got the Priority.
Next, an old Custom, our Fathers did name it
Poetical license, and alwayes did claim it.

By this we have power to change Age in Youth,
Turn *Non-sence* into Sence, and Falshood to Truth;
In brief, to make good whatsoever is faulty,
This art some *Poet*, or the *Devil* has taught ye:
And this our Property you have invaded,
And a *Privilege* of both Houses have made it:
But that trust above all in Poets reposed,
That *Kings* by them only are made and Deposed,
This though you cannot do, yet you are willing;
But when we undertake Deposing or Killing,
They're *Tyrants* and *Monsters*, and yet then the Poet
Takes full Revenge on the Villains that do it,
And when we resume a *Scepter* or a *Crown*,
We are Modest, and seek not to make it our own.
But is't not presumption to write Verses to you,
Who make the better *Poems* of the two,
For all those pretty Knacks you do compose,
Alas, what are they but *Poems* in prose,
And between those and ours there's no difference,
But that yours want the rhime, the wit and the sense:
But for lying (the most Noble part of a *Poet*)
You have it abundantly, and your selves know it,
And though you are Modest, and seem to abhor it,
'T has done you good service, and thank He'ven for it:
Although the old Maxime remains still in force,
That a Sanctified Cause, must have a Sanctified Course:
If poverty be a part of our Trade,
So far the whole Kingdome *Poets* you have made,
Nay even so far as undoing will do it,
You have made *King Charles* in manner a Poet,
But provoke not his Muse, for all the world knows,
Already you have had too much of his *Prose*.

The Parliaments Pedigree.

NO *Pedigrees* nor *Projects*
   Of after-times I tell,
Nor what strange things the *Parliament*
   In former times befell,
Nor how an *Emperour* got a *King*,
   Nor how a *King* a *Prince*,
But you shall hear what Progenies
   Have been begotten since.

The *Devil* he a *Monster* got,
   Which was both strong and stout,
This many-headed Monster
   Did strait beget a *Rout:*
This *Rout* begat a *Parliament*,
   As *Charles* he well remembers,
The *Parliament* got Monsters too,
   The which begot *Five Members*.

The *Members Five* did then beget
   Most of the House of *Peers*,
The *Peers* mis-understandings got
   All *Jealousies* and *Fears;*
The *Jealousies* got Horse and Men,
   Lest Warrs should have abounded,
And I dare say this *Horse* got *Pym*,
   And he begot a *Round-head*.

The *Round-head* got a *Citizen*,
   That great Tax-bearing *Mule*,
The *Mule* begot a Parliament *Asse*,
   And he begot a *Fool:*

Some say the *Fool* got *Warwick*,
  And *Rich* gave him his whole Land,
In zeal Lord *Rich* got God knows who,
  And God knows who got *H*———

This *H*——— *Surplices* got down,
  And those Church Rites that were,
He hath Petitions enough each day,
  No need of the *Lords* Prayer:
But it's no wonder that's cry'd down,
  And that indeed the rather,
'Cause *Pym* and he two Bastards are,
  And dare not say, *Our Father*.

Now since this is the chiefest thing,
  Hath got this great division,
Which *London* for to reconcile,
  Hath got this great Munition:
The City hath now been refin'd,
  From all her Drosse and Pelf,
They're now about for to new mold,
  And Coyn the *Common-wealth*.

To those who desire no Peace.

SHould all those various Gales, whose titles are
  Enrol'd within the Pilots Register,
Break from their drowsie Dens, where they have layn
Bound up in slumbers, and invade the Main,
They could not raise a storm like that which they
Raise in the *Common-wealth*, who would betray

Our Peace to Civil War, in which the State
Must bleed it self to death, and have the fate,
After its stock of life is spent, to lye
Buried i'th Rubbish of an Anarchy.
Should Ravens, Bats, and the shrill Owl conspire
To twist their Notes into a General Quire.
And chuse the Mandrake for the Chaunter, they
Could not shrill forth such an ill-boding lay,
Or strains so Jarring, as do those whose throats
Warble the clamorous and untunefull Notes
Of Blood and Death, some whirle-wind, Sirs, has ta'en
Its Lodging up in the Fanatick brain
Of these bold sons of tumult, I dare say
They moulded were of some distemper'd Clay,
Which from its Centre was by Earth-quake torn,
A Tempest shook the world when they were born;
Sure from its Sphere the Element of Fire
Is dropt, and does their bosomes now inspire,
The flame lockt up in bold *Ravillacks* urne,
Is snatcht from thence, and in their hearts does burn.
Night, open thy black wombe, and let out all
Thy dreadfull furies, yet these furies shall
Not chill my heart with any fear, since day
Has furies shewn, blacker by far than they.
Let *Vaux* now sleep untill the day of Doom,
Open his eyes, forgotten in his Tomb,
Let none revile his dust, his Name shall be
Extirpated from every History,
To yield a room for others, for 'tis fit
Their Names in place of his should now be writ,
Who think that no Religion can be good,
Unlesse't be writ in Characters of Blood,
No marvail if the Rubrick then must be
Blotted from out the Sacred Liturgie,

And those red Letters now no more be known,
They'le have no other Rubrick but their own.
But shall they thus impetuously roule on,
And meet not any Malediction?
Yes sure, may sleep, that milde and gentle balme,
Which all unkind distempers does becalme,
Be unto them a torture, may their Dreams
Be all of Murders, Rapes, and such like Theams;
And when they're spent, may Wolves approach and howle,
To break their slumbers; may the Bat and Owle,
Before their Gates, to usher in the dayes
Unwellcome light, stretch out their direfull layes;
'Mongst their disordered humors, may there be
A deadly Feud, and fatal mutiny;
May sudden flames their houses melt away,
And Feavers burn their houses too of Clay;
May all their faculties and sences be
Astonisht by some drousie Lethargie,
That there may be allow'd them only sence
Enough to feel the pangs of Conscience,
Griping their souls, that they who thought it sin
To have peace without, may have no peace within.

The French Report.

ME have of late been in *England*
Vere me have seen much sport,
De raising of de Parliament,
Have quite pull'd down de Court,

De King and Queen dey seperate,
  And rule in Ignorance,
Pray judge ye Gentlemen, if dis
  Be a la mode de France.

A vise man dere is like a Ship
  Dat strikes upon de shelves,
Dey Prison all, Behead and Whip
  All viser den demselves,
Dey send out men to fetch deyr King,
  Who may come home perchance,
Oh fye, fye, fye, it is be Gar
  Not a la mode de France.

Dey raise deyr Valiant Prentices,
  To guard deyr Cause with Clubs,
Dey root deyr Bishops out of doors,
  And Presh demselves in Tubs,
De Cobler and de Tinker too,
  Dey will in time advance,
Pox take dem all, it is (*Mort Dieu*)
  Not a la mode de France.

Instead of bowing to deyr King,
  Dey vex him with Epistles,
Dey furnish all deyr Souldiers out
  With Bodkins, Spoons, and Whistles,
Dey bring deyr Gold and Silver in,
  De Brownists to advance,
But if dey be cheat of it all,
  'Tiz a la mode de France.

But if when all deyr wealth is gone,
  Dey turn unto deyr King,

Dey will make all amends again,
  Den merrily we will sing,
VIVE LE ROY, VIVE LE ROY,
  Vee'le Sing, Carouse and Dance,
De English men have done fort Bon,
  And a la mode de France.

A Loyal Subjects Oath.

This is my Oath, for ever to despise,
  With heart and soul and all my Faculties
The Kings proud foes, and with my life subdue
All that to his Sacred Majesty are not true,
To execute his Precepts with my Blood,
So far as Conscience dictates it is good;
To make my body a Bullwark 'gainst his foes,
And to maintain his red and whitest Rose,
Venture Life and Living, Sword and Muse,
Still to uphold the Glorious Flower-de-luce:
To be the same to Prince, and Duke of *York*,
Or for a cursed Jew that eats no Pork,
Let me be Cursed, and receive the Curse
Hangs over *Pym*, and *Hotham*, and a worse
I cannot wish, he that denyes this Oath,
Let these, and my Curse, light upon them both.

Short and Sweet.

Wise men suffer, good men grieve,
Knaves devise, and Fools believe,
Help, O Lord, send ayd unto us,
Else Knaves and Fools will quite undoe us.

To the City of London.

Tell me Cittz, what ye lack,
That the Knaves of the Pack,
Ye do not see forth comming,
Love ye Treason so well,
That ye neither buy nor sell,
But keep a noise with your Drumming.

What is't that you guard,
With your double watch and ward,
Your own wares, or your wifes things,
If down come the Blades,
Then down go the Trades,
They'll not leave a dead or a live thing.

What doth your profit say,
When shall we see the day,
That money shall be paid in,
Great *Strafford* he is dead,
Ye have cut off his head,
And the Bishops all are laid in.

And yet you grow poor,
As any Common whore,
   That hath been long a fading;
There's no man will buy,
Ye may leave to swear and lie,
   As ye use to do in your trading.

There's something Behind
That lies in the winde
   And brings you thus to nothing,
What doth then remain?
O the Parliament must raign,
   And you'll have *A King and no King*.

But though their power can
From a VVoman turn a Man,
   If they please so to declare him;
Yet let them take heed,
The King is King indeed,
   And the Souldiers cannot spare him.

Is't nothing ye think
24. in a *Link*
   Kings that make his succession:
Besides for our Good,
Three Princes of the *Brood*,
   And three Kingdoms in Possession.

And all his Vertues too
Should be something to you,
   If they could ought amend you;
But 'cause Hee's Chaste and Just,
You'd have Cruelty and Lust,
   Another *King Harry* God send you.

But if you mean to thrive,
And keep your trades alive,
   And bring to your City treasure,
Give the King his full Rate,
As well as to the State,
   And let Him have *London* measure.

The Players Petition to the Parliament.

Heroick Sirs, you glorious nine or ten,
  That can depose the King, and the Kings men.
Who by your Sublime Rhetorick agree,
That prisons are the Subjects libertie :
And though we sent in silver at great rates,
You plunder, to secure us our Estates.
Your serious subtilty is grown so grave,
We dare not tell you how much power you have,
At least you dare not hear us ; how you frown
If we but say, King *Pym* wears *Charles* his Crown,
Such a word's *Treason*, and you dare not hear it,
Treason to speak it, and yet not to wear it.
O wise mysterious Synod, what shall we
Do for such men as you e're forty three
Be half expir'd, and an unlucky season
Shall set a period to *Triennial Treason,*
When the fields pitcht, and some, for all their skill,
Shall fight a Bloody Battel on *Tower-Hill ;*
Where Master *Pym*, your wise judicious Schollar,
Ascends his Throne, and takes his Crown in Coller ;
When *Canterbury* coming forth shall wonder
You have so long secur'd him from the Thunder

Oft King-hunting Prentices, and the Mayor
Shall jussel zealous *Isaack* from his Chair.
Fore-seeing *Brookes*, thou drewst a happy lot,
'Twas a wise Bolt, although 'twas quickly shot ;
But whilst you live, our loude Petition craves,
That we the true Subjects, and the true Slaves,
May in our Comick mirth and Tragick rage,
Set up the Theatre, and shew the Stage,
The shop of truth and fancy, and we Vow
Not to Act any thing you disallow :
We will not dare at your strange Votes to Jear,
Nor personate King *Pym* with his State-flear ;
Aspiring *Cataline* shall be forgot,
Bloody *Sejanus*, or who e're would Plot
Confusion to a State ; the Warrs betwixt
The Parliament, and just *Henry* the sixt,
Shall have no thought or mention, cause their power,
Not only plac'd, but left him in the *Tower ;*
Nor yet the Grave advice of Learned *Pym*,
Make a Malignant, and then Plunder him.
All these and such like actions as may mar
Your soaring Plots, and shew you what you are,
We will omit, lest that your mention shake 'um,
Why should the men be wiser then you make 'um.
Methinks there should not such a difference be
'Twixt our profession and your quality,
You meet, plot, talk, consult, with minds immense,
The like with us, but only we speak sense
Inferiour unto you ; we can tell how
To depose Kings, there we are more then you,
Although not more than what you would ; then we
Likewise in our vast Privilege agree,
Only yours are the longer ; and controules,
Not only Lives and Fortunes, but mens Souls,

For you declare by Ænigmatick sense,
A Privilege over mens Conscience,
As if the *Trinity* would not consent
To save a Soul without the Parliament.
Wee make the People laugh at some vain shew,
And as they laugh at us, they doe at you;
But then i'th Contrary we disagree,
For you can make them cry faster then wee:
Your *Tragedies* more really are exprest,
You murder men in *Earnest,* wee in *Jest.*
There we come short: But if you follow't thus,
Some wise men fear you will come short of us.
Now humbly, as we did begin, Wee pray,
Dear *School-masters*, you'd give us leave to play
Quickly before the King come, for we wou'd
Be glad to say y'ave done a little good
Since you have sate, your Play is almost done,
As well as ours, would it had ne'er begun;
For we shall see, e'er the last Act be spent,
Enter the King, *Exeunt* the Parliament.
And hey then up go we, who by the frown
Of guilty Consciences have been kept down:
So may you still remain, and sit and Vote,
And through your own beam see your brothers mote,
Until a legal trial do shew how
You us'd the King, and hey then up goe you:
So pray your humble *Slaves* with all their powers,
That they may have their due, and you have yours.

A Madrigall on Justice, alluding to the PARLIAMENT.

Justice is here made up of Might,
With two left hands, but ne're a right,
And men that are well-sighted, find
This Justice sits with both eyes blind:
Yet though the Matron cannot see,
She holds that edg'd Sword, *Cruelty*,
Which that it may not rust, she whets
In cutting off the Islands *Teats*,
Who long since did *Anathemize*
Englands too too much seeing eyes,
Because they have been found to be
Guilty of *Wit* and *Piety:*
   All this and more they rudely vent,
   By Privilege of Parliament.

All former Laws fall head-long down,
And are themselves now lawless grown;
Equity hath been lately try'd,
And Right it self been rectifi'd;
The rules that shew a Christian how
To live, must all be ruled now;
The lesson here to learn, is brought,
And *Ethicks* better manners taught;
Religion, and the Churches wealth,
Of late deprived of their health,
Were brought to th' House, that they might be
Cured of their Integrity;
   We found a seam for this great rent,
   By Privilege of Parliament.

Most men do now the Buttocks lick
Of their great body Politick;
For not the head, but breech, is it
By which the Kingdom now doth sit;
The world is chang'd, and we have Choyces,
Not by most Reasons, but most Voyces,
The Lion's trod on by the Mouse,
The lower is the upper House:
As once from Chaos order came,
So do their orders Chaos frame,
And smoothly work the Lands delusion,
By a Methodical Confusion;
   These are the things that lately went
   By Privilege of Parliament.

They would not have the kingdom fall
By an Ignoble Funeral;
But piously prefer the Nation
To a renowned Decollation,
The feet, and lower parts, 'tis sed,
Would trample on, and off the head,
What ere they say, this is the thing,
They love the *Charles*, but hate the *King*;
To make an even Grove, one stroke
Should lift the *Shrubb* unto the *Oake*;
Anew-found musick they would make,
A *Gamut*, but no *Ela* take.
   This is the pious good intent
   Of Privilege of Parliament.

In all humilitie they crave
Their Soveraign, to be their *Slave*;
Desiring him, that he would be
Betray'd to them most loyally:

For, it were *Meeknesse* sure in him
To be a *Vice-Roy* unto *Pym;*
And if he would a while lay down
His Scepter, Majestie, and Crown,
He should be made for time to come
The greatest Prince in Christendom.
Charles at this time not having need,
Thank'd them as much as if he did.
   This is the happy wish'd event
   Of Privilege of Parliament.

Pym, that ador'd *Publicola*,
Who play'd the base———
Who got a Lust to sacrifice
The *Heroë* to the Peoples Eyes,
Whose back-from-Hell-fetch'd-knaverie
By some is nick-nam'd policie,
Would be a *Lyon* with a pox,
When at the best hee's but a *Fox;*
And just like him that set on fire
The hallowed *Ephesian* Spire,
Hath purchas'd to be largely known,
In that he is an Addage grown:
   All this to honest *John* is lent,
   By Privilege of Parliament.

The Valiant House was not afeard,
To pull our *Aaron* by the Beard;
To hide dark deeds from *Gazers* sights,
Strove to blow out the Churches Lights,
That squares might run round as their head,
They long to have the Rochet sped:
They Vote down Universities,
Lest men from thence become too wise,

And their benighted deeds display,
Whose works of darknesse hate the day;
Hence they prefer in every Town,
The Petticoat before the Gown ;
 These blessings to the Land are sent
 By Privilege of Parliament.

They put forth Orders, Declarations,
Unacted Laws, and Protestations,
Of which all can be said, is this,
The whole is one Parenthesis,
Because the sence (without all doubt)
Were ne're the lesse, were all left out.
Petitions none must be presented,
But what are by themselves invented,
Else they not heal, but Cicatrize,
And from the cure a Scar doth rise,
Though Holy Cut, the fault commit,
Yet Long-tail must be paid for it;
 Unto this wound was laid a Tent,
 By Privilege of Parliament.

They paid the *Scottish* debt, and thus,
To be more honest, they rob'd us ;
They feed the poor, with what think ye,.
Why sure with large Calamity,
And once a month they think it fitting
To fast from sin, because from sitting,
They would have winde and storms supprest,
To drive the Hallcyon from her Nest ;
Charles is a Picture, they make bold
To use the Scepter he should hold :
They'd pull down one, but give as good
A Golden Crown, made up of Wood,

And thus is Justice justly rent,
By Privilege of Parliament.

The Call.

Hoe Yes,

IF there be any Traytor, Viper, or Wigeon,
That will fight against God for the true Religion,
That to maintain the Parliaments Votes,
Of all true Subjects will cut the throats,
That for the King and his Countries good,
Will consume all the Land with Fire and Blood.
    I say,
If any such Traytor, Viper, Mutineer, be born,
Let him repair to the Lord with the double gilt Horn.

Englands Woe.

I Mean to speak of *Englands* sad fate,
To help in mean time the King, and his Mate,
That's ruled by an Antipodian State,
                  Which no body can deny.

But had these seditious times been when
We had the life of wise Poet *Ben,*
Parsons had never been Parliament men,
                  Which no body can deny.

Had Statesmen read the Bible throughout,
And not gone by the Bible so round about,
They would have ruled themselves without doubt,
    Which no body can deny.

But Puritans now bear all the sway,
They'll have no Bishops as most men say,
But God send them better another day,
    Which no body can deny.

Zealous P—— has threatned a great downfall,
To cut off long locks that is bushy and small,
But I hope he will not take ears and all,
    Which no body can deny.

P—— *Burton*, sayes women that's lewd and loose,
Shall wear no stallion locks for a bush,
They'll only have private boyes for their use,
    Which no body can deny.

They'll not allow what pride it brings,
Nor favours in hats, nor no such things,
They'll convert all ribbands to Bible strings,
    Which no body can deny.

God blesse our King and Parliament,
And send he may make such K—— repent,
That breed our Land such discontent,
    Which no body can deny.

And blesse our Queen and Prince also,
And all true Subjects both high and low,
The Brownings can pray for themselves you know,
    Which no body can deny.

Upon Ambition.

Occasioned by the Accusation of the Earl of STRAFFORD, *in the year* 1640.

How uncertain is the State
   Of that greatnesse we adore,
When Ambitiously we sore,
   And have ta'en the glorious height,
'Tis but Ruine gilded o're,
   To enslave us to our fate,
Whose false Delight is easier got, then kept,
Content ne'er on its gaudy Pillow slept.

Then how fondly do we try,
   With such superstitious care,
To build Fabricks in the Ayr?
   Or seek safety in that sky,
Where no Stars but Meteors are,
   That portend a ruine nigh?
And having reacht the object of our ayme,
We find it but a *Pyramid* of flame.

The Argument.

When the unfetter'd Subjects of the Seas,
   The Rivers, found their silver feet at ease,
No sooner summon'd, but they swiftly went
To meet the Ocean, at a Parliament:

Did not the petty Fountains say their King,
The *Ocean*, was no *Ocean*, but a *Spring*?
As now some do the Power of Kings dispute,
And think it lesse, 'cause more is added to't.

Pale *Ignorance*, can the excesse of store
Make him seem poorer then he was before?
The Stars, the Heavens, inferiour Courtiers, may
Govern Nights Darknesse, but not rule the Day;
Where the Sun Lords it, should they all Combine
With *Lucia* in her brightest dresse, to shine,
Their light's but faint: Nor can he be subdu'd,
Although but one, and they a Multitude.

Say Subjects, are you Stars? be it allow'd,
You justly of your numbers may be proud,
But to the Sun inferiour; for know this,
Your *Light* is borrow'd, not your *Own*, but *His*:
And as all streams into the Ocean run,
You ought to pay your Contribution;
Then do not such Ingratitude oppresse,
To make him low, that could have made you lesse.

The Character of a Roundhead. 1641.

WHat Creature's this with his short hairs,
   His little band and huge long ears,
  That this new faith hath founded,
The Puritans were never such,
The Saints themselves, had ne'er so much,
  Oh, such a knave's a Roundhead.

What's he that doth the Bishops hate,
And count their Calling reprobate,
    Cause by the Pope propounded,
And saies a zealous Cobler's better,
Then he that studieth every letter,
    Oh, such a knave's a Roundhead.

What's he that doth high Treason say,
As often as his yea and nay,
    And wish the King confounded,
And dare maintain that Master *Pym*,
Is fitter for the Crown then him,
    Oh, such a rogue's a Roundhead.

What's he that if he chance to hear,
A piece of *London's* Common-Prayer,
    Doth think his Conscience wounded.
And goes five miles to preach and pray,
And lyes with's Sister by the way,
    Oh, such a rogue's a Roundhead.

What's he that met a holy Sister,
And in an Hay-cock gently kist her,
    Oh! then his zeal abounded,
Close underneath a shady willow,
Her Bible serv'd her for her pillow,
    And there they got a Roundhead.

A Curtain Lecture.

The Tune, *Cannot keep her Lips together.*

WILL you please to hear a Song,
    Through it want both rime and reason,
It was pend to do no wrong,
    But for description at this season,
Of he or she what e're they be,
    That wish Church-orders quite confounded,
Yet makes a shew, where e're they go,
    Of Fervent zeal: I mean a Roundhead.

First hee'l have a smoothing tongue,
    Next hee'l learn for to dissemble,
And when he hears of willfull wrong,
    He'll sigh and look as he would tremble,
The next of all then let him fall,
    To praise mens hearts in secret bravery,
A speaking still against all ill,
    That is the Cloak to hide their Knavery.

Let Charity be used much,
    In words at length and not in action,
It is the Common use of such,
    Not to do, but give direction,
They'l be loath to swear an Oath,
    By yea and nay, you may believe them,
But for their gains, they will take paines,
    To cheat and ly, and never grieve them.

The Common-Prayer they like it not,
    For they are wise and can make better,

And such a Teacher they have got,
   Confutes it all in word and letter;
For he can rayle mens hearts to quaile
   With deep damnation for their sinning,
But to amend they ne're intend,
   And to transgress they're now beginning.

But here is a very worthy man,
   That undertakes more than he is able,
That in a Tub sometimes will stand,
   In Hey-barn, Sheep-house, or a Stable,
That all the Rout that comes about
   To hear his Doctrines, *Saints* he calls them,
They vow and swear they nere did hear
   Such worthy things as he hath told them.

They will not hear of Wedding Rings
   For to be used in their Mariage,
But say they are Superstitious things,
   And doth Religion much disparage,
They are but vain, and things prophane,
   Wherefore now no Wit be-speaks them
So to be ty'd unto the Bride,
   But do it as the *Spirit* moves them.

No *Pater-Noster* nor no *Creed*
   In their Petitions never mention,
And hold there's nothing good indeed
   But what is done by their pretention,
Prayers that are old in vain they hold,
   And can with God no favour merit,
Therefore they will nothing say,
   But as they are moved by the Spirit.

The wisest Schools they count but Fools,
   Which do no more than they have taught them
For *Brownists* they can preach and pray
   With Wits their Fathers never bought them;
Then I perceive that wit they have
   They gather it by Inspiration,
No Books they need to learn to read,
   If all be true of their relation.

Only the Horn-book I would have
   Them practice at their beginning,
That you the better may perceive
   The Fruits that comes by fleshly sinning.
Neverthelesse I would express
   All other Books that now are used,
Least that the Ghost that leads you most
   By too much Art to be abused.

Their Hair close to their Heads they crop
   And yet not only for the fashion,
But that the Eare it should not stop
   From hearing of some rare Relation:
Therefore his Eares he will prepare
   To hearken to an Holy Brother,
That in regard he may be heard
   From one side of the Barne to th' other.

They count their Fathers were but Fools,
   Which formerly became such Debters,
To spend their Means upon the Schools,
   To teach their Sons a few fond Letters,
The Christ Crosse-row's enough to know,
   For 'tis the Horn that must exalt 'em,
Their Gen'ral Vows his Antler'd Brows
   Shall gore the Proudest dare assault 'em.

Part I. *Rump Songs.* 47

At the last when they must part,
  Male and Female go together
Joynd in hand, and joyn'd in heart,
  And joyn'd a little for their pleasure.
First for a Kisse they will agree,
  And what comes next you may conjecture,
So that the Wicked do not see,
  And so break up the *Roundheads* Lecture.

A Mad World My Masters.

WE have a King and yet no King,
    For he hath lost his Power,
For 'gainst his Will his Subjects are
    Imprison'd in the *Tower*.

We had some Laws (but now no Laws)
    By which he held his Crown,
And we had Estates and Liberties
    But now they're voted down.

We had Religion; but of late
    That's beaten down with Clubs,
Whilst that Prophanesse Authoriz'd
    Is belched forth in Tubs.

We were free Subjects born, but now
    We are by force made Slaves,
By some whom we did count our Friends,
    But in the end prov'd Knaves.

And now to such a grievous height
  Are our Misfortunes grown,
That our Estates are took away
  By tricks before ne're known.

For there are Agents sent abroad
  Most humbly for to crave
Our Almes : but if they are deny'd,
  And of us nothing have.

Then by a Vote *ex tempore*
  We are to Prison sent,
Mark'd with the Name of *Enemy*
  Of *King* and *Parliament*.

And during our Imprisonment,
  Their lawless Bulls do thunder
A Licence to their Souldiers
  Our Houses for to plunder.

And if their Hounds do chance to smell
  A man whose Fortunes are
Of some Account, whose Purse is full,
  Which now is somewhat rare.

A *Monster* now *Delinquent* term'd,
  He is declar'd to be,
And that his Lands as well as Goods
  Sequestred ought to be.

And as if our Prisons were too good,
  He is to *Yarmouth* sent
By vertue or a Warrant from
  The *King* and *Parliament*.

Thus is our Royal Soveraigns name
 And eke his Power infus'd,
And by the vertue of the same
 He and all His abus'd.

For by this Means his Castles now
 Are in the power of those
Who treacherously with Might and Maine
 Do strive him to depose.

Arise therefore brave *British* men,
 Fight for your King and State,
Against those Trayterous men that strive
 This Realm to Ruinate.

'Tis *Pym*, 'tis *Pym*, and his Colleagues,
 That did our woe engender,
Nought but their Lives can end our Woes,
 And us in safety render.

The Riddle.

S-Hall's have a Game at Put, to pass away the time,
 X-pect no foul-play; though I do play the Knave
I- have a King at hand, yea that I have:
C- Cards be ye true, then the Game is mine.
R-ejoyce my Heart, to see thee then repine.
A-that's lost, that's Cuckolds luck.
T-rey comes like Quater, to pull down the Buck.

An Answer to a Love-Elegy *(written from I.P. one of the Five Members, to his Delightfull Friend)* in Latin.

What *Latin* Sir? why there is no man
That e're thought you an *English-Roman.*
Your Father Horse could teach you none,
Nor was it e're your Mother tongue,
Your Education too assures
Me, that your *Poem* is not yours:
Besides, I thought you did detest
The Language of the *Latin Beast,*
But now your Impudence I see
Did hereby shew its Modesty;
Each syllable would blush you thought,
If it had bin plain *English* taught,
And that your foul debauched stuff
Might do its Errand fast enough,
Forsooth your Wisedom thought it meet
That Words might run to give 'em feet,
Pardon me, Sir, I'm none of those
That love *Love-verse*, give me your Prose,
I wish each Verse to make delay,
Had turn'd lame *Scazon* by the way,
I read a Hell in every line
Of your Polluted *Fescennine;*
Your Verses stunk; to keep 'em sweet
You should have put Socks on their Feet.
And that the Answer which I shall
Now write, may be Methodicall,

I'le briefly make ('tis not amiss)
An *Anacephalæosis*.
And first I look'd for *Nestor;* when
Mere *Cupid* trickl'd from your Pen,
Who was your Father, you make proof
By your Colt's tooth, though not your hoof,
She that was great with you, you hold
Did not lye in, but was with fole'd.
I wonder one so old, so grave
Should yet such Youth, such Lightnesse have;
Of the Five Members you alone
Shall be esteem'd the Privy One,
Who (like the *Gnosticks*) preach your *Text*,
Increase and Multiply, and next
Convincing Doctrines you deduce,
Put out the Lights, and make Use.
You say I am a Maid exceeding
Apt to be taught by you good breeding.
But where there's breeding, it is said
There's none, unlesse a broken Maid
Turn Papist, (*Stallion*) they'le dispence
With Whoredom, by an Indulgence,
Turn Fryer, that thou mayst be free
At once with a whole Nunnery,
There 'twill be vertue to ride on
The Purple Whore of *Babylon*
Thou mayst as soon turn *Turk*, as *King*,
And that, O that's the tempting thing
That thou mayst glut thy Appetite
With a *Seraglio* of Delight.
I am no *Proserpine*, that thus
I should desire an *Incubus:*
But you must vote (if Me you'le win)
No Fornication to be Sin,

You say the House takes it not well
The *King* 'gainst *Rebells* should Rebell;
And that's the reason why you stand
To be Dictator of the Land,
Which mov'd me to a mighty toyle
Of getting Vardygrease and Oyle.
'Cause such Itch-Med'cine is a thing
That's fittest to anoint you *King*.
You say youl'd undertake and do
Wonders, would I undergo you,
For my sake you would Cobler play,
Your *Trade* should be to underlay,
For Me you'd your chiefest blood,
Pray spend it on the Sisterhood,
You wish to dye in those great Fights
Of *Venus*, where each Wound delights,
And should I once to Heaven take wing,
Youl'd follow me, though in a string;
Thank you (good Sir) it is our Will
You your last Promise doe fulfill;
There's nothing spoke that pleaseth us
Like your (*In funes Cedulus*)
Next come those idle Twittle-twats,
Which calls me many God-knows-whats,
As hallowed, beautifull, and faire,
Supple and kind, and *Debonaire*.
You talk of Women that did wooe,
When I am mad I'le do so too;
Then that my Father may not spye
The coupling of you and I,
He shall be guiltlessly detected,
As a true Subject ill-affected,
And so the Protestant shall lye
In Gaol for fear of Popery.

Part I.   *Rump Songs.*   53

(From hence it is that every *Town*,
Almost is now a Prison grown,
Where Loyalty lies fetter'd, then
You do commit more sins than men.)
But those your words I have thought best,
Should punisht be by being prest;
And that this Body Politick
May then be well, which now lyes sick,
May the Greek Π, that fatal *Tree*,
This Spring bear all such fruit as thee.

The Penitent Traytor.

The Humble Petition of a Devonshire *Gentleman who was Condemned for* TREASON, *and Executed for the same, An.* 1641.

To the Tune of *Fortune my Foe, &c.*

Attend good Christian People to my story,
A sadder yet was never brought before ye;
Let each man learn here like a good Disciple,
To shun foul *Treason*, and the tree that's *Triple*.

Long time I liv'd in the Country next to *Cornwall*,
And there my Children were both breed and born all,
Great was my Credit, as my debts did speak,
And now I'le shew you why my neck must break.

There being a Parliament called in *September*,
I was for th' Commons an Elected Member,
And though there were besides above four hundred
Yet I at last was for the fifth part numbred.

For first, I join'd with some whom Piety
Made Knaves, lest such their Fathers prov'd should be ;
Their Ignorance to sin enjoyed many Voyces,
Which made bad Speeches, but Excellent Noyses.

Thus by my faction the whole House was sway'd,
All sorts of people flockt to me for Ayd ;
They brought me Gold and Plate in Huggar Muggar,
Besides eight hundred pounds worth in Loaf-sugar.

What e're the Grievance was, I did advise
They should Petitions bring in Humble wise,
Which I did frame my self, & thus did rook them,
They paid me when I gave, and when I took them.

By this I gained, and by the Money-Pole,
Which paid my debts, 10000 pounds i'th whole,
My Childrens Portions too, with much content,
I paid in State, by Acts of Parliament.

Thus though I make all Jesuits fly the Nation,
My self did practise much Equivocation,
For oft I Vow'd the Common-wealth as honey
Was sweet to me, but I, by wealth, meant money.

And lest my Plots should after be unmasked,
And how I got such Wealth, chance to be asked,
I cast about how I might gain such power,
As might from Justice safely me secure.

Part I.   *Rump Songs.*   55

Then first I labour'd to divest the Crown,
Of all Prerogatives, and bring them down;
First, to both Houses, and then but one should have them,
Five Members next, and last my self would have them.

Because I knew the State would not admit
Such Change, unlesse the Church did Usher it,
I left the old Religion for advantage,
Endeavouring to set up one that did want age.

Which when all Learned Levites did withstand,
(Regarding Gods Word more then my command)
I such suppress, and made (for which I woe am)
The basest people Priests, like *Jeroboam.*

Then each profession sent out *Teachers,* moe
Then both the Universities could doe
To handle a *Text* the Good-wifes fingers itches,
And vows she'll preach with her Husband for the Breeches.

By this new Godly lives but few did gain,
The rest for want of *Trading* they complain,
I told them 'twas a wicked Counsellors plot,
And till his head went off, their wares would not.

This Great mans guilt was Loyalty and Wisdom,
Which made me cast about to work his Doom;
The Sword of Justice was too short to do't,
2000. Clubs must therefore jerk it out.

He being knockt down, some others for the like Crime,
Were sent to Prison, some escapt in time;

Thus Law and Equity in awe was kept here,
And Clubs were taught how to controul the Scepter.

We took from th' Upper-house Votes five times five,
And they aym'd all the Kings Voyce Negative,
Which to effect we did an Order make,
That what he would not give, our selves would take.

Then we petition'd that the Forts and Towers,
And all the strength o'th Kingdom might be ours,
And thus to save the King from Soveraign dangers,
As if he had better Fall by Us than Strangers.

Whilst he denyes they Legally are stay'd on
By a Law call'd, *Resolv'd upon the Question*,
But still his Chief strength was above our Arts,
His righteous Cause, and loyal Subjects hearts.

Being Arm'd with these, by Heaven he was so blest,
That he soon honour Got, and all the rest,
Bringing all such to punishment endignant,
As were of my Contrived part, Malignant.

O *Tyburn, Tyburn;* O thou sad Tryangle,
A vyler weight on thee ne'er yet did dangle,
See here I am at last with Hemp to mew,
To give thee what was long before thy due.

How could I bless thee, could'st thee take away
My Life and Infamy both in one day;
But this in Ballads will survive I know,
Sung to that preaching tune, *Fortune my Foe*.

Then mark good Christian people, and take heed,
Use not religion for an upper weed,
Serve God sincerely, touch not his *Anointed*, .
And then your *Necks* shall never be disjoynted.

God bless the King, the Queen, and all the Children,
(And pardon me all, that I 'gainst them have ill done)
May one of that brave Race still rule this Nation,
And now I pray you sing the Lamentation.

The Passage of a Coach travelling to Dover.

THe Foundation of the Coach, a *Guilty Conscience.*
The Axeltree, *Ambition* and *Cruelty.*
The Wheels, *Fears* and *Jealousies.*
The Reins, *too much liberty and licentiousness.*
The six Horses, *five Members* and *K——*
The Postillion, *Captain Venne.*
The Coach-man, *Isaac Pennington* Lord Maior :
  In the two ends of the Coach sate *Essex* and *B——*
In the Boots sate *Say* and *Seal*, and the *silent Speaker.*
On the hinder part of the Coach was written this Anagram.

Robert Devereux General
Never duller Oxe greater Rebel.

After the Coach follows *Straffords* Ghost, crying, *Drive on, Drive on, Revenge, revenge.*

As this Coach was going through the City it was staid by a *Court of Guard*, who cry'd, *Where's our Mony? where's our Plate?* the Speaker said, *Ye have the Publick Faith for't.* Whereupon they passed towards *Gravesend*, where they stayed at the Sign of the *Hope*, where was the Earl of *Warwick*, with a Ship called the *Carry-Knave.*

The Five Members Thanks to the Parliament.

Now tend your ear a while
    To a tale that I shall tell,
Of a lusty lively Parliament
    That goes on passing well.

Which makes our Gratious King, a King
    Of so much worth and glory,
His like is not to be seen or found
    In any Humane Story.

Win him who knows how many Crowns,
    With losse of two or three,
Within so short a time as this,
    As Wonder is to see,

The Country eas'd, the Cit ypleas'd,
    O what a World is this!
When upright men did stand at Helme,
    How can we fail or miss?

And yet beyond all this, the King
   Doth in abundance swim,
Gramercy *K*—- and *Stroud* say I,
   Haslerigge, *H*—— *Hampden*, *Pym*.

And when as our Church Government
   Was fallen into Disorder,
As that upon Grosse Popery
   It seemed somewhat to border.

So sweet a Course is taken now,
   As no man need to fear,
For Bishops learn'd, and Learned men
   Have nothing to do here :

But every one shall teach and preach,
   As best becomes his Sense :
And so we'll banish Popery,
   And send it packing hence.

Now for that happy Church and State,
   Drest up so fine and trym :
Gramercy *K*—— and *Stroud*, I say
   Haslerigge, *H*—— *Hampden*, *Pym*.

For Arbitrary Government,
   Star-Chamber, High Commission,
They will themselves do all that work,
   By their good Kings permission.

If any else presume to do't,
   They weigh it not a straw,
They'll club such sawcy Fellows down,
   As Beasts debarr'd of Law.

And let no Wights henceforth presume
    To hold it Rime or Reason,
That Judges shall determine what
    Is Felony or Treason :

But what the Worthies say is so,
    Is Treason to award,
Albeit in Councel only spoke,
    And at the Councel-board.

I'le shew you yet another thing,
    Which you'll rejoyce to see,
The Prince and People know that these
    Men cannot Traytors be.

Then let our King, our Church and State
    Acknowledge as is due,
The Benefits they do receive
    From this right Divine crue.

And for this Sea of Liberty,
    Wherein we yet do swim,
Gramercy *K*—— and *Stroud* say I,
    Haslerigge, *H*—— *Hampden*, *Pym*.

Upon the Parliament Fart.

Down came Grave Antient Sir *John Crooke,*
And read his Messuage in a Book ;
Very well quoth *Will. Norris,* it is so,
But Mr. *Pym's* Tayle cry'd No.
Fye quoth Alderman *Atkins* I like not this passage,
To have a Fart inter voluntary in the midst of a Message.
Then upstarts one fuller of Devotion
Than Eloquence, and said, a very ill Motion.
Not so neither quoth Sir *Henry Jenking,*
The Motion was good but for the stinking.
Quoth Sir *Henry Poole* 'twas an audacious trick
To fart in the face of the Body Politick.
Sir *Jerome* in Folio swore by the Mass
This Fart was enough to have blown a Glass :
Quoth then Sir *Jerome* the Lesser, such an Abuse
Was never offer'd in *Poland* nor *Pruce.*
Quoth Sir *Richard Houghton,* a Justice i'th *Quorum*
Would tak't in snuff to have a Fart let before him.
If it would bear an Action quoth Sir *Thomas Holecraft,*
I would make of this Fart a Bolt or a Shaft.
Then qd. Sir *John Moor* to his great Commendation
I will speak to this House in my wonted fashion.
Now surely sayes he, For as much as, How be it,
This Fart to the Serjeant we must commit.
No quoth the Serjeant, low bending his Knees,
Farts oft will break Prisons, but never pay Fees.
Besides, this Motion with small reason stands,
To charge me with that I can't keep in my hands.
Quoth Sir *Walter Cope* 'twas so readily let,
I would it were sweet enough for my Cabinet.

Why then Sir *Walter* (quoth Sir *William Fleetwood*)
Speak no more of it, but bury it with Sweetwood ;
Grave Senate, quoth *Duncombe,* upon my salvation,
This Fart stands in need of some great Reformation ;
Quoth Mr. *Cartwright,* upon my Conscience
It would be reformed with a little Frankencense ;
Quoth Sir *Roger Aston* it would much mend the matter,
If this Fart were shaven, and washt in Rosewater ;
Per verbum Principis, how dare I tell it,
A Fart by hear-say, and not see it, nor smell it.
I am glad qd. *Sam: Lewknor* we have found a thing,
That no Tale-bearer can carry it the King,
Such a Fart as this was never seen
Quoth the learned Council of the Queen,
Yes quoth Sir *Hugh Breston* the like hath been
Let in a dance before the Queen,
Then said Mr. *Peak* I have a President in store
His Father Farted last Sessions before,
A Bill must be drawn then, quoth Sir *John Bennet,*
Or a selected Committee quickly to pen it,
Why quoth Dr. *Crompton* no man can draw
This Fart within Compass of the Civil-Law,
Quoth Mr. *Jones* by the Law't may be done
Being a Fart intayld from Father to Sonne,
In truth quoth Mr. *Brooke,* this Speech was no lye
This Fart was one of your *Post-Nati*
Quoth Sir *William Paddy* a dare-assuram
Though twere *contra modestum :* 'tis not *præter naturam,*
Besides by the Aphorismes of my art
Had he not been deliver'd, h'ad been sick of a Fart ;
Then quoth the Recorder, the mouth of the City,
To have smother'd that Fart had been great pity,

It is much certain quoth Sir *Humphrey Bentwizle*,
That a Round-fart is better than a stinking fiezle :
Have patience Gentlemen, quoth Sir *Francis Bacon*
There's none of us all but may be mistaken ;
Why right, quoth the great Attorney I confesse,
The Eccho of ones —— is remedilesse.

The old Earle of Bristol's *Verses on an Accommodation.*

THe *Parliament* cryes *Arme*, the *King* sayes *No*,
The New *Lieutenants* cry *Come on, let's go ;*
The *Citizens* and *Roundheads* cryes *So, so ;*
The *People* all amaz'd cryes *Where's the Foe ;*
The *Scots* that stand behind the Door cryes *Boe*,
Peace, Stay awhile and you shall know :
The *King* stands still faster than they can go.
If that the *King* by force of Armes prevail,
　He is invited to a *Tyranny ;*
If that by power of *Parliament* he fail,
　We heap continual Warre on our Posterity :
Then that is not for *Accommodation*,
Loves neither *God*, nor *Church*, nor *King*, nor *Nation*.

The Rump's Hypocricy.

WE fasted first, then pray'd that War might cease,
   When Praying would not serve, we paid for Peace,
And glad we had it so, and gave God thanks,
Which made the *Irish* play the *Scotish* Pranks.
Is there no God? let's put it to a Vote,
Is there no Church? some Fools say so by rote;
Is there no King, but *Pym*, for to assent
What shall be done by Act of Parliament?
No God, no Church, no King, then all were well,
If they could but Enact there were no Hell.

The Parliaments Hymnes.

O Lord preserve the Parliament,
   And send them long to reign,
From three years end to three years end,
   And so to three again.

Let neither King nor Bishops, Lord,
   Whilst they shall be alive,
Have power to rebuke thy Saints,
   Nor hurt the Members five.

For they be good and godly men,
   No sinfull path they tread;

They now are putting Bishops down,
  And setting up Round-head.

From *Holdsworth*, *Bromrigge*, and old *Shute*,
  Those able learned Scholars,
Good Lord deliver us with speed,
  And all our zealous Followers.

From *Fielding* and from *Vavasour*,
  Both ill affected men ;
From *Lunsford* eke deliver us,
  That eateth up Children.

Thy holy *Burton, Bastwick*, ⸺
  Lord keep them in thy Bosome ;
Eke him that hath kept out the King,
  Worshipfull Sir *John Hotham*.

Put down the King and *Hartford*, Lord,
  And keep them down for aye ;
Thy chosen *Pym* set up on high,
  And eke the good Lord *Say*.

For *Warwick* wee beseech thee Lord,
  Be thou his strong defence,
Holland, Brooks, and *S*⸺ shield,
  And eke his Oxcellence.

For *B*⸺ and *K*⸺ to
  That are both wise and stout,
Who have rebuk'd the King of late,
  And his ungodly Rout.

Once more we pray for Parliament,
  That they may sit secure,

And may their Consultations,
From Age to Age endure.

Let all the Godly say *Amen*,
And let them Praises sing
To God and to the Parliament,
And all that hate the King.

The Round-heads Race.

I Will not say for the Worlds store,
   The World's now drunk, (for did I)
The Faction which now reigns would roare,
   But I will swear 'tis giddy.

And all are prone to this same Fit,
   That it their Object make,
For every thing runs Round in it,
   And no form else will take.

To the Round-Nose Peculiar is
   The Ruby and the Rose;
The Round-lip gets away the Kisse,
   And that by Favour goes.

The Round-beard for Talke of State,
   Carry it at the Club;
The Round-Robin by a like fate
   Is Victor in the Tubb.

Hanworths Round-block speak pollicy,
   The Round-hose Riches draw.

The Round-heads for the Gospell bee
The Round Copes for the Law.

Tom his Round Garbe so rules all o're,
The pox take him for mee
That e're lookes for square dealing more,
And hears an health to thee.

On the Queens Departure.

UP, up wronged *Charls* his friends, what can you be
Thus Mantled In a stupid Lethargie,
When all the world's in Arms? and can there be
Armies of Fears abroad and none with thee?
Breath out your souls in sighs, melt into tears,
And let your griefs be equal to your fears;
The Sphæres are all a jarring, and their jarres
Seems counter-like to Calculate the Starres;
The Inferior Orbes aspire, and do disdaine
To move at all, unlesse they may attain
The highest Room, our Occedentall Sunne
Eclips'd by Starres, forsakes his *Horizon*,
Bright *Cinthia* too (they say) hath hid her face
As 'twere Impatient of her *Sol's* disgrace;
And our fears tell us, that unlesse the Sunne
Lend us his beams again, the World will run
Into another Chaos, where will be
Nought but the cursed Fruits of Anarchie;
Sedition, Murder, Rapine, and what's worse
None to Implore for Aid; Oh, hears the Curse,
But stay ye Starres, what will ye wish to bee?
More Sunns then one will prove a Prodigie:

5—2

To afright the Amazed World, will ye be-night
That glorious Lamp, that Fountain of all light,
Will none but *Sol's* own Chaire, please your desire?
Take heed bold Stars you'le set the world on fire.

Pyms *Anarchy.*

Ask me no more, why there appears
Dayly such troopes of Dragooners?
Since it is requisite, you know;
They rob *cum privilegio.*

Ask me no more, why th' Gaole confines
Our Hierarchy of best divines?
Since some in Parliament agree
Tis for the Subjects Liberty.

Ask me no more, why from *Blackwall*
Great tumults come into *Whitehall*?
Since it's allow'd, by free consent,
The Priviledge of Parliament.

Ask me not, why to *London* comes
So many Musquets, Pikes and Drums?
Although you fear they'll never cease;
'Tis to protect the Kingdoms peace.

Ask me no more, why little *Finch*
From Parliament began to winch?
Since such as dare to hawk at Kings
Can easie clip a Finches wings.

Ask me no more, why *Strafford's* dead,
And why they aim'd so at his head?
Faith, all the reason I can give,
'Tis thought he was too wise to live.

Ask me no more, where's all the Plate,
Brought in at such an easie rate?
They will it back to th' Owners bring
In case it fall not to the King.

Ask me not why the House delights
Not in our two wise Kentish Knights?
There Counsell never was thought good,
Because it was not understood.

Ask me no more, why *Lesley* goes
To seize all rich men as his foes?
Whilst Country Farmers sigh and sob,
Yeomen may beg when Kings do rob.

Ask me no more, by what strange sight
Londons Lord Maior was made a Knight?
Since there's a strength, not very far,
Hath as much power to make as mar.

Ask me no more, why in this Age
I sing so sharp without a Cage?
My answer is, I need not fear
Since *England* doth the burden bear.

Ask me no more, for I grow dull,
Why *Hotham* kept the Town of *Hull*?
This answer I in brief do sing,
All things were thus whem *Pym* was K——

To my Lord B. of S. he being at York.

My Lord,

WHen you were last at *London* 'twas our fear,
Lest the same *Rout* which threatned *Majesty,*
Might strike at *you*: 'tis but the same Career
To aime at *Crowns*, and at the *Miter* fly.
    For still the *Scepter* and the *Crosier staffe*
    Together *fall*, 'cause they're together *safe* :

Yet while the sence of Tumults deepest grow,
And presse in *us*, no doubts in *you* arise ;
There still dwelt *calm* and *quiet* in your *Brow,*
As our *Distractions* were your *Exercise:*
    And taught us, all *assaults*, all *Ills* to beare,
    Is not to fly from Danger, but from Fear.

That *Courage* waits you still, some merely rode
From Tumults and the Peoples frantick Rage,
Counting their *safety* by their *far abode,*
And so grew *safer still* at the next Stage :
    But 'tis not space that shelters you, the rest
    Secure themselves by *Miles*, you by your Breast.

And now my Lord, since you have *London* left,
Where Merchants wives *dine* cheap, & as cheap *sup,*
Where Fools themselves have of their Plate bereft,
And sigh and drink in the *course* Pewter cup.
    Where's not a Silver *Spoon* left, not that giv'n than
    When the first *Cockney* was made *Christian.*

No not a *Bodkin*, *Pincase*, all they send
Or carry all, what ever they can happe on,
Ev'n to the pretty *Pick Tooth*, whose each end
Oft purg'd the Relicks of *continual* Capon.
   Nothing must stay behind, nothing must tarry,
   No not the *Ring* by which dear *Joan* took *Harry*.

But now no *City-Villain*, though he were
Free of a *Trade* and *Treason*, dares intrude,
No sawcy Prentises assault you there,
Engag'd by their *Indentures* to be *rude*:
   Whom for the *two* first years their Masters use
   Onely to cry down *Bishops* and cleanse *Shooes*.

There as in silent Orbes you may ride on,
And as in *Charles* his *Wain* move without jarres,
Your *Coach* will seem your *Constellation*,
Not drawn about by *Horses*, but by *Stars*.
   Till seated near the *Northern Pole*, wee thence
   Judge your *seat Sphear*, *you* its *Intelligence*.

An Elegie on the Most Reverend Father in God William, Lord Archbishop of CANTERBURY.

Attached the 18. *of* December, 1640.
Beheaded the 10. *of* January, 1644.

Most Reverend Martyr,

THou, since thy thick Afflictions first begun,
Mak'st *Dioclesian's* dayes all *Calme*, and *Sun*,

And when thy Tragick Annals are compil'd,
Old Persecution shall be *Pity* styl'd,
The *Stake* and *Faggot* shall be Temp'rate names,
  And *Mercy* wear the Character of *Flames*:
Men knew not then *Thrift* in the Martyrs breath,
Nor weav'd their Lives into a four years Death,
Few antient *Tyrants* do our Stories Taxe,
That slew first by *Delayes*, then by the *Axe*,
But these (*Tiberius* like) alone do cry,
'*Tis to* be *Reconcil'd to let Thee dy.*
  Observe we then a while into what *Maze*,
Compasse, and *Circle* they contrive Delayes,
What *Turnes* and wilde *Perplexities* they chuse,
Ere they can forge their *Slander*, and *Accuse:*
The Sun hath now brought his warm Chariot back,
And rode his Progress round the *Zodiack*,
When yet no *Crime* appears, when none can tell,
Where thy *Guilt* sleeps, nor when 'twill break the shell.
Why is His *Shame* defer'd? what's in't that brings
Your *Justice* back, spoyles *Vengeance* of her Wings?
Hath *Mercy* seiz'd you? will you rage no more?
Are *Windes* grown tame? have *Seas* forgot to *roar*?
No, a wilde fiercenesse hath your minds possest,
Which *time* and *sins* must *cherish* and *digest*:
You durst not now let *His* clear Blood be spilt,
You were not yet grown up to such a guilt;
You try if *Age*, if *Seaventy years* can Kill:
Then y'have your *Ends*, and you are *harmlesse* still,
But when this fail'd, you do your Paths enlarge,
But would not yet *whole Innocence* discharge;
You'll not be *Devil All*, you fain would prove
Good at a *Distance*, within some *Remove*,

"Virtue hath sweets which are good Mens due gaine,
"Which Vice could not Deserve, yet would Retaine.
This was the Cause, why once it was your Care,
That *Storms* and *Tempests* in your *Sin* might share,
You did engage the *Waves*, and strongly stood
To make the *Water* guilty of his *Blood*.
Boats are dispatcht in haste, and 'tis his doome,
Not to his *Charge*, but to his *Shipwrack* come;
Fond men, your cruel project cannot doe,
Tempests and *storms* must learn to kill from *you*:
When this comes short, he must *Walke Pilgrimage*,
No *Coach* nor *Mule*, that may sustein his Age,
Must trace the *City* (now a *Desert rude*)
And combate salvage *Beasts* the *Multitude*.
But when his *Guardian Innocence* can fling,
Awe round about, and save him by that *King*.
When the *Just cause* can fright the *Beasts* away,
And make the *Tyger* tremble at her *prey*.
When nether *Waves* dare seize him, nor the *Rout*;
The storm with Reason, and the storm *without*:
Lost in their streights when *Plots* have vanquisht bin,
And *Sin* perplext hath no *Relief*, but *Sin*.
Agents and *Instruments* now on you fall,
You must be *Judges*, *People*, *Waves*, and *All*.

Yet 'cause the *Rout* will have't perform'd by *you*,
And long to see *done* what they dare not *Doe*.
You put the *Crime* to *use*, it swells your *Heape;*
Your *Sin's* your *own*, nor are you *Guilty cheap*,
You *Husband All*; there's no *Appearance* lost,
Nor comes he once to th' *Bar* but at your *cost*;
A *constant Rate* well *Taxt*, and *Levyed* right,
And a *Just value* set upon each *sight*.

At last they find the *Dayes* by their own *Purse*,
Lesse known from *him* than what they doe *disburse*:
But when it now strikes high for him *t'appear*,
And *Chapmen* see the *Bargain* is grown *dear*;
They *Muster hands*, and their hot suits enlarge,
Not to persue the *Man*, but save the *Charge*;
Then least you loose their *Custome*, (a just fear)
Selling your *Sinnes* and others *Blood* too dear.
You grant their Suits, the Manner, and the Time;
And he must Dye for what no *Law* calls *Crime*.
Th' *Afflicted Martyrs*, when their pains began,
Their *Trajan* had, or *Dioclesian*.
Their *Tortures* were some *Colours*, and proceed;
Though from no *Guilt*, yet 'cause they *disagreed*:
What *league*, what *friendship's* there? They could not joyn,
And fix the *Ark* and *Dagon* in one *Shrine*.
Faith, combats *Faith*; and how agree can they,
That still go on, but still a several way?
Zeal, *Martyrs Zeal*, and *Heat* 'gainst *Heat* conspires.
As *Theban Brothers* fight though in their *Fires*.
Yet as two diff'rent *Stars* unite their *Beams*,
And *Rivers* mingles *Waves* and mix their *Streams*;
And though they challenge each a several *Name*,
Conspire because their *moysture* is the *same*.
So *Parties* knit, though they be *diverse* known,
The *Men* are *many*, but the *Christian*, *one*.
Trajan no *Trajan* was to his own *Heard*,
And *Tygers* are not by the *Tygers* fear'd.
What strange excesse then? what's that *menstruous Power*
When *Flames* do *Flames*, and *Streams* do *Streams* devour?
Where the *same Faith* 'gainst the same *Faith* doth knock,
And *Sheep* are *Wolves* to *Sheep* of the same *Flock*?

Where *Protestant* the *Protestant* defies,
Where *both Assent* yet one for *Dissent dyes*?
Let these that doubt this, through his Actions *Wade*,
Where some must needs *Convince*, All may *perswade*.
   Was he *Apostate*, who your *Champion* stood,
Bath'd in his *Inke* before, as now in *Blood*?
He that unwinds the *subtle Jesuite*,
That Feels the *Serpents Teeth*, and is not *bit*?
Unites the *Snake* finds each *Mysterious knot*,
And turns the *Poyson* into *Antidot*.
Doth *Nicety* with *Nicety* undoe?
And makes the *Labyrinth* the *Labyrinth's* clew?
That *sleight* by *sleight* subdues, and clearly proves,
Truth hath her *Serpents* too, as well as *Doves*,
Now, you that blast his *Innocence*, Survey,
And view the *Triumph* of this *Glorious day*;
Could you (if that might be) if you should come
To seal God's cause with your own *Martyrdom*,
(Could all the blood whose Tydes move in their veins,
Which then perhaps were *Blood*, but now in stains)
(Yield it that *Force* and *strength*, which it hath took
Should we except his *Bloud*) from *this* his *Book*,
Your *Flame* or *Axe* would lesse evince to Men,
Your *Block* and *Stake* would prop lesse than his *Pen*;
   Is he *Apostate*, whom the *Baites* of *Rome*
Cannot seduce, though all her *Glories* come?
Whom all her specious *Honours* cannot hold,
Who hates the snare although the *Hook* be *Gold*?
Who *Prostituted Titles* can despise,
And from *despised Titles*, greater *Rise*?

Whom *Names* cannot *Amuse*, but seats withall
The *Protestant* above the *Cardinall* ?
Who *sure* to his own Soul, doth scorn to find
A *Crimson cap* the *Purchase* of his *Minde* ?
  " Who *is* not Great, may blame his Fate's Offence,
  " Who would not be, is Great in's Conscience.
Next these His *Sweat* and *Care* how to advance
The *Church* but to Her *Just Inheritance*,
How to gain back her *Own*, yet *none Beguile*,
And make her *Wealth* her *Purchase*, nor her *spoyle* :
Then, shape Gods worship to a *joynt consent* ;
'Till when the seamlesse Coat must still be *Rent* ;
Then, to repair the *Shrines*, as *Breaches* sprung,
Which we should *hear*, could we lend *Pauls* a *Tongue*,
  Speak, Speak great *Monument* ! while thou yet art *such*,
And Rear him 'bove their *Scandals* and their *Touch* ;
Had he surviv'd thou mightst in Time Declare,
Vast things may *comely* be, and *Greatest Fair*.
And though thy *Limbs spread high*, and *Bulk exceed*,
Thou'dst prov'd that *Gyants* are no *monstrous breed* :
Then 'bove *Extent* thy *Lustre* would prevaile,
And 'gainst *Dimension Feature* turn the Scale ;
But now, like *Pyrrah's half adopted Birth*.
Where th' issue part was *Woman*, Part was *Earth*,
Where *Female* some, and some to *stone* was Bent,
And the *one half* was t'others *Monument*,
Thou must imperfect lye, and learn to Groan,
Now for his *Ruine*, straightway for *thine own* :
But *this* and *Thousand* such *Abortives* are ;
By *Bloody Rebels* Ravisht from his care ;
But yet though some miscarried in their *Wombe*,
And *Deeds Still-born* have hastned to the *Tombe*,

God (that Rewards him now) forbad his store,
Should all lye hid, and he but give ith' *Ore.*
Many are *Stampt,* and *shapt,* and do still shine,
Approv'd at *Mint,* a firm, and *Perfect Coyne.*
Witness that *Mart* of *Books* that yonder stands.
Bestow'd by him, though by *anothers* Hands :
Those *Attick Manuscripts,* so *rare a Piece,*
They tell the *Turk,* he hath not conquer'd *Greece.*
Next these, a second *beautuous Heap* is thrown,
Of *Eastern Authors,* who were *all his own.*
Who in so *Various Languages* appear,
Babel, would scarce be their *Interpreter.*
  To *These,* we may that *Fair-Built Colledge* bring,
Which proves that Learning's no such *Rustick* thing ;
Whose *structure* well contriv'd doth not relate
To *Antick fineness,* but *strong lasting state :*
Beauty well mixt with *strength,* that it complyes
Most with the *Gazer's* use, much with his *Eyes,*
On *Marble Columns* thus the *Arts* have stood,
As wise *Seth's Pillars* sav'd 'em in the *Flood.*
But did he leave here *Walls,* and only Own
A Glorious *Heap,* and make us rich in *Stone?*
Then had our *Chanc'lour* seem'd to fail, and here
Much honour due to the *Artificer :*
But *this* our *Prudent Patron* long fore-saw,
When he Refin'd *rude Statutes* into *Law ;*
Our *Arts* and *Manners* to his *Building* falls,
And he erects the *Men,* as well as *Walls :*
  " Thus *Solons Laws* his *Athens* did Renown,
  " And turn'd that *throng of Building* to a *Town.*
Yet neither *Law* nor *Statute* can be known
So *strickt,* as to *Himself* he made his *own,*

Which in his Actions *Inventory* lyes,
Which *Hell* or —— can never scandalize :
Where every Act his rigid eye surveyes,
And *Night* is *Barre* and *Judge* to all his Dayes;
Where all his secret Thoughts he doth comprize,
And every *Dream* summon'd to an *Assize* ;
VVhere he *Arraigns* each *Circumstance* of care,
VVhich never parts dismiss'd without a *Prayer* :
See ! how he *sifts* and *searches* every part,
And ransacks all the Closets of his heart ;
He puts the hours upon the *Rack* and *Wheel*,
And all his *minutes* must *confess* or *feel*;
If they reveal one Act which forth did come.
VVhen *Humane frailty* crept into the *Loome*,
If one Thread stain, or sully, break, or faint,
So that the *Man* does Inteerrupt the *Saint*,
He hunts it to its *Death*, nor quits his feares,
Till't be *Embalm'd* in *Prayers*, or *drown'd* in *Teares*.
    The *Sun* in all his journeys ne're did see
One more *devout*, nor one more *strict* than He.
    Since his *Religion* then's *Vnmixt* and *Fine*,
And *Works* do *warrant* Faith, as Ore the Mine :
VVhat can his *Crime* be then ? Now you must lay
The *Kingdoms Laws subverted* in his way :
See ! no such *Crime* doth o're his *Conscience* grow,
(VVithout which *Witness* ne're can make it so ;)
A clear Transparent *White*, bedecks his mind,
VVhere nought but *Innocence* can shelter find,
Witnesse that *Breath* which did your *stain* and *blot*
Wipe freely out, (though *Heaven* I fear will *not*)
Witnesse that *Calme* and *Quiet* in His *Breast*,
Prologue and *Preface* to his *Place* of *Rest* ;
When with the *VVorld* He could undaunted part,
And see in *Death* not *meagre Looks* ; nor *Dart* :

When to the *Fatal Block* His *Gray Age* goes
With the same *Ease*, as when he took *Repose*.
"He like old *Enoch* to His Blisse is gone,
"'Tis not his Death, but his Translation.

A Mock Remonstrance referring to the Porters Petition.

To Pym *King of the Parliamented,*
The Grievances are here presented
Of Porters, Butchers, Broom-men, Tanners,
That fain would fight under your Banners;
Weavers, Dyers, Tinkers, Coblers,
And many other such like Joblers,
As Water-men, and those call'd Dray-men,
That have a long time sung Solamen, *&c.*

WHereas, *Imprimis*, first, that is, the Porters,
The heavy burthens laid on their four Quarters
Is not complain'd of here; nor of Us, any,
Although We have good Causes, and full many,
As yet unknown; but there's a day will come
Shall pay for all, We say no more but Mum.'
It is well said by some, You are about
To give the Church and Government a Rout,
Let it be so cry VVe, for it is known,
To do't, you will want more hands than your own.
And since you are * necessitated to
Raise war, 'ifaith (Sirrevence) do, do, do;
'Tis fit that Old things should grow out of date,
Like *Hampden's* Sister, or the Beldame *Kate.*

* *Their Declaration.*

Old things in course do commonly decay,
When New perhaps may last full many a day ;
Old Frocks, old Shirts, old Brooms, old Boots, old Skins
Are much addicted to the Venial sins
Of wearing out; and why not then the Church,
That has left many a simple man ith' lurch.
Besides, the Porters so the Surplice hate,
Their very Frocks they have casheer'd of late ;
And rather than endure 'em you may see,
They wear the Rope, the Hang-mans Livery.
The Butchers too, inspired are at least,
And know the very Intrails of the Beast
That wears those * Smocks, and though they love a Whore,
A *Babilonish* one they do abhor.
In fine, in this great work of Reformation,
Which you intend shall stigmatize the Nation,
We pray to be Fellow-labourers, and
That you our Vertues right may understand,
Know that the Porters shall for Eighteen-pence
Carry the Dreggs of *Rome* in Bottles hence
To any Foreign part you'l think upon,
And bring the Juyce of the *Turks Alcaron*
In lieu of it ; the Butcher kill'd in Slaughter
Shall send Gods, and the Laws Disciples after :
There shall not a Religious Relique be
Left in the Church, or in the Library,
But shall be swept away by the Nice hand
Oth' Broom-mens Art, who nothing understand
More than *Kent-street* ; If any them deride,
The *Tanners* come, and then beware their Hide ;
And for the Weavers, they can preach, or pray,
As is well known to the Lords, *Brooks* and *Say*.

* *Surplices.*

The Dyers they delight you know in Scarlet,
And care no more for Blood, than any Varlet;
Like Archers good they will come on so powring,
That who escapes them will escape a scowring.
The Tinkers they can both make Holes, and mend 'em
In Church or State; if you will but befriend 'em
With Mettle; They care not for God or Divell;
A Pack of Sturdy Rogues inur'd to Evill.
The Cobler vows, and that you'l say is News,
To venture All, what over Boots, o're Shooes?
And likewise undertakes at a Cheap rate
The Government, though Crabbed, to Translate.
The Water-men more slye than any Otters,
Knowing 'tis good fishing in troubl'd Waters,
If any do Oppose them, though their Betters,
They will betake themselves unto their Stretchers,
And so belabour 'em in Church and Cloysters,
Their Bones shall rattle, like a Sacke of Oysters,
In their thin Skins. The Dray-men likewise shall
With Crusted Fists, fling 'um and fling 'um all.
 Thus in Our several Functions We can serve ye,
Men fit for your Employment, pray observe ye,
And therefore list Us, where your best defence is,
In th' Yealow Regiment of's *Oxcellencies*:
So taking leave, resting at your Commands,
We do subscribe either Our Horns, or Hands.

The Caution.

A SONG.

To the Tune of *Oh Women, Monstrous Women.*

YOu Sep'ratists that Sequister
    Your selves from Laws are good,
Your Courses so irregular
    Shall now be understood ;
Your fond Expounding corrupts the Bibble,
Yet you'l maintain it with your Twibble.
*Oh Roundheads, Roundheads, damnable Roundheads,
What do you mean to do?*

He that does swear, though to a Truth,
    You count him far worse than a Lyer,
Yet you will firk your Sister *Ruth*,
    So it may edify her ;
You, like the Devil, abhor a Crosse,
But I'le have as good Reason from *Pyms* Stone-horse.
*Oh Roundheads, Roundheads, damnable Roundheads,
What do you mean to do?*

Our Churches Hierarchy you hold
    Within a foul Suspition ;
And say the Prelates Sleeves are old
    Reliques of Superstition ;
The very Ragges of *Rome* they are
Such as the Whores of *Babilon* wear.
*Oh Roundheads, Roundheads, damnable Roundheads,
What do you mean to do?*

Therefore in Zeal and Piety,
   You'l dy their Lawn in blood,
And root out their Society,
   A work you think is good ;
The Malice is, some of your Eares
Were cropt far shorter than your hairs.
*Oh Roundheads, Roundheads, damnable Roundheads,
What do you mean to do ?*

When you the Miter have pull'd down,
   You'l be hang'd before contented,
Your next Pluck must be at the Crown,
   A Plot long since invented ;
But *Grigge* swears *Tyburn* shall have her due,
Hee'l behang'd himself, if he hang not you.
*Oh Roundheads, Roundheads, damnable Roundheads,
What do you mean to do ?*

The Coblers were astonished,
   The Porters eke, also ;
To hear the Noyse that ecchoed
   From your vast *Tubb* below :
But let him be hang'd will never mend,
The Cobler thinks upon his end.
*But you to whom my Lines do tend
Have a care of what you do.*

Lilly contemn'd.

A SONG.

WHy art thou sad ? Our Glasses flow
   Like little Rivers to the Mayne ;

And ne're a man here has a Shrew,
  What need'st thou then complain?
  Then Boys mind your Glass,
  And let all News pass
That treats not of this our Canary,
  Let Lawyers fear their Fate,
  In the turn of the State,
We suffer if this do miscarry,
Chor. *'Tis this will preserve us 'gainst* Lillies *predictions.*
    And make us contemn our Fate and his Fictions.

'Tis this that setts the City Ruff;
  And lynes the Aldermen with Fur;
It makes the Watchmen stiff and tuff
  To call, *where go you Sir?*
    'Tis this doth advance
    The Cap of Maintenance,
  And keeps the Sword sleeping or waking;
    It Courage doth raise
    In such Men now adaies,
  That heretofore cry'd at Head-aching,
Chor. *'Tis this doth infuse in a Miser some pity,*
    And is the Genius, and Soul of the City.

Then why should we dispair, or think
  The Enemy approacheth near?
Let such as never used to drink
  Sack, be enslav'd to Fear.
    Then to get Honor,
    And that waits on her,
  Strange Titles, *Illustrious* and *Mighty.*
    Wee'l have a smart Bout
    Shall speak us men and stout,
  And I'le be the first that shall fight ye.

Chor. *He that stifly can stand to't, and hath the best Braine;*
Shall be styl'd Son of Mars *and God of the Mayne.*

A Monster to be seen at VVestminster.
1642.

Within this House is to be seen
Such a Monster as hath not been
At any time in *England,* nay
In *Europe, Africk, Asia.*
'Tis a Round body, without a Head
Almost three years, yet not dead.
'Tis like that Beast I once did see,
Whose Tayle stood where his Head should be;
And, which was never seen before,
Though't want a head, 'thas Horns good store,
It has very little hair, and yet
You'l say it has more hair than wit,
'Thas many Eyes and many Eares,
'Thas many Jealousies and Fears,
'Thas many Mouths, and many Hands,
'Tis full of Questions and Commands.
'Tis arm'd with Muskets, Pikes, it fears
Naught in the World but Cavaliers;
'Twas born in *England,* but begot
Betwixt the *English* and the *Scot.*
Though some are of Opinion rather
That the Devil was its Father,
And the City, which is worse,
Was its Mother, and its Nurse.

Some say (though perhaps in scorn)
That it was a *Cretan* born,
And not unlike, for't has the fashion
Just as may be of that Nation,
For 'tis a Lyer, none oth' least ;
A slow Belly, an Evil beast ;
Of what Religion none can tell,
It much resembles that in Hell.
Some say it is a Jew disguis'd,
And why, because 'tis circumcis'd ;
For 'twas deprived long ago
Of many a Member wee well know,
In some points 'tis a Jesuited Priest,
In some it is a Calvinist :
For 'tis not Justify'd, it saith
By Good-works, but by Publick Faith.
Some call't an Anabaptist : Some
Think now that Antichrist is come.
A Creature of an uncouth kind,
Both for its Body, and its mind :
Make hast and see't, else 'twill be gon,
For now 'tis sick, and drawing on.

London sad *London*.

AN ECCHO.

WHat wants thee, that thou art in this sad taking ?
    A King
What made him first remove hence his residing ?
    syding.

Did any here deny him satisfaction?
Faction.
Tell me whereon this strength of Faction lyes?
On lyes.
What didst thou do when the King left Parliament?
Lament.
What terms would'st give to gain his Company?
Any.
But how wouldst serve him, with thy best endeavour?
Ever.
What wouldst thou do if here thou couldst behold him?
Hold him.
But if he comes not what becomes of *London*?
Undone.

Upon bringing in the Plate.

A LL you that would no longer
    To a *Monarch* be subjected,
Come away to *Guildhall*, and be there liberall,
    Your Wish shall be there effected.
Come come away, bring your Gold, bring your Jewells,
    Your silver Shap't, or Molten,
If the King *you'l have down, and advance to the Crown*
    Five Members *and* K———

Regard no Proclamations,
    They're Subjects fit to Jest on,
Henry Elsing's far better than *C. R.*
    Resolv'd upon the Question.
        Come, come away, &c.

You *Aldermen* first send in
   Your *Chaines* upon these Summons,
To buy Ropes ends, for all the Kings Friends,
   They're *Traytors* to the Commons.
      Come, come away, &c.

Your *Basons* large, and *Ewers*,
   Unto this use alot them,
If ere you mean your hands to clean
   From th' Sins by which you got them.
      Come, come away, &c.

Bring in your *Cannes* and *Gobletts*,
   You Citizens confiding,
And think it no scorn, to drink in a *Horn*
   Of your own Wives providing.
      Come, come away, &c.

Ye Bretheren strong and lusty,
   The Sisters *Exercise* yee,
Get *Babes* of Grace, and *Spoons* apace,
   Both Houses do advise yee.
      Come, come away, &c.

Let the Religious *Sempstress*
   Her silver *Thimble* bring here,
'Twill be a fine thing in deposing a King,
   To say you had a Finger.
      Come, come away, &c.

Your Childe's redeemed *Whistle*
   May here obtain Admittance,
Nor shall that Cost be utterly lost,
   They'le give you an Acquittance.
      Come, come away, &c.

The Gold and Silver *Bodkin*,
  The Parliament woo'd ha both,
Which oft doth make, the House to take
  A Journey on the Sabboth.
    Come, come away, &c.

You that have store of Mony
  Bring't hither, and be thrifty,
If th' *Parliament* thrive, they'le so contrive
  You shall have back *Four* for *Fifty*.
    Come, come away, &c.

If when the Councell's ended,
  Your Plate you will recover,
Be sure you may the chief Head that day
  On the *Bridge* or *Tower* discover.
    Come, come away, &c.

The Prentices Petition to the Close Committee.

TO you close Members, wee the Young men come
  (If Justice in this house has any Room?)
With a Petition, but it is for peace;
If you are vext, pray let all Quarrells cease;
First, for Religion. (If't be no offence,
Nor hinder things of greater Consequence)
We hope you do suppose there's some such thing,
'Cause 'thas bin often mention'd by the King.
Wee'l hav't establisht, and do hold it fit
That no Lay-Levites ought to meddle with't.

Next, that in spight of Treason, we may have
A happy peace, but that we need not crave,
For when our bodkins cease 'twil be your pleasure
That arms may cease, not wanting wil, but treasure;
Else you'le but put the King to farther trouble,
To beat you to't, and make you Subjects double.
We know y'are powerfull, and can wonders do
Both by your Votes and Ordinances too ;
In case all those Murther'd Innocent men
May by your Votes be made alive again,
Then your admiring Spirits shall perswade us
That neither War nor Famine can invade us :
Till then you'le give us leave to trust our Eyes,
And from our sad Experience, now grow wise :
Let not the Collonell's gaping son o'th' City
Be made the Mouth unto this close Committe ;
Whose gaudy Troope, because they're boyes, he boasts
They are the Children of the Lord of Hosts ;
And knows no reason, (for indeed tis' scant)
Why States are not like Churches Militant.
Next, that Truth, Wisedome, Justice, Loyalty,
And Law, five Members of our Faculty
(Who not by the King ; but you, have been so long
By Votes Expell'd from your Rebellious throng)
May be restored; and in spight of *Pym*
Be heard to speak their mind as well as him.
Which if not granted, we do tell you this,
Your Lord (whose head's in a Parenthesis)
Shall not secure you, but we shall unty
That twisted Rabble of the Hierachy,
Clubs are good payments, and 'mongst other things
Know we are as many Thousands as you Kings.
In the Interim pray tell your fore-horse *Pym*,
Just as he loves the King, so we love him.

Londons *Farewell to the Parliament.*

Farewell to the Parliament, with hey, with hey,
Farewell to the Parliament, with hoe,
　Your dear delight the City,
　Our wants have made us witty,
　And a ——— for the Close Committee,
With a hey trolly, lolly, loe.

Farewell the Lord of *Essex*, with hey, with hey,
Farewell the Lord of *Essex*, with hoe,
　He sleeps till eleven,
　And leaves the Cause at six and seven,
　But 'tis no matter, their hope's in Heaven,
With hey trolly, lolly, loe.

Farewell the Lord *Wharton*, with hey, with hey,
Farewell the Lord *Wharton*, with hoe,
　The Saw-pit did hide him,
　Whilst *Hastings* did out-ride him,
　Then came *Brooks* and he out-ly'd him,
With hey trolly, lolly, loe.

Farewell *Billy Stroud*, with hey, with hey,
Farewell *Billy Stroud*, with hoe,
　He swore all *Whartons* lyes were true,
　And it concern'd him so to do,
　For he was in the saw-pit too,
With hey trolly, lolly, loe.

Farewell the Lord *Brooks*, with hey, with hey,
Farewell the Lord *Brooks*, with hoe,

He said (but first he had got a Rattle)
That but one hundred fell in the Battle,
 Besides Dogs, Whores, and such Parliament
With hey trolly, lolly, loe.   (Cattle,

Farewell *Say* and *Seale*, with hey, with hey,
Farewell *Say* and *Seale*, with hoe,
 May these Valiant Sons of *Ammon*,
 All be Hang'd as high as *Haman*,
 With the old Anabaptist they came on,
With hey trolly, lolly, loe.

Farewell *K*——— with hey, with hey,
Farewell *K*——— with hoe,
 Thy Father writ a Godly Book,
 Yet all was fish that came to the hook,
 Sure he is damn'd though but for his look.
With hey trolly, lolly, loe.

Farewell *K*——— with hey, with hey,
Farewell *K*——— with hoe,
 Thy House had been confounded,
 In vain he had compounded,
 If he had not got a Round-head,
With hey trolly, lolly, loe.

Farewell *D*—— *H*—— with hey, with hey,
Farewell *D*—— *H*—— with hoe
 Twas his Ambition, or his need,
 Not his Religion did the deed,
 But his Widow hath tam'd him of the speed.
With hey trolly, lolly, loe.

Farewell *John Hampden*, with hey, with hey,
Farewell *John Hampden* with hoe,
  Hee's a sly and subtile Fox,
  Well read in *Buchanan* and *Knox*,
  And hees gone down to goad the Oxe,
With hey trolly, lolly, loe.

Farewell *John Pym*, with hey, with hey,
Farewell *John Pym* with hoe,
  He would have had a place in Court,
  And he ventur'd all his partie for't,
  But bribing proves his best support.
VVith hey trolly, lolly, loe.

Farewell *John Pym* with hey, with hey,
Farewell *John Pym* with hoe,
  For all the feign'd disaster
  Of the *Taylor* and the Plaster,
  Thou shalt not be our Master,
VVith hey trolly, lolly, loe.

Farewell Major *Skippon*, with hey, with hey,
Farewell Major *Skippon* with hoe,
  Ye have ordered him to kill and slay,
  To rescue him and run away,
  Provide you vote fair weather, and pay,
VVith hey trolly, lolly, loe.

Farewell our VVorthies all, with hey, with hey,
Farewell our VVorthies all with hoe,
  For they instead of dying,
  Maintain the truth by lying,
  And get victories by flying,
VVith hey trolly, lolly, loe.

Farewell our *Scotch* Brethren, with hey, with hey,
Farewell our *Scotch* Brethren, with hoe,
 They March but to the border,
 But will be brought no farther,
 For neither Ordinance nor Order,
With hey trolly, lolly, loe.

Farewell my little Levites, with hey, with hey,
Farewell my little Levites, with hoe,
 Though you seem to fear him,
 Yet you can scarce forbear him,
 And when you thank him, you but jeer him,
With hey trolly, lolly, loe.

Farewell fears and jealousies, with hey, with hey,
Farewell fears and jealousies, with hoe,
 Which, with lying Declarations,
 Tumults, traytors, and protestations,
 Have been the ruine of two Nations,
With hey trolly, lolly, loe.

Farewell little *Isaack*, with hey, with hey,
Farewell little *Isaack*, with hoe,
 Thou hast made us all, like Asses,
 Part with our Plate, and drink in Glasses,
 Whilst thou growst rich with 2s. Passes,
With hey trolly, lolly, loe.

Farewell to Plate and Money, with hey, with hey,
Farewell Plate and Money, with hoe,
 'Tis going down by water,
 Or something near the matter,
 And a Publique Faith's going after,
With hey trolly, lolly, loe.

Farewell Members five, with hey, with hey,
Farewell Members five, with hoe,
   Next Petition we deliver,
   Sends you packing down the River,
   And the Devil be your driver,
With hey trolly, lolly, loe.

A Song.

*N*Ew-England* is preparing a-pace,
  To entertain King *Pym*, with his Grace,
And *Isaack* before shall carry the Mace,
    For Round-heads Old Nick stand up now.

No surplisse nor no Organs there,
Shall ever offend the Eye, or the Ear,
But a Spiritual Preach, with a 3. hours Prayer,
    For Round-heads, &c.

All things in Zeal shall there be carried,
Without any Porredge read over the buried,
No Crossing of Infants, nor Rings for the Married,
    For Round-heads, &c.

The Swearer there shall punisht be still,
But Drunkennesse private be counted no ill,
Yet both kind of lying as much as you will,
    For Round-heads, &c.

Blow winds, Hoyse sailes, and let us be gone,
But be sure we take all our Plunder along,
That *Charles* may find little when as he doth come,
    For Round-heads Old Nick stand up now.

Sir John Hotham's *Alarm*.

Come Traytors, March on, to the Leader Sir *John*,
    Though King *Charles* his friends disaffect you,
Do not obey him, but obey Devil *Pym*,
    And the Parliament will protect you.

Let us plead that we Fight, for the King and his Right,
    But if he desire for to enter,
Let us Armed appear, and let us all sweare
    Our lives for his sake we will venter.

But if he give Command, to disarm out of hand,
    As we our *Allegiance* do tender,
Let us presently Sweare, that Commanded we are
    By the Parliament not to surrender.

If he desire for to see, what Command that may be,
    We then will resolve him no further,
But intreat him to stay, while we send Post away,
    He shall have a Copy of the Order.

But if he Proclaime, me a Traytor by Name,
    And all you that adhere to my Faction,
What an Honour it will be, when my Country see me,
    Second *Pym* in a Trayterous Action.

But when the King sends, to require amends
    Of the Parliament for such denyal;
Whether Treason or no, the Law shall ne're know,
    I must be put to your Vote for a Tryal.

Part I.   *Rump Songs.*   97

And to put it to the Voice, or the Parliaments choice,
   The House being now so empty ;
If there be such a thing, as God or a King,
   We'll carry it by five in the twenty.

If so please the Fates, as to change our Estates,
   That the King his own Rights doth recover,
We will turn to their way, and the Town will betray,
   Though a Ladder for our pains we turn over.

The Publique Faith.

SOme tell of *Africk* Monsters, which of old,
Vain Superstition did for God-heads hold,
How the *Ægyptians*, who first knowledge spread,
Ador'd their *Apis* with the white Bulls head ;
Apis still fed with Serpents that do hiss,
Hamon, *Osiris*, Monster *Anubis*.
But Sun-burnt *Africk* never had, nor hath
A Monster like our *English Publique Faith* ;
Those fed on Snakes, and satisfi'd, did rest,
This, like the Curtain Gulf, will have the best
Thing in the City, to appease its still
Encreasing hunger, Glutting its lewd will
With Families, whose substance it devours,
Perverting Justice and the Higher Powers ;
Contemning without fear of any Law,
Preying on all to fill its ravenous Maw ;
Whose *Estrich* stomack, which no steele can sate,
Has swallowed down Indies of Gold and Plate :

7

This is the *Publique Faith*, which being led
By th' Cities wealth, has in this Kingdom bred
Such various mischiefs with its viperous breath,
Blasting its peace and happinesse to death ;
And yet this Idoll which our world adores,
Has made men prostitute their truth like Whores,
To its foul Lust, which surely may as well
And soon be satisfi'd, as th' Grave, or Hell;
This preys on Horses, yet that will not do,
Unlesse it may devour the Riders too :
This takes up all the Riches of the Land,
Not by intreaty, but unjust Command,
Borrowing extortively without any day
But the *Greek Calends*, then it means to pay ;
This 'gainst the Law of Nations does surprise
The Goods of Strangers, Kings, & in its wise
Discretion, thinks (though its not worth their note)
They're bound to take the *Publique Faiths* trim Vote
For their security, when this *Publique Faith*
Has broke more Merchants then e're Riot hath,
And yet, good men o'th City, you are proud
To have this Bankrupt *Publique Faith* allow'd
More credit then your King, to this you'll lend
More willingly then ever you did spend
Money to buy your Wives and Children bread,
By such a strange Inchantment being misled
To your undoings ; you who upon Bond,
Nay scarcely upon Mortgage of that Land,
Treble your Moneys value, would not part
With your lov'd Coine, vanquish'd by th' powerfull art
Of this *Magician Publique Faith*, justly install
Him Master of your Bags, the Devil and all
That taught you get them by deceitfull wares,
And sucking in (like Mornings draughts) young Heirs :

Well, certainly if this fine humour hold,
Your Aldermen will have no other Gold
But what's in Thumb-rings, for their ponderous Chains,
They'le be the *Publique Faiths* just lawfull gains,
And have the Honour afterwards to be
Hang'd in them for its Publique *Treachery*.
What will become of you then, Grave and Witty
Inhabitants of this Inchanted City?
Who is't shall those vast Sums to you re-pay,
When Master *Publique Faith* is run away?
Or who shall those prodigious heaps renew,
Which were prodigally decreas'd by you?
Whom the whole world imagin'd men of thrift,
What will your Orphans do? How will they shift,
Whose whole Estates in th' City Chamber, hath
Been given a spoyle to ruin'd *Publique Faith*?
Perhaps you'le pawn your Charter to supply
The worthy wants of your Necessity.
Who is't will take't, when all (but men misled
Like you) know 'tis already forfeited?
Who is't will then into New Coine translate
Such monstrous Cupboards of huge antick Plate?
To *Publique Faiths* vast *Treasury* bring in,
From the Gilt Goblet, to the Silver Pin,
All that was Coinable, and what to do?
Even to create you *Knaves*, and *Traytors* too.
Faith if you chance to come off with your *Lives*,
Your way will be to live upon your *Wives*,
Their *Trading* will be good, when *Fortune* wears
Your Colours in the Caps of th' Cavaliers,
Whose Cuckolds you'll be then, & on your brow,
Wear their Horns, as you *Publique Faith's* do now;
Then, then you'll howle, when you shall clearly see
That *Publique Faith*, was *Publique Treachery*:

Then you'll confess your selves to 've been undone
By *Publique Faith's* man, *Isaack Pennington*;
Then you'll repent that ever you did fling
Such monstrous Sums away against your King;
When he in *Triumph*, with his *War-like Train*,
Shall to your terrour view your *Town* again;
Unlesse his Mercy mittigate his wrath,
Justly conceiv'd 'gainst you and *Publique Faith*;
That Reverent Alderman which did defile
His Breeches at the Mustering ere while,
Shall then again those Velvet Slops bewray,
Cause *Publique Faith* did make him go astray:
Pauls shall be opened then, and you conspire
No more against the Organs in the Quire,
Nor threat the Saints ith' Windows, nor repair
In Troops to kill the Book of Common-Prayer;
Nor drunk with Zeal, endeavour to engrosse
To your own use, the stones of *Cheap-side Crosse*:
Then, then you'll bow your heads, your horns and all,
That so exalted were to save from thrall
Your ruin'd Liberties, and humbly pray
For Mercy, more then upon each *Fast-day*;
When your Seditious Preachers to the throng,
Make Prayers *Ex Tempore* of five hours long;
Lest you by early penitence prevent
Your certain danger, if not punishment,
Which you by no means may so safely do,
As quitting *Publique Faith*, and *Treason* too:
Then, then, though late, you to your grief will find,
That you have walkt (as Moles ith' Earth do) blind
Of your fair reason, and obedient light,
Involv'd in Mists of black Rebellious Night:
If these Instructions will not make you see
Your Errour, may you perish in't for me,

And to your Ruine walk in deathfull path,
That leads to'th Gallows with the *Publique Faith*.

The Sence of the House, or the Reason why those Members who are the Remnant of the two Families of Parliament cannot consent to Peace, or an Accommodation.

To the Tune of *The New-England Psalm,
Huggle Duggle, ho ho ho the Devil he
laught aloud.*

Come come beloved *Londoners*, fy fy you shame us all,
Your rising up for Peace, will make the close Committee fall ;
I wonder you dare ask for that, which they must needs deny,
There's 30. swears they'l have no Peace, and bid me tell you why.

First I'le no Peace quoth *Essex*, my Chaplain sayes 'tis Sin
To loose 100 *l.* a day, just when my Wife lyes in ;
They cry God blesse your Excellence, but if I loose my Place
They'l call me Rebel, Popular Asse, and Cuckold to my face.

You Citizen Fools, quoth *W*—— d' ye talk to me of Peace,
Who not only stole his Majesties Ships, but rob'd him of his Seas,
No no I'le keep the Water still, and have my Ships well man'd,
For I have lost and stole so much, I know not where to land.

Do Brother do, says *H*—— for Peace breeds us no quiet,
Besides my Places to have lost, with sixteen Dishes dyet,
I play'd the *Judas* with the King, which makes the World detest me,
Nay should his Majesty pardon me, 500. would arest me.

K—— said, these *Londoners* deserve to loose their Eares,
For now they'l all obey the King, like Citizen Cavaliers;
Let's vote this Peace a desperate Plot, and send them a denyal,
For if they save the Kingdom, they'le give us a Legal tryal.

The *Welsh-men* rage quoth *S*—— and call me villanous Goat
For plundering *Hereford*'s Aldermens Gownes to make my *Besse* a Coat,
'Tis true the Town did feed me well, for which I took good Fleeces,
But if Peace come they'le tear me and all my Whores in pieces.

Fight fight quoth *Say*, now now hold up these Jealousies
 and Fears,
The work will shew I laid the Plot above these 17.
 years ;
'Tis I that am your Engineer, but if for Peace you vote,
Oh then they'le make me go to Church, or else they'le
 cut my Throate.

My Father *Goodwin* quoth *W———* calls me a silly
 Lad,
And wonders theyl'e ask Peace of me who have been
 lately mad ;
You chuse me *Irish* General, and I chuse to stay
 here,
For should we fight among the Boggs, there's never a
 Sawpit near.

Those Heathen Prentices quoth *Brooks*, that made my
 Coach-man stay,
Bid me be bare, although I spoke but 13. Bulls that
 day,
But if Peace lop off my learned Skull, then all my House
 you'le see
The Sword of *Guy*, the Dun-cows rib, the Asses tooth,
 and me.

I made a *Speech* quoth *R———* when his Excellence first
 began,
For which he swore by a *Pottle of Sack* to make me a
 Gentleman :
But if the King get to *Whitehall* then all my hopes are
 past,
My Father was first Lord of the House, and I shall be
 the last,

Keep Silence, quoth Mr. *Speaker*, but do not hold your peace,
Let's sit, and vote, and hold them too't, for I'le do what you please;
I have had but poor 6000 *l.* besides some Spoons and Bowles,
Nay, grant a Peace, and how shall I be Master of the Rolles?

Then spake 5. Members all at once; who for an Army cry'd,
Last year, quoth they, you rescu'd us, else we had all been try'd:
What though you be almost undone, you must contribute still,
Or wee'le convey, our Trunks away, and then do what you will.

My Venome swells, quoth *H——* that his Majesty full well knows,
And I, quoth *Hampden*, fetcht the *Scots*, from whence this Mischief flows.
I am an Asse quoth *Haslerigg*, but yet I'me deep ith' Plott,
And I, quoth *Stroud*, can lye as fast, as Mr. *Pym* can trott.

But I, quoth *Pym*, your Hackney am, and all your drudgery do,
Have made good Speeches for my self, and Priviledges for you:
I can sit down and look on men, whilst others bleed and fight,
I eat their Lordships meat by day, and giv't their Wives by night.

Then *Vane* grew black ith' face, and swore there's none
    so deep as I,
The Staff and Signet slipt my hand, my Son can tell you
    why,
The name of Peace they say 'tis sweet, but oh it makes
    me shrink,
Straffords Ghost doth haunt me so, I cannot sleep a
    wink.

Were *Strafford* living, *Mildmay* said, he would do me no
    ill,
I hid my self ith' Privy, when the House did pass his
    Bill:
But all my Gold and Silver thread *Gregory* calls his
    own,
Though in a Ship I made my will, I was not born to
    drown.

You found me, quoth Sir *R——— P———* I had been long
    a Knave;
You promis'd I should be so still, if you my Vote might
    have.
And I, quoth *Laurence Whittaker*, agreed to doe so too,
But if you serve old Courtiers thus, they'le do as much
    for you.

This Peace, quoth *Michael Oldsworth*, will bring me never
    a Fee,
Although my Lord have sworn for Peace, and will not
    follow me.
Down, down with Bishops, *Wheeler* said, for I have rob'd
    the Church:
Oh base, will you conclude a Peace, and leave me in
    the lurch.

Who speaks of Peace quoth *Ludlow*, hath neither Sence
    nor Reason,
For I ne're spoke ith' House but once, and then I spoke
    High Treason,
Your meaning was as bad as mine, you must defend my
    Speech,
Or else you make my mouth as foul as was my Fathers
    breech.

I'le plunder Him, quoth *Baynton*, that mentions Peace
    to Me,
The Bishop would not grant my Lease, but now I'le have
    his Fee.
A Gunpowder Monopoly quoth *Evelyn* rais'd my Father,
But if you let this War go down, they'le call me *Powder
    Traytor*.

Oh *Jove*, quoth Sir *John Hotham*, is this a time to treat?
When *Newcastle* and *Cumberland* me to the Walls have
    beat?
You base-obedient Citizens d' ye think to save your
    Lives?
My Sonne and I will serve you all as I have serv'd Five
    Wives.

Indeed, quoth Sir *Hugh Cholmley*, Sir *John* you speak
    most true,
For I have sold, and morgaged, most of my Land to
    you;
My Brother would have serv'd the King, but was forbid
    to stay;
The King fore saw at *Keynton-field*, Sir *Harry* would run
    away.

I went down, quoth Sir *Ralph Stapleton*, with Musquet,
    Pike and Drum,
To fetch Sir *Francis Wortley* up, but truly hee'd not
    come.
Oh Lord, Sir *Robert Harlow* said, how do our Foes
    increase?
I wonder who the Devil it was that first invented
    Peace.

Treason, Treason, Treason, Sir *Walter Earle* cryes out,
Worse than blowing up the *Thames*, the Dagger, or the
    Clout.
Hang me, quoth *Miles Corbet* then, for we are all con-
    founded,
And *Cavaliers* will Cuckold me, as well as did the
    Roundhead.

Quoth Sir *John Wray*, Mr. *Speaker*? I'le end this matter
    streit,
For this which is my Ninth Speech, I'm sure is none of
    my Eight;
I try'd it at my Tables end, my Neighbours know 'tis
    right,
But Peace will make me speak lesse wit, and then fare-
    well your *Knight.*

A-vengeance, quoth *Harry Martin* then, I'le ha no
    Accommodation,
For it was I, that bravely tore his Majesties Proclama-
    tion;
Ith' House I spoke High Treason, I have sold both Land
    and Lease;
I shall not then keep but 3. Whores, A pox upon your
    Peace.

You see beloved Londoners, *your Peace is out of season,*
For which you have the sence of the House, and every Members reason:
Oh do not stand for Peace then, for trust me if you doe,
Each County in the Kingdome will rise and doe soe too.

Essex *Petition to the Best of Princes.*

Sir,

THat *All-Majesty* (from whom you take
Your Heaven-Anointed Scepter) for whose sake
You drink the Dregs of Bitternesse, which turns
Your Crown of Glory, to a Crown of Thornes;
View'd sinfull *Sodom, Sodom* that offended
Even him, as we do you, that vilely blended
His gracious Promises, did wrest his Powers,
And violate his Laws, as we do yours;
Yet urg'd by him whose Zeal brookt no denyal,
Would have sav'd all, if ten were found but loyal.
Great Prince, to whom the Breath of Heaven hath read
The Principles of Mercy, in whose stead
You sit as God to punish, or to spare,
Whose equal Hand can ruine, or repair
Our staggering Fortunes. Pity, and behold
Rebellious *Essex*! People now grown old
In Dis-obedience, who deserv'dly stand
Like Calves, expecting Death from your Just hand.

Part I. *Rump Songs.*

'Twas we that bleated first Rebellion out,
Who being Pulpit-led, not apt to doubt
Our Lecturing Zealots, and but green in reason,
Were made too wise, and frighted into *Treason* :
We are a Cock-brain'd Multitude, a Rabble
Of all Religions, and we daily squabble
About vain shades, and let the substance passe,
Hating good Manners as we hate the Masse ;
Our new discretions every day convince,
Our old Rebellions, 'gainst so mild a Prince
Were scarcely fixt, but a fresh Ordinance comes,
And damns our Conscience into deeper Sums ;
Breaks ope our Houses, Rifles all our Stuff,
Nay more, as if we had not yet enough,
Plunders our very wits ; nay if we do
Shew but a sorry shrug, Malignants too ;
That in so much our people now obeys
As many *Tyrants* as the Year hath dayes :
But we have ten, ten, ten times multiply'd,
And thousands more to that, which have deny'd
To bend their knees to *Baal*, whereof some lye
Cloystered in Grates, where they unpittied, cry
For Superannuated Crusts, and there remain,
Even taking Gods and *Charles* his Name in vain :
Some scorning to be aw'd by Subjects, fled
From their dear *Wives* and *Children* ; led
Like *Theeves* to *Gaols*, saluted with the Curse
Of every Dunghill scurfe, with durt and worse,
Where they are sadly, but yet dearly fed,
Some ag'd, some weak, some dying, and some dead :
For their dear sake (great *Charles*) they undertake
Deaths willing Martyrdome, for *Charles* his sake ;
Be gracious to their County, let her know
That she, a miserable Land, doth owe

Her sweet Redemption to their Congruous merit,
And least they'le abjure what now they scarce inherit,
Let that accustom'd Sun-shine of your Eye
Enrich her soyle, that she may still out-vye
Her Neighbouring Shires, & let that brand which now
She wears, be set on th' Epidemick brow;
And let the Loyal Gentry still be known
By this firm Mark from the perfidious Clown;
Let them, like treacherous slaves, be alwaies bound
To pay Rack-rents, and only Till the ground;
Let neither them nor their base off-spring dare
To be so rich as buy a Purchase there.

Dread Soveraign,
Forgive, Forget, Remember, and Relent,
Resemble him you so much represent,
And when pleas'd Heavens shall set thy Scepter free,
Triumph in *him*, and wee'll triumph in *thee*.

The Cryer.

O Yes, if any Man or Woman,
    Of what degree soever,
Lord, Knight, Esquire, Gentleman, or *Yeoman,*
  Felt-maker, Button-maker, or *Weaver,*
  Coach-man, Cobler, or *Brick-layer,*
    Sheriff, Alderman, or *Mayor,*
     In *City, Town,* or *Country,* hath
    Lost his *Religion,* or his *Faith,*
Let him forthwith repair to th' Cryer
    Of *Westminster,* where let him bring

Part I.   *Rump Songs.*   111

The Mark of what he doth require,
   And he shall hear on't, if *God blesse the King.*

O Yes, if any Man or Woman,
   Of what degree soever,
From the *Marquis,* to the *Yeoman,*
   From the *Straw-hat,* to the *Beaver,*
From the *Land-lord,* to the *Dray-man,*
Whether the *Clergy,* or the *Layman,*
Hath lost a *War-horse-Armes,* or *Dragoones,*
That were the *Treasure* of *Buffoones;*
Jewells, Money, Pearle, or Plate,
Cups for *Service,* or for *State;*
Come to the Cryer, and you then
Shall find them he knows where, but God knows when.

The Cavaliers Prayer.

God blesse the *King* and *Queen,* the *Prince* also,
And all his *Loyal Subjects* both high and low,
For *Roundheads* can pray for themselves we know;
   Which no body can deny.

The Devil take *Pym* and all his Peers,
God blesse Prince *Rupert* and his Cavaliers,
For if they come hither *Pym* will stink with fears;
   Which no body can deny.

God blesse *Rupert* and *Maurice* withall,
That gave the Roundheads a great downfall,
And knockt their Noddles 'gainst *Worcester* wall;
   Which no body can deny.

Lawn sleeves and Surplices must go down,
For why, King *Pym* doth sway the Crown ;
But all are Bishops that wears a Black Gown ;
   Which no body can deny.

Let the Canons roar, and the Bullets flye,
King *Pym* doth swear he'll not come nigh,
He sayes, its a pittyfull thing to dye ;
   Which no body can deny.

The *Horners* they are brave Blades,
I do not know, but it is said
The stout Earl of *Essex* is free of that trade ;
   Which no body can deny.

The Baker over *Burton* cannot domineer,
For it is most firmly reported here,
He's as free of the Pillory as ever they were ;
   Which no body can deny.

There is *Isaack Pennington* both wise and old,
I do not know, but 'tis for truth told
That he is turned poor Sexton of *Pauls.*
   Which no body can deny.

There is a *Lord W*——— both wise and round,
He will meet *Prince Rupert* upon any ground,
And if that his hands behind him be bound ;
   Which few people will deny.

To whom it concerns.

COme, come, ye Cock-brain'd Crew, that can suppose
No truth, but that which travells through the Nose;
That looks on Gods Anointed with those Eyes,
You view your Prentices; ye that can prize
A Stable with a Church; that can Impeach
A Grave Devine, and hear an Hostler preach:
Are ye all mad? has your Fanatick zeal
Stifl'd your stock of Sences at a Meal?
Have ye none left to look upon these Times?
With Grief, which you, and the unpunisht Crimes
Have brought upon this miserable Land?
Are ye all Bruits? not apt to understand
The neighbouring stroke of Ruine, till't be past?
And you become the Sacrifice at last?
What would you have? can Reformation border
On Sacriledge? or Truth upon Disorder?!
Can Rifleing, and Religion dwell together?
Can the way hence be said the next way thither?
Go, ply your Trades, *Mechanicks*, and begin
To deal uprightly, and Reform within;
Correct your prick-ear'd Servants; and perswade
Your long lov'd Arm-fulls; if you can thus trade
In Pigges and Poultry: let them cease to smooth
Your Rumpled Follies, and forbear to sooth
Your pious Treasons, thus to kick and fling,
Against the *Lords Anointed*, and your *King*.

8

By the Author.

That neither loves for *Fashion* nor for *Fear*,
As far from *Roundhead*, as from *Cavalier*.

To the City.

DRaw near you factious Citizens ; prepare
To hear from me what hideous Fools you are ;
What lumps of sordid Earth ; in which we find
Not any least Resemblance of a Mind ;
Unlesse to Baseness and Rebellion bent
Against the King, to ayde the Parliament ;
That Parliament, whose Insolence will undoe
Your Cities Wealth, your Lives, and Safety too :
Are you so stupid, dull, you cannot see
How your best Vertues now are Treachery ?
Apparent Treason, Murder, and the like :
How with unhallowed hands you strive to strike
Him, whom you should your Loyalty afford,
(*Great Charles*) the *blest Anointed of the Lord* ?
How you do daily contribute, and pay
Mony, your Truths and Honours to betray ?
Bigg with Phanatique thoughts, and wilde desire :
'Tis you, that blew up the increasing Fire
Of foul Rebellion, you that only bring
Armies into the *Field* against your *King*;
For were't not for supportment from your Baggs,
That *Great* and *Highest Court* that only braggs

Of your vain folly, long ere this had bin
Punish'd for their bold Sacrilegious sin,
Of *Actual Treason*, there had never come
Upon this Kingdom such a *Martyrdom*.
Armes hang'd up as uselesse, and the State
Retain'd his freedom; had you kept your Plate,
No *Keinton-Battails* had with Mothers curse,
Made Childless there the Treason of your Purse;
The *Publick Purse* o'th *City*; which must be
Esteem'd the Cause of *Publick Misery*;
No *Drums* had frighted *silken Peace* from out
The *Neighbouring Countries*, nor need you about
Your *City* with your *guilded Musquets* goe
Trayning, not for good Service, but for Shew;
That the whole Town may see your *Feathers* spread
Over your *Hatts*, as th' *Hornes* doe o're your *Head*;
The *Humble Parliament* had never dar'd
To have prescrib'd *Laws* to their *King*, but spar'd
Their Zeal in bringing *Innovations*, and
Distractions o're the beautious face oth' *Land*,
They would not then have so Supreamly brought
Their Votes, to bring the Kingdomes *Peace* to nought;
Nor with so sleight a value lookt on Him,
King Charles, and only doted on *King Pym;*
Nor for Authentick doctrine, have allow'd
As Law, the Precepts of Ingenuous *Stroud*;
Hampden nor *Martyn* had not then lookt bigge
Upon their *King*, nor *Arthur Haslerigge;*
Nor yet *K——* on whom we now confer
The style of *Trayterous Earle* of *M——*
Secur'd by you, the *Patrons* of the Cause,
Condemn'd his *Loyalty*, and the *Kingdoms Laws*;
Nor mis-led *Essex*, had not you been, nere

8—2

Had acted on this *Kingdoms Theater*
So many *Tragedies*; nor *Warwick* sought
T" ingrosse the Naval Honours, no nor thought
On any Action so unjust, unmeet,
As keeping from his Majesty his *Fleet;*
Tis you have done all this, y'ave been the Head,
The very Spring from whence this River spread
The streams of foul *Rebellion;* which we know
At last will drown'd you with its over-flow;
You the *Arch-Traytors* are, you, those that slew
The Kingdoms happinesse, and th' Allegiance due
Unto his *Sacred Majesty:* you, you that have
Betray'd this Nations Honour to the Grave
Of lasting Obloquy; you that have destroy'd
The smiling wealth of th' *City*, and made void
The good Opinion, which the *King* before
Had of your Loyalties, and th' Faith you bore
To th' *Royal Stem*; which still has to your great
Advantage made this *City* their *Chief Seat*.
Fond and seditious Fools, d'ye think, yee
Are wiser than Times *numerous Progeny?*
That have Ador'd your *City*, when did *They*
Your harmlesse *Ancestors*, strive to give away
Their Wealth, and Duty from their *Sovereigne Lord*,
To make themselves *Traytors* upon *Record?*
When did they their *Plate* and *Coine* bring in?
To be the Cause of their own *Ruyning?*
They never us'd to fright their *King*, nor draw
Tumults together, to affront the *Law*.
No, nor good *Houses*, their *Corslets* slept, and all
The Armes they us'd hung up in each mans Hall.
They did not then *enamel'd Musquets* carry
To *Train* in *Moor-fields*, and in *Finsbury*:

But did in *Comely Archery excell*,
Like honest grave Children of *Adam Bell*,
And *Climme oth' Clough*, now each of you will be
More than a furious *William Cloudeslee* ;
And trace the Streets with terror, as if *Ven*,
With *Fulk* and *Mannwaring*, were the only Men
Whom you did owe *Allegiance* to ; as if *They*
Could give you priviledge to disobey
The *Royal Mandate*, which does them proclaim
Guilty of *Treason*, and you of the *same* ;
As deeply stand Impeacht, and will at last
Pay dearly for't, when your *vain hopes* are past.
All *succours*, which you *credit* for your *Merit*,
Will be afforded you, by the *help* oth' *Spirit*,
That is the *Devil* ; sure the *Heavenly Powers*,
Will never *Patronize* such *Acts* as *yours*.
Poor baffl'd *City* ! baffled by a *Crue*
Of Men, which are as arrant Fools as you ;
Surely your *Brains* can never be so *dull*
As not *conceive this*, which each *empty Skull*
Must needs *resent* ; how that *their only Ayme*
Is, *to create your City all one Flame*,
And as the *Smoak* and *Sparks* do *up aspire*,
They'le *sit* and *laugh* (like *Nero*) at the *Fire*
Themselves have made ; unlesse your *Heads* be all
Horns and no *Flesh*, you needs must see the *Fall*
That threatens *you*, like *Lightning* : To *eschew*
Which *Ruine*, 'twould be Wisedome to *renue*
Your *lost Allegiance*, and *Repentance* bring,
As a *fresh Victim*, to *appease your King* ;
For be assur'd, *Who to the King's untrue*,
Must in their Nature needs be false to you.

The MONSTER.

Peace, *Vipers* peace, let *Crying blood* nere cease
To haunt your *bloody Souls*, that love not *Peace*.
And curst be that *Religion*, that shall cry,
A *Reformation* with *Phlebotomye*;
Your *Impious Firebrands*, whom the very *Tears*
Of *Growning England*, buried in their *Fears*,
Cannot extinguish; whom the *bleeding Veins*
Of *desperate Ireland*, which even now remains
A very *Golgotha*, cannot asswage
Those *Stripes*, the earnest of *Another Age*
Taste of your *salvage Piety*, and ly
The *Lamb-less Martyrs* of your *Cruelty*;
Whilst you lye softly emb'red, to encrease
The *flames* of *Christendome*, and cry *no Peace*,
Let *Sampsons* coupled *Messengers* convey
Those *Firebrands* hence, and let them make their way
To their own *Houses, consume* and *devaste*,
Burn down their Barnes, and lay their *Graynards waste*,
Demolish all within *doors*, and *without*,
Make havock there, *destroy both Branch and Root*.
Let all their *Servants* flee *amaz'd*; and cry,
Fire, Fire, and let no helping hand be nigh;
Let their *Wives* live, but only live t' appear
Thornes in their *Sides*, and *Thunder* in their *Ears*;
May all their *Sons* run mad into the Street,
And seeking *Refuge* there, there may they meet
Th' *encountering Sword*, and whom it spares to *kill*,
May they be *Slaves*, and labour at the *Mill*:
Let all their *Daughters beg*, and *beg* in *vain*;
Let them be *ravisht* first, and then be *slain*;

Let all their *Kindred* wander up and down,
Like *Vagabonds* be lasht, from *Town*, to *Town*:
Let *basenesse* be Entituled on their *Names*,
Too firm for all recoveries: O let *Shames*,
Reproach, and *Lasting Infamy*, remain
In *deeper Characters* than that of *Cain*;
Let *Caitiff P——* and that *Bloody Plot*,
Be *Sanctified* now, or at least forgot;
And let those *Vipers* vindicate their *Crimes*
In every *Almanack* to after times;
Where may there *Treason* live among their sences,
More firm then Reigns of either *Kings* or *Princes*.
Thus may these *Firebands* thrive, and if this *Curse*
Succeed not, let it yield unto a worse.
For them, let them burn still, till Heaven thinks good,
To *Quench* them in their *Generations Blood*;
So that the *World* may hear them hisse and cry,
Who lov'd not *Peace*, in *Peace* shall never dye.

The Earl of Essex *his Speech to the Parliament after* Keinton *Battle.*

Hail to my *Brother Round-heads*, you that sit
At home, and study *Treason*, 'bove my *Wit*
Or *Valour* to maintain; it's you whose hearts
And brains are stufft with all Devillish darts
Of *Rapine*, and *Rebellion*; yet whose dark
Religious Villanies, hates the least spark
Of Justice or Obedience to the King;

To you, and none but you, true News I bring,
With all my *Fellow Rebells* that survive,
'Mongst whom in faith my self scapt scarce alive :
For when the Cavaliers, and Popish Schollers
Charg'd us so hot, my Coach full of *Rex-dollers*
I could have given to have been ten miles off ;
And though the Zealots of our Party scoff,
And taunt the King's well-wishers, take't from me,
Happy were all the Round-heads that did flee ;
They scapt a scowering, which through very fear
Took me and all my Regiment in th' Rear,
At the first Charge ; for that when we should fight,
We sneakt away, and had more mind to ———
For had I dard, to venture my dear life,
I should have fought once for the *Whore my Wife* ;
Yet I dare swear that we had won the day,
Had not so many fallen and run away :
And yet for all this Blood that hath been spilt,
My Sword is guiltlesse, for fast by the hilt
I held it in my Scabbard, and still cry'd
Well done, Fight on, unto the Fools that dy'd ;
Whilst I stole towards *Warwick*, to avoyd
The Field, with the sad Spectacle quite cloyd :
I lost my Coach, and (which doth make me fret)
I lost *Blake's* Letter in my Cabinet,
That reveal'd all our *Treason*, he good man
Suffer'd at *Oxford*, and unlesse I can
Repent, 'tis said, that I must dye like him,
Be Hang'd and Quarter'd, and you Mr. *Pym* :
We must be cautious, for the Cavaliers
Have desperate souls, concerning those base fears
That brought mee back again ; besides, the King
Has a Just Cause you know, and though we bring

Part I. *Rump Songs.*

The silly Multitude into the Noose,
Our own hearts tell us we are like to loose
Our heads, if *Charles* prevail; which we must do
If he proceeds thus, to kill ten for two
You must provide new Armour, and more Armes,
And a new Generall, that dares hear *Alarms*
Of *Drums* and *Trumpets;* one that may have sence
And valour to excell my Excellence.
The *Peevish Women* as I pass'd the *Strand*,
Blesse me knee deep, and would have kiss'd my hand,
As King, whilst I most curteously vayl'd
My Hat, and Feather to them, others rayl'd;
And them as wisht, or knew I had the worst,
For one that pray'd for me, devoutly curst.
The truest News of all I hope to tell ye,
Is that I have more mind to fill my belly,
Then fight again, for that same *Dutchland Devil*,
Rupert, the Prince of mischief, and all evil,
My Victuals took away, and burst my *Waggons*,
Whilst the *Kings Forces* fought with fiery *Dragoons*,
And beat me out o'th' *Field*; although we blind
The Multitude, and say w' had sea and wind,
Yet I protest the Elements themselves
Conspir'd to ruine us, *Rebellious Elves*:
And to conclude, from *Jeering Cavalier*,
Has put upon us, in a *Song*, this Jeer,
Rather than they should have the betters,
That you and I were drawn and hang'd, &c.

A Dialogue between two ZEALOTS upon the &c. in the Oath.

Sir *Roger* from a zealous piece of Freeze,
Rais'd to a Vicar of the Children threes;
Whose yearly Audit may, by strict account,
To twenty Nobles, and his vails Amount;
Fed on the common of the female charity,
Untill the *Scots* can bring about their parity,
So shotten, that his Soul like to himself,
Walks but in *Querpo* : this same Clergy Elf,
Encountring with a Brother of the Cloth,
Fell presently to Cudgels with the Oath :
The Quarel was, a strange mis-shapen Monster
&c. (God blesse us !) which they conster
The brand upon the buttock of the Beast,
The Dragons tayle ty'd on a knot, a neast
Of young *Apocraphas*, the fashion
Of a new mental Reservation.
    While *Roger* thus divides the text, the other
Winks and expounds, saying, My pious Brother,
Hearken with reverence ; for the point is nice,
I never read on't, but I fasted twice ;
And so by revelation know it better,
Than all the Idolaters o'the Letter.
With that he swell'd, and fell upon the Theam,
Like great *Goliah* with his Weavers beam :
I say to thee, *&c.* thou ly'st,
Thou art the curled lock of Antichrist :
Rubbish of *Babel*, for who will not say,

Tongues were confounded in &c?
Who swears &c. swears more Oaths at once
Than *Cerberus* out of his triple Sconce :
Who views it well, with the same eye beholds
The old half Serpent in his numerous folds.
Accurst &c. thou, for now I scent,
What lately the prodigious Oysters meant.
Oh *Booker*, *Booker*, how cam'st thou to lack
This Sign in thy prophetick Almanack?
It's the dark Vault wherein th' infernal plot
Of Powder 'gainst the State was first begot.
Peruse the Oath, and you shall soon descry it,
By all the Father *Garnets* that stand by it ;
'Gainst whom the Church, whereof I am a Member,
Shall keep another fifth day of *November* :
Yet here's not all, I cannot halfe untrusse
&c. it's so abominous.
The *Trojan* Nag was not so fully lin'd !
Unrip &c. and you shall find
Og the great Commissary, and which is worse,
Th' Apparatour upon his skew-ball'd horse.
Then (finally my Babe of Grace) forbear,
&c. will be too far to swear ;
For 'tis (to speak in a familiar style)
A *York-shire* wea-bit, longer than a mile.
 Then *Roger* was inspir'd, and by Gods-diggers,
Hee'l swear in words at large, and not in Figures.
Now by this drink, which he takes off as loath
To leave &c. in his liquid Oath.
His Brother pledg'd him, and that bloody wine,
He swears shall seal the Synods *Cataline*.
So they drunk on, not offering to part
Till they had quite sworn out th' eleventh quart :

While all that saw and heard them, joyntly pray,
They and their tribe were all, &c.

The Publique Faith.

STand off my Masters : 'Tis your pence apeece,
Jason, Medea, and the Golden Fleece ;
What side the line good Sir ? Tigris, or Po ?
Lybia ? Japan ? Whisk ? or Tradinktido ?
St. Kits ? St. Omer ? or St. Margaret's Bay ?
Presto begon ? or come aloft ? what way ?
Doublets ? or Knap ? the Cog ? low Dice ? or high ?
By all the hard names in the Letany,
Bell, Book and Candle, and the Pope's great toe
I conjure thy account : Devil say no.
   Nay, since I must untruss, Gallants look to't,
Keep your prodigious distance forty foot,
This is that *Beast of eyes* in th' *Revelations*,
The *Basilisk* has twisted up three Nations.
Ponteus Hixius doxius, full of tricks,
The *Lottery* of the vulgar lunaticks.
The *Knapsack* of the State, the thing you wish,
Magog and *Gog* stew'd in a Chaffendish
A bag of Spoons and Whistles, wherein men
May whistle when they see their Plate agen.
Thus far his Infancy : his riper age
Requires a more mysterious Folio page.
Now that time speaks him perfect, and 'tis pity
To dandle him longer in a close Committee,
The Elf dares peep abroad, the pretty Fool
Can wag without a truckling standing-stool ;

Revenge his Mother's infamy, and swear
Hee's the fair Off-spring of one half-score year;
The Heir of the House and hopes, the cry
And wonder of the Peoples misery.
'Tis true, while as a Puppy it could play
For Thimbles, any thing to passe the day;
But now the Cub can count, arithmetize,
Clink *Mascnello* with the *Duke* of *Guise*;
Sign for an *Irish purchase*, and traduce
The *Synod* from their Doctrine to their Use;
Give its Dam suck, and a hidden way
Drinks up arrears *a tergo mantica*.
An everlasting Bale, Hell in Trunk-hose,
Uncased, the Divel's *Don Quixot* in prose.
The Beast and the false Prophet twin'd together,
The squint-eyed emblem of all sorts of weather.
The refuse of that Chaos of the earth,
Able to give the World a second birth.
Affrick avaunt! Thy trifling Monsters glance
But Sheeps-eyed to this Penal Ignorance.
That all the Prodigies brought forth before
Are but Dame Natures blush left on the score.
This strings the Baker's dozen, christens all
The cross-leg'd hours of time since *Adam's* fall.
 The Publick Faith? why 'tis a word of kin,
A Nephew that dares *Cozen* any sin.
A Term of Art, great *Bohemoth's* younger Brother,
Old *Machiavel*, and half a thousand other.
Which when subscrib'd writes *Legion*, names on truss,
Abaddon, Belzebub, and *Incubus,*
All the *Vice-Royes* of darkness, every spell
And Fiend wrap'd in a short Trissillable.
 But I fore-stall the Show. Enter and see,
Salute the Door, your *Exit* shall be free.

In brief 'tis call'd Religions ease, or loss ;
For no one's suffer'd here to bear his crosse.

A Committee.

Cast *Knaves* my *Masters*, fortune guide the chance,
No packing I beseech you, no by-glance
To mingle pairs, but fairly shake the bag,
Cheats in their spheres like subtile spirits wag.
Or if you please the Cards run as they will,
There is no choyce in sin and doing ill.
Then happy man by's dole, luck makes the ods,
He acts most high that best out-dares the gods.
These are that *Raw-bon'd Herd* of *Pharaoh*'s Kine,
Which eat up all your Fatlings, yet look lean.
These are the after-claps of bloudy showres,
Which, like the *Scots*, come for your guide and yours.
The Gleaners of the Fielde, where, if a man
Escape the sword, that milder frying-pan ;
He leaps into the fire, cramping the claws
Of such can speak no English but the Cause.
Under that foggy term, that Inquisition,
Y' are wrackt at all adventures *On suspition :*
No matter what's the crime, a good estate's
Delinquency enough to ground their hate.
Nor shall calm innocence so scape, as not
To be made guilty, or at least so thought.
And if the spirit once inform, beware,
The flesh and world but renegadoes are.

Part I. *Rump Songs.*

Thus once concluded, out the *Teazers* run,
And in full cry and speed till *Wat*'s undone.
So that a poor *Delinquent* fleec'd and torn
Seems like a man that's creeping through a horn,
Finds a smooth entrance, wide, and fit, but when
Hee's squeez'd and forc'd up through the smaller end,
He looks as gaunt and pin'd, as he that spent
A tedious twelve years in an eager Lent;
Or bodies at the *Resurrection* are
On wing, just rarifying into aire.
The *Emblem* of a man, the pitied *Case*
And shape of some sad being once that was.
The *Type* of flesh and blood, the Skeleton
And superfices of a thing that's gone.
The winter quarter of a life, the tinder
And body of a corps squeez'd to a cinder;
When no more tortures can be thought upon,
Mercy shall flow into oblivion.
   Mercifull Hell! thy Judges are but three,
Ours multiform, and in plurality!
Thy calmer censures flow without recall,
And in one doom souls see their finall All.
We travel with expectance: Suffrings here
Are but the earnests of a second fear.
Thy plagues and pains are infinite; 'tis true;
Ours are not only infinite, but new.
So that the dread of what's to come, exceeds
The anguish of that part already bleeds.
   This only difference swells 'twixt us, and you,
Hell has the kinder *Devils* of the two.

The Model of the New Religion.

Whoop! *Mr. Vicar* in your flying frock?
What news at *Babel* now? how stands the *Cock!*
When wags the floud? no *Ephimerides*?
Nought but confounding of the languages?
No more of th' Saints arival? or the chance
Of three pipes two pence and an ordinance?
How many Queer-Religions? clear your throat,
  May a man have a peny-worth? four a groat?
Or do the *Jansto* leap at truss-a-fayle?
Three Tenents clap while five hang on the tayle?
No *Querpo model*? never a knack or wile?
To preach for Spoons and Whistles? cross or pile?
No hints of truth on foot? no sparks of grace?
No late sprung light? to dance the wilde-goose chase?
No *Spiritual Dragoones* that take their flames
From th' inspiration of the City Dames?
No crums of comfort to relieve your cry?
No new dealt mince-meat of Divinity?
  Come lets's project: by the great late *Eclipse*
We justly fear a famine of the lips.
For Sprats are rose an *Omer* for a sowse,
Which gripes the conclave of the lower House.
Let's therefore vote a close humiliation
For opening the seal'd eyes of this blind Nation,
That they may see confessingly, and swear
They have not seen at all this fourteen year;
And for the splints and spavins too, tis said
All the joynts have the *Riffcage*, since the head

Swell'd so prodigious, and exciz'd the parts
From all *Allegiance*, but in tears and hearts.
  But zealous *Sir*, what say to a touch at Prayer?
How *Quops* the spirit? In what garb or ayre?
With *Souse* erect, or pendent, winks, or haws?
Sniveling? or the extention of the jaws?
Devotion has its mode: *Dear Sir*, hold forth,
Learning's a venture of the second worth.
For since the peoples rise and its sad fall,
We are inspir'd from much, to none at all.
  Brother adieu! I see y'are closely girt,
A costive *Dover* gives the *Saints* the squirt.
Hence (Reader) all our flying news contracts
Like the *States Fleet*, from the *Seas* into *Acts*:
  But where's the Model all this while, you'll say
'Tis like the Reformation, run away.

To a Fair Lady weeping for her Husband Committed to Prison by the Parliament. 1643.

TUsh, let them keep him if they can,
  He's not in hold while you are free,
Come, sigh no more, but pledge the man,
  What though in Fetters, yet can he
  Be Prisoner unto none but thee;
Then dry your Eyes, for every tear
Makes them like drowned worlds appear.

Post through the Aire, my fancy went,
  With wings disguis'd, and there stood by
When he was brought to th' Parliament,
  And streight *to th' Bar, to th' Bar*, they cry,
  The smiling Captain asked, *Why?*
With that they soon drew up his Charge,
Which Lady you shall hear at large.

Imprimis, he was married late,
  With a Gold Ring, unto a Dame,
Would make the best of us a Mate;
  Witty, Pretty, Young, and Quaint,
  And fairer then our selves can Paint:
Her lips do set mens teeth on edge,
Sure 'tis a Breach of Priviledge.

And her Malignant beauty, can
  Provoke our Members up to rise,
Nay make our General prove a man;
  And the Star-Chamber of her Eyes,
  Robs Subjects of their Liberties:
And then her voice keeps Eares in awe,
Even like the High-Commission Law.

Nay more, the fair Delinquent hath
  A pair of Organs in her throat,
Which when she doth inspire with breath,
  She can command in every noat,
  More then both our Houses Vote
Her very Hair, put in Array,
Can fetter our Militia.

Her Cheeks still Natures Pattent have,
  Not yet call'd in, for only she

In them ingrossed all that's brave,
  And other Ladies Hucksters be,
  Her Beauty's the Monopolie;
When theirs is spent, to her they come,
And chaffer with her face for some.

She keeps an Alter on her brow,
  Her Eyes two Tapers on each side,
There Superstitious Lovers bow;
  Her Name is *Mary* too beside,
  Who owns a Faith that's sanctifi'd;
Let's clap up him till further leisure,
And send for her to wait our pleasure.

Then go fair Lady, follow him,
  Fear no *Trumpet*, fear no *Drum*,
Fair Women may prevail with *Pym*,
  And one sweet smile when there you come,
  Will quickly strike the *Speaker* dumb:
If not, then let one tear be spent,
And 'twill dissolve the Parliament.

Mr. Fullers *Complaint*.

ENgland once *Europes* joy,
    Now her scorn;
  Ambitious to be forlorn,
    Self, by self torn;
      Stand amaz'd?
      Thy woes are blaz'd,
    By silence best,
And wanting words, even wonder out the rest.

Help Gracious King,
The source and spring
  Of all our bliss,
    Alas the fault's not his;
Good Prince how is he griev'd,
  That he's mistook?
  Or what's a Curse,
Far worse, he is not believ'd.

Help long-wisht for Parliament,
If so good by your intent;
  And will,
  And skill,
Why ill is your successe?
  Alas Malignant humors lurk,
  And cause the Physick not to work,
To give our woes redresse.

Help in the Law, ye Learned Sages,
Studied well in former ages:
  But our Rents
  Are above all Presidents;
    In fight, what's might,
    That's right:
For Statutes are by Lawyers awed,
And Common-law by Canon-law out-lawed.

Help ye Divines our souls to plaister,
Settle the Legacy which your Master
  Bequeath'd to his own at his decease,
  Even Peace:
    Alas alas in *Gilead*,
    Where is no balm for to be had;

O Cruell,
They that should holy water bring, bring fiery fuell.

No help, no help,
    Why then 'tis vain
    For to complain;
        And why men sin with all their heart,
        Sorrow only but in part;
    And still they cry
        That all is ill,
And love to make't and keep't so still.

Since then our wounds
    Are grown so wide,
    And all means try'd,
    And all deny'd;
        Good God help us at last,
        Before all help be past,
For this is sure,   (cure.
Men made the wounds, but God alone can help the

Upon wearing the Kings Colours.

Alas, what take ye pepper in the Nose
To see King *Charles* his Colours worne in Pose?
'Twas but an Ornament to grace the Hat,
And must we have an Ordinance for that?
O serious worthies! how can you dispence
With so much time to draw a Grievance thence?
But you do very well to make it known,
When others Liberties surmounts your own;

You can and will suppresse it, well, you may
Do even what you please, we must obey;
I hope you'll take in hand the *Taylors Trade*,
And teach us how our *Apparell* must be made,
That women in a Vote shall plainly see
How wider their Smocks and Petticoats shall be;
If this continue, faith turn *Barbars* too,
And cut our hair of the same length you do;
And let it be no less a Crime then *Treason*,
To wear, do, or speak any thing that's reason:
As for the King, you'll say he's King, 'tis true,
But he can rule himself, and order you:
What, can he so? he's mightily too blame,
And faln into displeasure for the same;
He will not grant that you're his Friends 'tis true,
Should you rule two Kingdoms as a third does you.
Lest from a Ribbin then, should spring a Faction,
'Twas wisely done to stop its growth i'th' Action;
Yet in despight of you, that this controule,
I'le wear my Soveraigns Colours in my *Soul*.

A Western Wonder.

D O you not know, not a fortnight agoe,
    How they brag'd of a Western wonder?
When a hundred and ten, slew five thousand men,
    With the help of Lightning and Thunder.

There *Hopton* was slain, again and again,
    Or else my Author did lye;
With a new *Thanksgiving*, for who are living,
    To God, and his Servant *Chudleigh*.

But now on which side, was this Miracle try'd,
  I hope we at last are even ;
For Sir *Ralph* and his Knaves, are risen from their Graves,
  And Cudgel'd the Clowns of *Devon*.

And now *St.*—— came, for his Honour was lame
  Of the Gout three months together ;
But it prov'd when they fought, but a running Gout,
  For his heels were lighter then ever.

For now he out-runs, his Armes and his Guns,
  And leaves all his money behind him ;
But they follow after, unlesse he take water
  At *Plymouth* again, they will find him.

What *Reading* hath cost, and *St.* —— hath lost,
  Goes deep in the Sequestration ;
These wounds will not heal, with your new Great Seal,
  For *Jepsons* Declarations.

Now *Peters*, and *Case*, in their Prayer and Grace,
  Remember their new *Thanksgiving;*
Isaack and his *Wife*, now dig for their life,
  And shortly must do't for their living.

A SONG.

THe world is now turn'd upside-down,
  'Tis thought K. *Charles* will keep his Crown,
The *Roundheads* now shall all be put down,
    And alas poor Parliament now, now, now.

Prince *Rupert* made fair work t'other day,
He kild all the Troopers that durst to stay,
The rest he kild, their Horses running away:
    And alas poor Parliament now, now, now.

And *Essex* his hornes hung so in his light,
Alas poor Cuckold, he could not see to fight,
And both Houses they were all ready to ⸺
    And alas poor Parliament now, now, now.

Then send for *W*⸺ and give him good pay,
He'le hoise up his Sayles and carry you away,
In hopes you'le stand his Friend another day:
    And alas poor Parliament now, now, now.

Upon *Alderman* Atkins *bewraying his Slops on the great Training day.*

I Sing the strange adventures and sad Fate,
That did befall a Collonel of late,
A portly Squire; a Warlike hardy wight,
And pity 'tis, we cannot call him Knight,
A stout man at Custard, and Son of *Mars*,
But oh the foul disaster of his ⸺
Before the *Worthies*, and the rest beside,
Who saw how he his Courser did bestride,
Weilding his *Truncheon*, like a *Weavers* beam,
And yet ⸺ his hose in every seam;
I cannot tell how fair he was i'th' Cradle,
But sure I am he was foul enough i'th' Saddle:

For feats of *Armes* none could come near him then,
He smelt so strong, and when eight thousand men
Discharg'd their Musquets, he discharged too,
But what? his Office and his Guts? what though
He made a House of Office of his Hose?
Stand further off, if it offend your Nose:
Belike he meant to hansell his New Satten,
Or, like fat Oxen, in his dung to batten;
But when in triumph he from *Finsbury*
Came home to *Leaden-hall*, he call'd to see
His *Hellena*, his Sultanesse, when she
At's first approach smelt out his Knavery;
And lest by the hot skirmish of the day,
Her *Paris* might miscarry in the way,
Or mett with some wounds, sends for in all haste
Shambrook the skilfull Chirurgion, who begins at th' waste
T'untruss, and as he stumbling downwards tends,
He had the businesse at his fingers ends;
Foh, quoth the Chirurgion, call the Kitchin Quean
With clout in hand to make his Worship clean;
Then about the Master all the Servants shuffl'd,
He, like old *Lockwood* in the Counter, scuffl'd,
Shew'd two broad mighty Hanches all bewray'd,
Nay then, quoth *Shambrook*, how shall I be paid;
The Devil a wound I see, is this the prime
Of six City Colonels in good time?
They say that shitten luck is good, and I
Will put it to the Vote of Chivalry,
Whether all be not likely well to jump
In th' New Militia, when a ——— is trump.

The Downfall of Cheapside-Crosse,
May 2, 3, 4. 1643.

WHat hast thou done poor *Crosse*, that this hard doome
Is laid upon thee? what is now become
Of all the gilded Images? for behold,
That now is Stone and Brick, which once seem'd Gold,
The City-Rulers, in their Graver wit,
And late got Power, have now thought it fit,
That thou shouldst be demolisht, and pluckt down
By th' warrant of Lord *Isaack Pennington*;
London's chief (*ut vis*) who thinks store of good
He doth, in prisoning, hanging, shedding blood,
In robbing, plundering each that's good to's King,
Because no Plate, nor Mony, they will bring
Into *Guildhall*: nay then it is no wonder,
If by his Order thou art pluckt asunder,
When first the top of thee with many a knock
They did beat down, (Lord) how the silly flock
Of Round-heads shouted, looking up to th' Skies,
Giving God thanks for the great Victories
They had got 'gainst thee, whilst the Drums did beat,
And Trumpets sounding; truly it was meet:
They threw their Hatts up, and their Muskets shot,
They shook their Heads, and clapt their Hands, what
    not?

And thus when any Picture, Legge, or Arme
Was thrown to th' Ground, the Roundheads all did swarme,
And sundry heaps tumbling one on another,
Striving who first should see it, then a Brother
A long Prayer made for thanks, that now they might,
Doe what they list, be it nor Just, nor Right;
For now they keep the whole City in awe,
With wrong-expounded, and misconstrued Law,
Doing what they think fit, what's good i'th eyes
Of them, being led even as their Spirits rise.
But for their Misdemeanours let this Curse
Light upon them, or a ten-times far worse:
May they no Silver have, nor yet no Gold,
Because there's Crosses in't: and, to be bold,
May they lead Lives so crost with grief and care,
That, at the last, may bring them to despair,
May they no good thing quietly enjoy,
May they even perish as they walk, and dye,
And may they still crost be, and crost again,
May Crosses mixt with Losses be their pain,
Nay, because *Crosses* they desire none,
May they have ever Crosses two for one,
May all their Noses rot, that we may know
Them, may their Eares as long as Asses grow,
May their Hair nere be long, and may their hands
Even pine away, may they stink as they stand:
And to conclude, may they all lead crosse Lives,
Nay, which is worse, be troubled with crosse Wives.

A Vindication of Cheapside-Crosse against the Roundheads.

Must I then down? is an eternal doome
Past out against me? must I needs to *Rome*?
And why? it is contrary to the Laws,
To judge th' offendor e're they hear the Cause.
Why come you arm'd against me? what may be
The cause of difference 'twixt you and me?
Have I transgrest the Law? or did I ever
Our gracious Soveraign from his People sever?
Did I to a factious Covenant subscribe,
Or turn a *Jack*-on-both-sides for a bribe?
Rebells have long our wisht for blisse defer'd,
All rose in armes, but yet I never stir'd.
When such a *Prick-ear* troop upon me gaz'd,
Crying (no *Crosse*) good faith I stood amaz'd:
I was struck dumb with wonder, and which worse,
Because I'de gold about me, fear'd my Purse.
This zealous rabble came not to adore me,
Yet (thanks to th' Butchers) some fell down before me,
Others ran quite away, the rest disputed,
Mis-using Scripture phrases, but confuted,
Wisedome they call'd Apocriphal, threw dirt on
All Fathers faces, but Saint *P*—— and *Burton*.
Was God ith' middle of this Congregation?
Or were they led by instinct, or revelation?
Kings doft their Crowns, and Cardinals their Copes,
All must be bare unto a crew of Crops.

But do's Religion such a hatred bring,
To hate the very picture of a King?
Brethren what would you have? or what d'ye fear?
I draw no sword, nor do I wear long hair.
I'le do no wrong (though arm'd with Pikes about)
Would you know why? 'twas to keep Roundheads
 out,
Who have not sworn, but tane a Protestation
To leave no golden Crosse to blesse our Nation,
They will divide my Coat, my Flesh, my Bones,
Theyl'e share the Gold, and give their Wives the
 Stones.
They say they'le pluck the Tower of *Babel* down,
All things go right when there's no Crosse it'h
 Town.
But who can live without them? Crosses are
The good mans blessings, and his certain share.
He that would win an everlasting Crown,
Must elevate his Crosse, not throw it down.
They'le have no Common Prayer, but do abhor
All that is common, but a common W———
Will you hear reason? that's not common to ye,
Will Prayers prevail? Ile pray *ex tempore.*
You think 'tis justice that your factious crew
Are crosse to me 'cause I am Crosse to you.
You will have flesh for flesh, It's very dear
That *Peters* nose should pay for *Malchas* ear,
If he should snuffle now, that were a jest,
That very thing would make him full blest:
You'l run to hear him, and cry's doctrine strong,
Though non-sense, in regard he stands so long.
Put out his eyes next time, and you may find
A second like the first, and doctrine blind.

Some call me Popish, and report they see
Divers adore me, what's all that to me?
Because they worship me shall I fall down
Unto such Calves, Mechanicks of the Town.
'Tis Popery, let them kneel that list, Ile stand?
Before Ile bow, Ile fly to some new Land.
Be sorry Brethren, I am pleas'd to think
'Twas from too little wit, or too much drink.
Ile be a Roundhead spiritually sent
To pardon your affronts, if youl repent.
I am a foe to *Rome*, for you shall find
When I am gone, there's the more room behind.

A Song in defence of Christmass.

NOw Christmass is come, let us beat up the Drum,
   And call our good Neighbours together.
And when they appear, let us make them good chear,
   That will keep out the wind and the weather,
To feast at this season, I think 'tis no treason,
   I could give you a reason why,
Though some are so pure, that they cannot endure to see
   a Nativity Pye.

I cannot but wonder, that the Souldiers should plunder,
   For keeping our Saviours birth,
For all Christians then, or I cannot tell when,
   Should shew forth their joy and their mirth,

But our Saints now adayes, despise good old wayes,
   'Gainst which they both preach and pray,
But to give them their dues, they're no better than
      Jewes,
That speak against Christmass day.

These like the good chear, all times oth' year,
   'Tis the birth day that doth them annoy,
Plumb-porrage and brawn, and the Doe and the Fawne,
   With the Creature, they love to enjoy,
They often have meetings, and then there's such greetings,
   Such traceing of Sisters about,
They preach and they pray, but I must not now say
   What they do when their Candles are out.

Yet I cannot forbear, to tell in your ear
   What befell at a breaking of bread,
How a Virgin full neat, went thither to eat,
   But it cost her, her Maiden-head;
These men of high merit, though much for the spirit,
   Are yet for the Flesh now and than,
For a new Babe of Grace, was got near the Place,
   By a Congregational man.

The Dippers and Ranters, and our Scotch Covenanters,
   That bragge of their Faith and their Zeale,
These abound in their fainings, but I'le make no com-
      plainings,
Nor will I their Secrets reveale,

The poor Cavaliers, that still lives in fears
  Of Prisons, and Sequestration,
Though they keep Christmasse day, are more honest than they,
But Honesty's quite out of fashion.

If you view our great Cities, and our Countrie Committees,
  You will not find overmuch there,
Our Divines, though they preach it, themselves do scarce reach it;
  And our Lawyers have little to spare.'
I could tell of some more, that have no great store,
  Of our Gentry, both Old and New,
But I think it is best, with edge tools not to jest,
  Nor to speak all we know to be true.

But the poor Cavalier, as to mirthe and good cheere,
  But now bid Christmass adieu,
If the Taxes hold on, their Money will be gone,
  They will want both to bake and to brew,
Their Healths are put down, who adher'd to the Crown,
  'Tis they that must fast and pray,
For to any mans thinking, both their eating and drinking,
  Is like to be taken away.

The Bishop of Ossery on the Rebells.

Let proud *Babilon* cease to boast
    Of her *Pyramid's* stately spires,
This Rebellion is more strange,
    Surmounting all Infernal fires.
No Age the like hath ever bread,
Nor shall when these Rebells be dead.

A Bill on St. Paul's Church Door.

This House is to be let,
    It is both wide, and fair;
If you would know the price of it,
    Pray ask of Mr. Maior.
                  Isaack Pennington.

A SONG.

What though the Zealots, pull down the Prelates,
    Push at the Pulpit, and kick at the Crown,
Shall we not ever, strive to endeavour
    Once more to purchase our Royal Renown?
Shall not the Roundhead first be confounded?
    Sa, sa, sa, sa boyes, ha, ha, ha, ha boyes,

Then wee'le return home, with Triumph and Joy,
Then wee'le be merry, drink Sack and Sherry,
   And we will sing Boys, *God blesse the King* Boys,
   Cast up our Caps, and cry, *Vive le Roy*.

What though the wise, make Alderman *Isaack*,
   Put us into Prison, and steal our Estates;
Though we are forced, to be un-horsed,
   And walk on foot, as it pleaseth the Fates,
In the Kings Army, no man will harm ye;
   Then come along Boyes, valiant and strong Boys,
   Fight for your Goods, which the Roundheads enjoyes;
And when you venter, *London* to enter,
   And when you come Boys, with Phife and Drum Boyes,
Isaack himself shall cry, *Vive le Roy*.

If not then, chuse him, 'twill not excuse him,
   Since honest Parliaments never made them Theeves;
Charles ne're did furder, Theeves dipt in Murder,
   Never by Pardon, long Lease, or Reprieves;
For such Conditions, and Propositions
   Will not be granted, then be not daunted,
   We will our honest old Customes enjoy:
Pauls now rejected, shall be respected,
   And in the Quire, Voyces sing hire,
   Thanks to *Jehovah*, then *Vive le Roy*.

On two Parliaments dissolved.

TWo Parliaments dissolv'd ! then let my heart,
As they in Faction, it in fraction part,
And, like the Levite sad with rage, ascribe
My piece-meal Portion to each broken Tribe,
And say, that *Bethlehem, Judahs* love, hath been
Wrong'd by the Fag-end crue of *Benjamin*,
O Let such High presumption be accurst,
When the last Tribe shall wrong the best, and first ;
While, like the Levite, our best *Charles* may say,
The Ravenous Wolf hath seiz'd the Lions prey.
Thus oft Inferiour Subjects are not shye,
A love to mock at Sacred Majesty.
What Faculty should not be injured,
If that the Feet had Power to spurn the Head ?
And Kings Prerogative may soon fall down,
When Subjects make a Footstool of a Crown :
The Starrs, the Heavens Inferiour Courtiers might,
Command the Darknesse, but not rule the Light,
Nor him that made it ; should they all combine
With *Luna* at the full, our Sun should shine
Brighter than they, nor can he be subdu'd,
Though he but one, and they a Multitude.
Say, Subjects ye were Starrs, and 'twere allow'd,
You justly of the Number might be proud ;
Yet to your Sun be humble, and know this,
Your Light is borrowed, not your own, but His.
When the unfettered Subjects of the Seas,
The Fountains, felt their feet, and ease,

No sooner summon'd, but they nimbly went
To meet the Ocean at a Parliament.
Did then these petty Fountains say their King,
The Ocean, was no Ocean, but a Spring?
Let me alone, if fresh excess of store
Can make me poorer than I was before.
And shall we then the power of Kings dispute?
And count it lesse, when more is added to't?
No, let the Common body, if it can,
Be not a River, but an Ocean,
And swell into a Deluge, till it hide
The top of Mountains in its teeming pride.
Kings, like *Noahs Ark*, are nearer to the Skies,
The more the Billows underneath them rise.
You then, who if your hearts were first in love,
Might sit in Counsell with the Gods Above:
You, that do question your Kings Power Below,
If you come there, will you use Heavens King so?
Do not aspire, you must take up you rest
More safe Below, than in the Eagles nest.
Hath Clemency offended? will you harm
And pluck the Sun from Heaven that makes you warm?
No King nor Bishops please? what, have we got
An Outside *English*, and an Inside *Scot?*
If Faction thus our Countries Peace distracts,
You may have want of Parliaments, not Acts.
Ill-ended Sessions, and yet well begun,
Too much being spoke hath made too little done.
So Faction thrives, Puritanism bears sway,
None must do any thing but only *Say*.
Stoop, stoop, you baren-headed Hills, confess
You might be fruitfuller, if ye were lesse.

Tremble ye thred-bare Commons : are you vext
That lambs feed on ye? Lions will come next.

Collonel Vennes *Encouragement to his Souldiers.*

A SONG.

Fight on brave Souldiers for the Cause,
    Fear not the Cavaliers,
Their threatnings are, as sencelesse as
    Our jealousies and fears.
'Tis you must perfect this great Work,
    And all Malignants slay,
You must bring back the King again
    The clean contrary way.

'Tis for Religion that you fight,
    And for the Kingdoms good,
By robbing Churches, plundering them,
    And shedding Guiltlesse blood.
Down with the Orthodoxal Train,
    All Loyal Subjects slay,
When these are gone, we shall be blest
    The clean contrary way.

When *Charles* we have made Bankrupt,
    Of Power and Crown bereft him,
And all his Loyal Subjects slain,
    And none but Rebells left him,

When we have beggar'd all the Land,
  And sent our Trunks away,
Wee'le make him then a Glorious Prince
  The clean contrary way.

'Tis to preserve his Majesty,
  That we against him fight,
Nor ever are we beaten back,
  Because our Cause is right.
If any make a scruple at
  Our Declarations, say
Who fight for us, fight for the King
  The clean contrary way.

At *Keinton*, *Brainsford*, *Plymouth*, *York*,
  And divers Places more,
What Victories we Saints obtain,
  The like nere seen before.
How often we Prince *Rupert* kill'd,
  And bravely wonne the day,
The wicked Cavaliers did run
  The clean contrary way.

The true Religion we maintain,
  The Kingdoms Peace and Plenty,
The Priviledge of Parliament,
  Not known to One of twenty.
The antient Fundamental Laws,
  And teach men to obey
Their lawfull Soveraign; and all these
  The clean contrary way.

Wee, Subjects Liberties preserve
  By Imprisonment and Plunder,

And do enrich our selves and State,
  By keeping th' Wicked under,
Wee must preserve Mechanicks now,
  To Lectorize and pray,
By them the Gospel is advanc't
  The clean contrary way.

And though the King be much misled
  By that Malignant Crew,
Hee'le find us honest at the last,
  Give all of us our due.
For we do wisely plot, and plot
  Rebellion to allay,
He sees wee stand for Peace and Truth
  The clean contrary way.

The Publique-Faith shall save our Souls,
  And our good Works together,
And Ships shall save our Lives that stay
  Only for Winde and Weather.
But when our Faith and Workes fall down,
  And all our Hopes decay,
Our Acts will bear us up to Heaven
  The clean contrary way.

A Second Western Wonder.

YOu heard of that wonder, of the *Lightening* and
   Thunder,
Which made the lye so much the louder ;
Now list to another, that Miracles Brother,
   Which was done with a *Firkin of Powder*.

h what a damp, struck through the Camp,
   But as for Honest Sir *Ralph*,
It blew him to the *Vies*, without beard, or eyes,
   But at least three heads and a half.

When out came the book, which the *News-monger* took
   From the *preaching Ladies* Letter,
Where in the first place, stood the *Conquerors* face,
   VVhich made it shew so much the better.

But now without lying, you may pains him flying,
   At *Bristoll* they say you may finde
Great *William* the *Con.* so fast he did run,
   That he left half his name behind.

And now came the Post, saves all that was lost,
   But alas, we are past deceiving,
By a trick so stale, or else such a tayl
   Might mount for a new *Thanks-giving*.

This made Mr. *Case*, with a pittifull face,
   In the Pulpit to fall a weeping,
Though his mouth utter'd *lyes*, *truth* fell from his eyes,
   VVhich kept our *Lord Maior* from sleeping.

Now shut up shops, and spend your last drops,
   For the Laws of your Cause, you that loath 'um,
Lest *Essex* should start, and play the *Second part*,
   Of *Worshipfull* Sir *John Hotham*.

The Battel of Worcester.

ALl you that be true to the King and the State,
   Come listen, and Ile tell you what happen'd of late,
In a large field near *Worcesters* gate.
              Which no body can deny.

Brave *Sir John Byron*, true to the Crown,
VVith forces too few, 'tis very well known,
VVent thither, 'tis said, to keep the *Town*,
              Which no body can deny.

But whether 'twas true, ye have learn'd to guess,
As for my own part I think no lesse,
To give you a taste of our Future successe,
              Which no body can deny.

Thither came *Fines* with armes Complete,
The *Town* to take, and *Byron* defeat,
Provisions were made, but he staid not to eat,
              Which no body can deny.

But as soon as he heard our great Guns play,
VVith a Flea in's ear, he ran quite away,
Like the lawfull begotten *Son* of Lord *Say*,
              Which no body, &c.

Nay had the old Crop-ear'd his Father dar'd
To approach the walls, his design had bin marr'd,
For *Byron* would not have proved a VVard.
     Which no body can deny.

Pox on him he keeps his Patent yet,
But I hope next Term he shall not sit,
'Twas but *quam diu se bene Gesserit*,
     Which no body, &c.

But now behold, increased in force,
Hee comes again with ten Troups of Horse,
Oh bloudy-Man he had no remorse,
     Which no body, &c.

They marched up boldly, without any fear,
Little thinking Prince *Rupert* was come so near,
But alas poor souls it cost them dear,
     Which no body, &c.

The Prince like a Gallant man of his trade,
Marcht out of the *Town* till this quarter was made,
Sir, the Enemies are near at hand it is said :
     Which no body, &c.

Where, where are they ? Prince *Rupert* cryes,
And looking about with fiery eyes,
Some thirty behind a hedge he spyes.
     Which no body, &c.

This Forlorn-hope he no sooner saw,
But 4. or 5. more did towards them draw ;
He asked, who's there ? one answer'd him, haw,
     Which no body, &c.

Part I. *Rump Songs.*

The man you'll say was rudely bred;
The Prince shot a Bullet into his head,
His haw had been better spared than said,
     Which no body, &c.

Prince *Maurice* then, to second his Brother,
Discharg'd his Pistol, and down fell another,
'Twere pitty but news were sent to his Mother,
     Which no body, &c.

Lord *Digby* slew one to his great fame,
So did Monsieur de *Lisle*, and Sir *Rich. Crane*,
And another *French* man, with a harder name,
     Which no body, &c.

Prince *Rupert* to his own Force retired,
And bad them not shoot till their Doublets were fired,
His Courage and Conduct were both admired,
     Which no body, &c.

He Charged but twice, yet made them shrink,
'Twere hard to get off now one would think,
Yet both can do it as easie as drink.
     Which no body, &c.

Then have amongst ye, quoth Sir *Lewes Dives*,
For a good Cause you know alwayes thrives,
His heart in his shoulders cost many mens lives,
     Which no body, &c.

John Byron did as bravely fight;
To the *Prince of Wales* his great delight,
He came home in safety and was made a Knight.
     Which no body, &c.

My Friend *David Walter* in Doublet white,
Without any Armes either rusty or bright,
Charg'd through them twice like a little spright,
     Which no body, &c.

But oh Prince *Maurice*, where was he?
Where one of us would be loath to be,
Surrounded with Butchers three times three,
     Which no body, &c.

These men of *East-cheap* little said,
But all their blows at his head they made,
As if they had been at work at their Trade,
     Which no body, &c.

Then came a *French-man* fiery and keen,
He broke the Ring and came in between,
Ere a man let a —— not a Butcher was seen.
     Which no body, &c.

Brave Lord *Wilmot*, by whose hands did fall
Many a Rebell stout and tall,
Came to him without any Armes at all,
     Which no body, &c.

Their Horses then close up they spur'd,
The wounds they gave were all with the Sword,
Their Pistols proved not worth a ——
     Which no body, &c.

But the Parliament having quite forgot
To Vote that *Sandys* should not be shot
By the hand of a *Mounsier* he went to the pot.
     Which no body, &c.

Part I. *Rump Songs.*

Douglas a *Scotch-man* of great fame
Was slain that day for want of the same;
The Houses in this were much to blame,
     Which no body, &c.

Of all their chief Commanders that day,
I hold it fit I should something say,
His name was *Brown*, and he ran away,
     Which no body, &c.

If a few more o'em should shew such a freak,
Both Houses surely would quickly break,
And honester men would have leave to speak,
     Which no body, &c.

They fly, they fly, Prince *Rupert* cry'd,
No sooner said, but away they hy'd;
The force of his Armes they durst not abide,
     Which no body can deny.

Smectymnuus, *or the Club-Divines.*

S*Mectymnuus!* the Goblin makes me start!
I'th' Name of Rabbi *Abraham*, what art?
Syriack? or *Arabick?* or *Welch?* what skilt?
Ap all the Brick-layers that *Babel* built!
Some Conjurer translate, and let me know it,
Till then 'tis fit for a *West-Saxon* Poet.
But do the Brother-hood then play their Prizes
Like Mummers in Religion with disguises?
Out-brave us with a name in Rank and File,
A name, which if 'twere train'd, would spread a Mile;

The Saints monopolie, the zealous cluster,
Which, like the Porcupine, presents a muster,
And shoots his quills at Bishops and their Sees,
A Devout litter of young *Maccabees*.
Thus Jack of all trades hath devoutly shown
The twelve Apostles on a cherry-stone,
Thus fashion's Al-a-Mode in Treasons fashion;
Now we have heresie by Complication
Like to *Don Quixots* Rosary of slaves
Strung on a chain; a Murnival of Knaves
Packt in a trick, like Gypsies when they ride,
Or like Colleagues, which sit all on a side:
So the vain *Satyrists* stand all a row,
As hollow teeth upon a Lute-string show:
Th' *Italian* Monster, pregnant with his Brother,
Natures *Diæresis*, half one another,
He, with his little sides-man *Lazarus*,
Must both give way unto *Smectymnuus*.
Next *Sturbridge Fair* is *Smecks*, for lo his side
Into a five-fold *Lezar's* multipli'd.
Under each arm there's tuckt a double gyssard,
Five faces lurk under one single vizard:
The *Whore of Babylon* left these brats behind,
Heirs of confusion by *Gavelkind*.
I think *Pythagoras's* soul has rambl'd hither,
With all the change of Rayment on together:
Smec is her general Ward-robe, shee'l not dare
To think of him as of a thorough fare;
He stops the Gossiping Dame; alone he is
The purlew of a *Metempsichosis*.
Like a *Scotch* Mark, where the more modest sense
Checks the loud phrase, and shrinks to 13. pence:
Like an *Ignis fatuus*, whose flame,
Though sometimes tripartite, joynes in the same:

Like to nine *Taylors*, who if rightly spell'd,
Into one man are Monosyllabel'd:
Short-handed zeal in one hath cramped many,
Like to the Decalogue in a single penny.
    See, see! how close the curs hunt under sheet,
As if they spent in Quire, and scann'd their feet;
One Cure, and five Incumbents leap a truss:
The title sure must be litigious!
The *Sadduces* would raise a question,
Who must be *Smec* at th' Resurrection.
Who coop'd them up together were to blame,
Had they but wire-drawn, & spun out their name,
'Twould make another Prentices Petition
Against the Bishops and their Superstition.
    Robson and *French* (that count from five to five,
As far as nature fingers can contrive,
She saw they would be sessors, that's the cause
She cleft her hoof into so many claws,)
May tire their Carret-bunch, yet ne're agree
To rate *Smectymnuus* for Pole-money.
    Caligula, whose pride was mankinds bail,
(As who disdain'd to murther by retail)
Wishing the world had but one general neck.
His glutton blade might have found game in *Smec*,
No eccho can improve the Author more,
Whose lungs pay use on use, to half a score:
No Felon is more letter'd, though the brand
Both superscribes his shoulder and his hand.
Some *Welsh-man* was his Godfather, for he
Wears in his name his Genealogy,
The Banes are ask'd, would but the time give way,
Beewixt *Smectymnuus* and *Et cætera;*
The Guests invited by a friendly Summons,
Should be the Convocation and the Commons;

The Priest to tye the Foxes tayles together,
Mosely, or *Sancta Clara*, chuse you whether.
See, what off-spring every one expects!
What strange pluralities of men and sects?
One sayes hee'l get a Vestery, another
Is for a Synod: But upon the Mother:
Faith! cry St. *George*, let them go to't, and stickle,
Whether a Conclave or a Conventicle;
Thus might Religions catterwaul, and spight,
Which uses to divorce, might once unite.
But their crosse Fortunes interdict their trade,
The Groom is Rampant, but the bride displaid.
 My task is done, all my Hee-Goats are milkt,
So many Cards i'th' stock, and yet be bilkt?
I could by Letters now untwist the Rabble,
Whip *Smec* from Constable to Constable.
But there I leave you to another dressing,
Only kneel down and take your Fathers blessing,
 May the *Queen Mother* justifie your fears,
And stretch her Patent to your leather ears.

A Lenten Letany.

Composed for a confiding Brother, for the benefit and edification of the Faithfull Ones.

FRom Villany drest in the Doublet of Zeal,
From three Kingdomes bak'd in one Common weal,
From a gleek of *Lord Keepers* of one poor Seal,
     Libera nos, &c.

From a Chancery-writ, and a whip and a bell,
From a Justice of Peace that never could spell,
From *Collonel P.* and the *Vicar of Hell,*
     Libera nos, &c.

From Neat's feet without socks, and three-peny Pyes.
From a new sprung Light that will put out ones eyes,
From Goldsmiths-hall, the Devil, and Excise,
     Libera nos, &c.

From two hours talk without one word of sense,
From Liberty still in the future tense,
From a Parliament long-wasted Conscience,
     Libera nos, &c.

From a Coppid Crown-tenent prick'd up by a Brother,
From damnable Members, and fits of the Mother,
From Ears like Oysters that grin at each other,
     Libera nos, &c.

From a Preacher in buff, and a Quarter-staff-steeple,
From th' unlimited Soveraigne Power of the People,
From a Kingdom that crawles on its knees like a Creeple,
     Libera nos, &c.

From a vinegar Priest on a Crab-tree stock,
From a foddering of Prayer four hours by the Clock.

From a holy Sister with a pittifull Smock,
>> *Libera nos, &c.*

From a hunger-starv'd Sequestrators maw,
From Revelations and Visions that never man saw.
From Religion without either Gospel or Law,
>> *Libera nos, &c.*

From the Nick and Froth of a Peny Pot-house,
From the Fiddle and Crosse, and a great *Scotch* Louse,
From Committees that chop up a Man like a Mouse,
>> *Libera nos, &c.*

From broken shins, and the blood of a Martyr,
From the Titles of Lords, and Knights of the Garter,
From the teeth of mad-dogs, and a Country mans quarter,
>> *Libera nos, &c.*

From the Publique Faith, and an Egg & Butter,
From the *Irish* Purchasers, and all their clutter,
From *Omega's* nose, when he fettles to sputter,
>> *Libera nos, &c.*

From the zeal of Old *Harry* lock'd up with a Whore,
From waiting with Plaints at the Parliament dore,
From the death of a King without why or wherefore,
>> *Libera nos, &c.*

From the French disease, and the Puritan fry,
From such as nere swear, but devoutly can lye,
From cutting of capers full three story high,
Libera nos, &c.

From Painted glass, and Idolatrous cringes,
From a *Presbyters* Oath that turns upon hinges,
From *Westminster Jews* with Levitical fringes,
Libera nos, &c.

From all that is said, and a thousand times more,
From a Saint, and his Charity to the Poor,
From the Plagues that are kept for a Rebel in store,
Libera nos, &c.

The Second Part.

THat if it please thee to assist
Our *Agitators*, and their List,
And *Hemp* them with a gentle twist,
Quæsumus te, &c.

That it may please thee to suppose
Our actions are as good as those
That gull the People through the Nose,
Quæsumus te, &c.

That it may please thee here to enter,
And fix the rumbling of our center,
For we live all at peradventure,
Quæsumus te, &c.

That it may please thee to unite
The flesh and bones unto the sprite,
Else Faith and literature good night,
>   *Quæsumus te, &c.*

That it may please thee O that wee
May each man know his Pedigree,
And save that plague of Heraldry,
>   *Quæsumus te, &c.*

That it may please thee in each Shire
Cities of refuge Lord to rear,
That failing Brethren may know where,
>   *Quæsumus te, &c.*

That it may please thee to abhor us,
Or any such dear favour for us,
That thus have wrought thy peoples sorrows,
>   *Quæsumus te, &c.*

That it may please thee to embrace
Our dayes of thanks and fasting face,
For robbing of thy holy place,
>   *Quæsumus te, &c.*

That it may please thee to adjourn
The day of judgement, least we burn,
For lo it is not for our turn,
>   *Quæsumus te, &c.*

That it may please thee to admit
A *close Committee* there to sit,
No Devil to a Humane wit!
>   *Quæsumus te, &c.*

That it may please thee to dispence
A little for convenience,
Or let us play upon the sense,
    Quæsumus te, &c.

That it may please thee to embalm
The Saints in *Robin Wisdom's Psalm*,
And make them musical and calm,
    Quæsumus te, &c.

That it may please thee, since 'tis doubt
Satan cannot throw Satan out,
Unite us and the Highland rout,
    Quæsumus te, &c.

AN ELEGIE

On the Death of Sir Bevile Grenvile.

TO build upon the merit of thy *Death*,
  And raise thy Fame from thy *expiring Breath*,
Were to steal Glories from thy *Life*, and tell
The World, that *Grenvil* only did *dye* well.
But all thy Dayes were fair, the same Sun rose,
The Lustre of thy *Dawning*, and thy *Close*.
Thus to her Urn th' *Arabian* wonder flyes,
She lives in *Perfumes*, and in *Perfumes* dyes:
  E're stormes, and tumults (Names undreaded here)
Could in their Bloome and Infancy appeare;

He in the stock and treasure of his mind
Had heaps of Courage, and just heat combin'd.
Where, like the thrifty Ant, he kept in store
Enough for *Spring*, but for a *Winter* more.
In Peace he did direct his thoughts on Warrs,
And learn't in *silence* how to combat *Jarres*.
And though the Times look't smooth and would allow
No track of Frown or Wrincle in their Brow:
Yet his quick sight perceiv'd the Age would low'r,
And, while the *Day* was *faire*, fore-saw the *Show'r*.
  At this the prudent Augur did provide
Where to *endure* the *storme*, not where to *hide*,
And sought to shun the Danger now drawn nigh,
Not by *Concealment* but by *Victory*.
As valiant *Seamen*, if the Vessel knock,
Rather *sayle o're it*, than avoid the Rock.
And thus Resolv'd, he saw on either hand,
The *Causes*, and their bold *Abettors* stand.
The *Kingdoms Law* is the pretence of each,
Which these *by Law preserve*, these by its *breach*,
The *Subjects Liberty* each side maintains,
These say it consists in *freedom*, these in *Chaines*,
These love the *decent* Church, but these not pass
To dresse our *Matron* by the *Geneva Glass*?
These still *enshrine* their God; but these adore
Him most at some *Araunah's Threshing-floor*.
Each part defends their King a several way,
By true *Subjection* these, by *Treasons* they.
But our Spectatour soon unmask't the sin,
And saw all *Serpent* through that *specious skin*.
And midst their best Pretext did still despair,
In any dresse to see their *Moor look fair*.

And though the *Number* weigh'd ith' *popular scale*,
As light things float still with the *tyde* and *gale*,
He with the *solid* mixt, and did conclude,
Justice makes Parties *great*, not *Multitude*.
And with this constant Principle possest,
He did alone expose his single Breast,
Against an *Armies* force, and bleeding lay,
The *great Restorer o'th' Declining Day*.
  Thus slain thy *Valiant Ancestor* did lye,
When his one *Bark* a *Navy* durst defie,
When now encompass'd round, he Victor stood,
And bath'd his *Pinnace* in his conquering Blood.
Till all his Purple current dry'd and spent,
He fell, and left the *Waves* his *Monument*,
    Where shall next *famous Grenvills* Ashes stand?
    Thy Grandsire fills the *Seas*, and Thou the *Land*.

To my Lord Bishop of S. *on* New-years day.

Though with the course and motion of the year,
    Not only *Starres* and *Sun*
    Move where they first begun;
    But *Things* and *Actions* do
    Keep the same *Circle* too,
Return'd to the same point in the same *Sphear*.

Griefs and their *Causes* still are where they stood,
    'Tis the same *Cloud* and *Night*
    Shuts up our *Joyes* and *Light :*
    Warres as remote from *Peace,*
    And *Bondage* from *Release,*
As when the *Sun* his last years Circuite rode.

Though *Sword* and *Slaughter are not parted* hence,
    But we like *years* and *times,*
    Meet in *unequal chimes,*
    Now a *Cloud* and then a *Sun,*
    Undoe and are *undone,*
Let loose and stopt by th' Orbes intelligence.

Though *Combates* have so thick and frequent stood,
    That we at length may raise
    A *Calendar* of dayes,
    And style them foul or fair,
    By their *success,* not *Aire :*
And sign our Festivals by *Rebels blood.*

Though the sad years are cloath'd in such a dress,
    That *times* to *times* give place,
    And *seasons* shift their *grace,*
    Not by our *Cold* or *Heat,*
    But *Conquest* or *Defeat :*
And Losse makes *Winter, Summer, happiness.*

Nay though a greater Ruine yet await;
    Such as the *Active* curse,*
    Sent to make *worst* times *worse,*
    Deaths *keen* and *secret* dart,
    The shame of Hearths and Art
Which proves at once our *Wonder* and our *Fate.*

    * *The new disease.*

Though these conspire to sully our request,
　　And labour to destroy,
　　And kill your *New-years* joy,
　　Yet still your wonted Art
　　　Will keep our wish in *heart*.
Proportion'd not toth' times but to your breast
Thus in the Storme you *Calme* and *Silence* find,
Nor *Sword* nor *Sickness* can approach your mind.

A SATYR,

Occasioned by the Author's Survey of a Scandalous Pamphlet, intituled

The Kings Cabinet opened.

WHen *Lawes* and *Princes* are despis'd and cheap,
　　When *High patcht* Mischiefs all are in the heap;
Returns must still be had: *Guilt* must strive more
Though not to' *Enoble*, yet to *Enlarge her store.*
Poor *cheap Design !* the *Rebell* now must flie
To *Packet Warre*, to *Paper-Treacherie.*
The *Basiliskes* are turn'd to *Closet-Spies,*
And to their *Poys'nous* adde *Enquiring eyes:*
As *Snakes* and *Serpents* should they cast their sting,
Still the same *Hate*, though not same *Poyson* fling;
And their *Vain teeth* to the same point addresse,
With the like *Rancor*, though unlike *Successe:*

So those that into undiscerning veines,
Have thrown their *Venom deep*, and their dark stains,
By *frail Advantages*, still find it good,
To keep th' Infection high ith' Peoples Blood.
   "For *Active Treason* must be *doing* still :
   "Lest she *unlearn* her *Art* of *doing ill*.
Who now have waded through the *Publick* aw,
Will break through *Secrets* and prophane their Law.
Know you, that would their *Act* and *Statute* see
Nature kept *Court*, and made it her *Decree*.
   When *Angells* talke, all their *Conceipts* are brought
From *Minde* to *Minde*, and they discourse by *Thought*.
A *Close Idea* moves, and *Silence* flies
To *post* the *Message*, and *dispatch Replies*.
And though *Ten Legions*, in the Round are bent,
They only *hear* to whom the *Talk was meant*.
Now, though in *Men* a different Law controules,
And *Soules* are not *Embassadours* to *Soules :*
Nature gave Reason power to find a way,
Which none but these could venture to betray.
   "Two close safe Pathes she did bequeath to men,
   "In *Presence, Whisper;* and at *Distance, Penne*.
Publick *Decrees* and *Thoughts* were else the same,
Nor went it to *Converse*, but to *Proclaim*.
Conceipts were else but *Records*, but by this care
Our *Thoughts* no *Commons*, but *Inclosures* are :
What bold *Intruders* then are, who assail
To cut their Prince's *Hedge*, and break his *Pale ?*
That so *Unmanly gaze*, and dare be seen
Ev'n then, when He converses with his *Queen ?*

Yet, as who breaks the tall Bank's rising Side,
And all the Shore doth levy with the Tyde,
Doth not confine the Waves to any Bound,
But the whole Streame may gain upon the Ground;
So these *streight* Prospect scorn, and *Private* View,
" The Crime is small that doth engage a Few.
These print their Shame, they must compleat their Sinne:
Not take some *Waves*, and shut the *Sluce* agen.
But, to the *Raging of their Sea*, they do
Let in the *Madnesse of the People too*.

But, 'cause their *Crime* must wear a *Mask* and *Vail*,
And fain the Serpent would conceal his *Tail*.
No sooner comes the *Libell* to our view,
But see a *stay'd demure, grave Preface* too:
Which seems to show they would not thus intrude,
Nor presse so far, but for the *Publick* good:
But as some *London Beggers* use to stand,
In *Grecians Coats* with Papers in their hand,
Who are (as them indifferent Parts we meet)
English at Home, but solemn *Greeks* ith' street.
Of whom *uncloath'd*, and when the truth is heard,
Constantinople only knows the *Beard*.
So this *sly Masker*, lay its *Tinsell* by,
Is only *Painted Zeal*, and *Pageantry*.

We need not let our *Satyr* here compute,
How it prophanes God in His *Attribute*.*
But for its *Light* it need no *Bushell* call,
A *Sempstresse Thimble* will *Eclypse* it all.

O! in what meeknesse it pretends to creep!
How well the *Tyger* personates the *Sheep!*
It not Returns ill Language to the King,
Though the next Lines the *Psalms* against Him bring.

* *See the Preface.*

Then it to th' *Business* comes, and lets us know,
Who reads it either is its *Friend* or *Foe*.
If *Friend*, the Scandals all must true appear:
If *Foe* (alack the man is ne're the near.)
Foe no Light moves, no *Miracles* like these,
Hee'le say they're not the *Kings* too, if he please.
And tell us pray? what, may'nt your last words stand?
You counterfeit his *Seal*, why not his *Hand*?
But to admit, We now deduce and bring,
What *after-notes* clearly imply oth' King
 First, They His Comfort from His *Secrets* wrest.
They doe allow the *King*, but not the *Breast*,
The Sacred Knot must have a Tye, and Force,
To joyne their Hands, but yet their Thoughts Divorce.
And, as the Ivye weddes her Consort-Tree,
Though join'd, and close their chast Embraces be,
Yet in those *Twinnes* and *Circuits* we can find
No Traffique, no Commerce of mind with mind:
So must the Sacred Laws of Marriage pierce;
Here she may *Sprout* and *Grow*, but not *Converse*.
And, like a Plant remov'd by Grafters toyle,
She finds not Nuptials, but a change of Soyle.
England to th' Queen transplanted thus must prove,
No *Forraigne Kingdome*, but a *Forraigne Grove*.
 But, least this groundlesse seem, they reasons vex,
And tell the World Shee's of the Weaker Sex.
In what wilde Braines this Madnesse first began!
They're wondrous angry, 'cause the Queen's no Man.
Fond Sirs forbear, do not the world perplex:
Reason and *Judgement* are not things of *Sex*.

Souls and their Faculties were never heard
To be confin'd to th' *Doublet* and the *Beard*.
Consult one Age from this, and you shall find
A Queen the Glory of your Annals shin'd.
But who to farre and distant Objects flies,
Must say the *Sun* wants *Lustre*, or he *Eyes*.
Our *Present injur'd* Queen returns that store,
And doth again, what could be done before:
By the *King's* Judgement, shews Her *own* is Right,
And still she meets His Ray with her own Light.
  Thus the *wise King* to *Shebah's Queen* was known,
  Who knew *Him wise* by *Wisedom* of *her own*.
But as all *Publick* Knowledge barr'd must be,
So *Houshold-Acts* must have their *Mysterie:*
No Circumstance can passe, no Servant made,
But must be wrapt in *silence* and close *shade*.
One *Place* in Court a Riddle must afford,
Worthy a secret *Sybil's* dark Record.
As the *Kings Acts* must all their limits prove,
So their *Restraint* and *Reins* must check his *Love*.
Esteems of 's Comfort by their *pitch* must fly,
Nor must He *rate* his Dear Queen's Health *too high*.
He must affect thus *far*, and then no *more*,
His *Tydes* must be proportion'd to their *shore;*
His *Tenderness* their *Weights* and *Ballance* weare,
By *Graines* and *Scruples* they Confine His Care,
But (Savage) know, there can no ransome be
Poys'd with the Health of such a Queen as *She*.
She that at once such *weighty* Acts can do,
That can be *Queen* and yet *negotiate* too:
Send and be *sent*, and without more demurre,
Be both the *Queen* and her *Embassadour*.
That gives dispatch for Ships, and when she please,
Divides the Empire with the Queen o'th Seas:

Who dares the threats of any danger stand,
The stubborn Rock, or the Devouring Sand.
And though the Sea swell like Her *fate* and *Grave*,
Look at Her Consort, and despise the *Wave*.
 The Captive Queen did (thus) the *Tyrant* tell,
 I am no Captive so my *King* be well.*
By these her worth and rate is faintly known,
Past stories *blush* when she erects her *own*.
Search *old gray* Annals, you may find at length,
Some Queen in *Vigour*, and her *mid-day strength;*
Who in her injured Consorts cause, referres
To Copies glancing at these Acts of *Hers*.
But if *Infirm* and *Sickly* Queens we *scanne*,
No story patterns her, None ever can
Shew us a Queen fraught with such wide Affairs,
Here private *Weaknesse*, there a *Kingdom*'s care,
Perplext and tortur'd from her rest and ease,
By a *Rebellion here*, there a *Disease:*
Advice and *Medcines* at one time we view,
A *Counsel-board*, *Board of Physicians too.*
Yet her Capacious Soul both these defeats,
While this hand holds *Instructions*, that *Receipts*.
These are our fam'd Queens Crimes, but yet one more
Must be the main *Ingredient* of the store.
Which seems to presse so *deep*, there's nought so bright,
But this may sully all its lustre quite :
'Tis her *Religions Care:* She tryes Her Pow'rs
To keep that still, do not we so for *Ours*?
Why to one *Face* so diff'rent *shapes* have bin,
What *Virtue* is in *Us*, in Her is *Sin*.
Our diff'rent Faiths did long together grow,
And neither suffer'd, neither losse did know;

   * *Q. Curtius, lib.* 3.

And like a stream, which 'twixt two fields doth flow,
Which as it *Moistens*, so *Divides* them too:
So did the Kingdoms Law throw *Dew* and *growth*,
In *Weight* and just *proportion* unto both,
And like a parting Current, slide along
To keep them *wide*, that neither neither *Wrong*.
Our Faiths were then but *Two*, but since a sp'rit
So many *Mushrome Sects* rais'd in a Night:
The *Protestant* (as she could Parties gain
Who unconcern'd were in the *Dregs* and *staine*)
Did recommend her *Votaries*, and bring
Her Faith to *its Defender*, our *Just King*.
Who with such *Zeal* hath kept her Rites entire,
As well from *Languishing*, as from *strange* Fire:
That still the Censer savours its true scent,
Without *Accession*, yet no *Perfume spent;*
The happy *Martyrs* find their Faith had stood
In *Him*, as when they bath'd it in their blood.
They joy to see that *He* his God adores,
Not at *High-places*, nor at *Threshing-floores*,
But spight of *Scandals*, pays his homage still
In the *Just* Beauty of the *Sion-Hill*.
 The *Other Sects*, though as in Common-fields,
Which *Swine*, and *Horses*, *Mules* and *Oxen* yields,
Who though at *Distance fed*, *Approaching clash*,
And disproportion'd shapes together dash.
So they, though one *Rebellion* them sustain,
Themselves *Accuse*, and are *Accus'd again*.
Could they comply, then possibly might dwell
Some *faint Agreement*, though no *Peace* in Hell:
Now, these nice tasts no *Forraigne* aids indure,
(Their *Rebell Scots* are *English Rebells* sure,)
No, nor the *Papists:* much it with them sticks,
Lest these Men's *Punniards* should be *Hereticks:*

Their souls would be *prophan'd*, and clean *undun*,
Should they be slain by an *Idolatrous* Gun.
Go lay your *Vizar* by, your Masking stuff,
The Devil is *tyr'd*, and Hell hath *laugh'd* enough :
The world descryes the *Cheat*, 'tis quickly known
They no Faith *hate*, who have *Resolv'd* on None.
These may not fight: that is, the King you'd have
Tamely forsake his *Crown*, and be your *Slave*.
His Easier *Subjects* long agoe you gat,
All who approv'd your *Baite*, and swallowed *that*.
Indeed, *Discerning* souls the snare forsook,
And through the *Wave* did still descry the *Hook :*
But yet so *close* designs were cast about,
Your Race was *half runne* e're the King *set out*.
Yet you *complain*, and guilty fears do *gnaw*,
Lest you should *scanted* be for *Space* and *Law :*
Conscious, though you your cause did forward meet,
Its *Guilt* and *Sin* hangs *Plummets* at its feet.
  Are not the *Jews*, *Walloones*, the *Turks*, and all
Whom from as *Diff'rent Gods* as *Lands* you call,
An *Army strong* to keep the cause in heart,
But that the *King* must with His *Subjects* part?
Can no Accession so much safety send,
But you will *Dread* Him still before you end?
  Sometimes at Ebbes his God doth let Him stand,
That so the Rescue may declare His hand.
But, what (you hope) may make the King's side pause,
Is what he writes about the *Penall Laws*.
Poor shallow souls, I deem it one from hence
To forfeit *Loyalty*, and forfeit *Sence*.
  Shall such as wast their *Blood* be quite debarr'd,
And kept without the *Pale* from all *Reward ?*
Shall fame report, shall after Ages tell,
So just a King regards not who do dwell?

Part I. *Rump Songs.*

But you pretend, this was a *State-Decree*,
Nor without Pow'r which *made* may cancel'd be
The King *nev'r* sayes it shall: but cannot doubt
That when his God hath brought his work about,
And shifted *Jarres* and *Tumults* into *Ease*,
And set him 'midst his Counsell in High peace:
Their *joynt* united suffrage will think fit
To give *this* Act, or something Great as it.
  But see, His *Pardon* then to *Ireland* came,
(Wild *Rebells*) offers he not you the *same?*
He holds still out the *same* fresh chearfull Ray,
You shut your *Windows* and *exclude* the Day:
  Embrace the *shine*, or else expect the stroak,
  The Flint the Sun ne're *melts*, at last is *broke*.
But now the Flood-gates ope, and a free sluce,
Lets in all sencelesse Doctrines, and wild use;
And by *Comparing* what's said *long agoe,*
Finds *Disproportion* in the *King's Acts now.*
His *past* Resolves it up to *Present* brings,
His *Vowes* to *Vowes*, and *Things* to combat *Things.*
A *Different* face throughout, and a *fresh* Scene
Succeed: and all his Acts *seem* shifted clean.
Weak men! who are depriv'd by *Guilt* or chance,
Of all the *lights* of Common Circumstance;
That have unlearn't that *Actions shift* their *Face*,
And date their worth from *Persons, Time,* and *Place.*
And *sundry such,* from *whose Neglects* appear
Acts as *Sinnes there*, which are *Try'd Virtues here.*
For instance then, oft as the King reflects
His *Oath's enjoyn,* His *People he protects.*
Which *Oathes extent, and Circuit* we may view
Spread ore th' *Five Execrable Members* too.
Yet (far *as't them concerns*) that *Chain* is *broke,*
That *Oath* left *Him,* because they left *His Yoake.*

Now of this *Pitch*, and *Size*, do still appear
All *Aiery* Scruples which are started there.
The King *Declared*, He thought you meant no ill,
Say, would you have the King *Declare so still?*
  Allow but *Different* Circumstance, and we
  Find all your *Scandalls* will his *Glories* be.
Now, as the *worst* things have *some* things of *stead*,
And some *Toades* treasure *Jewells* in their Head.
So doth this *Libels womb Girt*, and *contain*.
What though it *compasse Round?* it cannot *stain*
Lines of so *cleare*, yet so *Majestick* straine;
A most *Transparent*, yet a *close-wove* Veine;
Which when we reach its *Sense*, we may descry,
We see more by *its Light*, then *our own Eye*.
  So *Phœbus* (when the *Cloud* and *Night* is done)
  Lends us his Light, to know he is the *Sunne*.
Yet this expressive clearnesse is but *barke*,
An *Out-side Sunne* which guards us from the dark.
Here the *Bright* Language shuts in *Brighter* sense,
Rich Diamonds sleep within a *Crystall* Fence.
Gemmes of that rate, to *Tully* they'd appear
Fit purchase *for his Critick Senates Ear:*
And their whole *Shine* in a full Lustre tends
To *God*, His *Conscience*, *Comfort*, and his *Friends*.

THE CLOSE.

No *winding* Characters, no *secret* Maze,
Could so *perplex*, but they have found their wayes.
They *thred* the Labyrinth, and what to do?
Whe'r *tends* the Guide? what *purchase* in this Clew?
Rash *Alexander* forc't King *Gordius Knot*,
And so in hand found he a *Rope* had got.*

    * *Q. Curtius, lib.* 2.

*A New Diurnal of Passages more
Exactly drawn up then heretofore.
Printed and Published, 'tis order'd to be,
By* Henry Elsing *the Clerk of the P.*

1 *June* 1643.

Since many Diurnals (for which we are griev'd)
Are come from both Houses, and are not believ'd;
The better to help them for running and flying,
We have put them in Verse to Authorize their lying.
For it has been debated, and found to be true,
That lying's a Parliament Priviledge too:
And that they may the sooner our Conquests rehearse,
We are minded to put them in Galloping Verse;
But so many Maim'd Souldiers from *Reading* there came,
That in spight of the Surgeons, make our Verses go lame.
We have ever us'd Fictions, and now it is known,
Our Poverty has made us Poetical grown.

Munday.

On *Munday* both Houses fell into debate,
And were likely to fall by the ears as they sate;

Yet would they not have the businesse decided,
That they (as the Kingdom is) might be divided.
They had an intention to Prayers to go,
But *Ex tempore* Prayers are now Common too.
To Voting they fall, and the key of the work,
Was the raising of Money for the State and the Kirk.
'Tis only Free-loan, yet this Order they make,
That what Men would not lend, they should Plunder and take;
Upon this, the word *Plunder* came into their minds,
And all of them did labour a new one to find;
They call'd it distraining: yet thought it no shame,
To persist in the Act, which they blusht for to name.
They Voted all Persons from *Oxford* that came,
Should be apprehended: and after the same,
With an Humble Petition, the King they request,
He'd be pleas'd to return, and be serv'd like the rest.
A Message from *Oxford* conducing to Peace,
Came next to their hands, that Armes might cease;
They Voted and Voted, and still they did vary,
Till at last the whole sense of the House was contrary
To reason; they knew by their Armes they might gain,
What neither true reason, nor Law can maintain.
Cessation was Voted a dangerous Plot,
Because the King would have it, both Houses would not.

But when they resolv'd it, abroad must be blowne,
(To baffle the World) that the King would have none.
And carefully muzzled the mouth of the Press,
Least the truth should peep through their jugling dress.
For they knew a Cessation would work them more harmes,
Then *Essex* could do the Cavaliers with his Arms.
While they keep the Ships and the Forts in their hand,
They may be Traytors by Sea, as well as by Land.
The Forts will preserve them as long as they stay,
And the Ships carry them and their Plunder away.
They have therefore good reason to account War the better,
For the Law will prove to them but a Killing Letter.

Tuesday.

A Post from his Excellence came blowing his Horn,
For Money to advance, and this spun out the Morn;
And strait to the City some went for relief,
The rest made an Ordinance to carry Powder-Beef.
Thus up go the Roundheads, and *Essex* advances,
But only to lead his Souldiers new dances,
To *Reading* he goes, for at *Oxford* (they say)
His Wife has made him Bull-works to keep him away.

Prince *Rupert*, for fear that the Name be confounded,
Will saw off his Horns, and make him a Round-
    head.
The news was returned with General fame,
That *Reading* was taken ere ever he came.
Then away Rode our Captains, and Souldiers did
    run,
To shew themselves valiant, when the Battail was
    done,
Preparing to plunder ; but as soon as they came,
They quickly perceived it was but a flam :
An Ordinance of Parliament *Essex* brought down,
But that would not serve him to batter the Town.
More Mony was rais'd, more Men and Ammunition,
Carts loaded with Turnips, and other Provision.
His Excellence had Chines, and Rams-heads for a
    Present,
And his Councel of Warre had Woodcock, and
    Pheasant.
But *Ven* had 5000. Calves-heads all in Carts,
To nourish his Men, and to chear up their Hearts.
This made them so valiant that that very day,
They had taken the Town but for running away.
'Twas ordered this day, that thanksgiving be made,
To the Roundheads in Sermons, for their Beef and
    their Bread.

Wednesday.

Two Members this day at a Conference sate,
And one gives the other a knock on the Pate.
This set them a voting, and the Upper House swore,
'Twas a breach of Priviledge he gave him no more.
The lower the breaking their Members head vo‿ted
A breach of their Priviledge; for it is to be noted,
That Reason and Priviledge in it did grow,
'Twas a breach of his Crown and Dignity too,
Then came in the Women with a long long Petition,
To settle Militia, and damn the Commission.
For if fighting continue, they say they did fear,
That Men would be scarce, and Husbands be dear.
So plainly the Speaker the Businesse unties,
That presently all the Members did rise.
They had hardly the leisure all things to lay ope,
But some felt in their Bellies if they had not a Pope.
Some strictly stood to them, and others did fear,
Each carried about them a fierce Cavalier.
This Businesse was handled by the close Committee,
That privately met at a Place in the City.
So closely to voting the Members did fall,
That the humble Sisters were overthrown all.
But they and their Helpers came short at the last,
Till at length the whole Work on Prince *Griffith* was cast.

And he with his troup did handle the matter
He pleased every Woman, as soon as he came at her.
The Businesse had like to have gone on her side,
Had not *Pym* perswaded them not to confide.
For rather than Peace, to fill the Common-Wealth,
He said hee'd do them every night himself.

Thursday.

This Day a great Fart in the House they did hear,
Which made all the Members make Buttons for fear;
And One makes nine Speeches while the Businesse was hot,
And spake through the Nose that he smelt out the Plot.
He takes it to task, and the Articles drawes,
As a breach of their own Fundamental-laws.
Now Letters were read, which did fully relate
A Victory against *Newcastle* of late;
That hundreds were slain, and hundreds did run,
And all this was got ere the Battel begun.
This they resolv'd to make the best on;
And next they resolv'd upon the Question,
That Bonfires and Prayses, the Pulpit and Steeple,
Must all be suborned to couzen the People.
But the policy was more Mony to get,
For the Conquest's dear bought, and far enough set;
Such Victories in *Ireland*, although it be known
They strive to make that Land as bad as our Own.

No sooner the Mony for this was brought hither,
But a croud of true Letters came flocking together,
How *Hotham* and's Army, and others were beaten,
This made the blew members to startle and threaten.
And these by all means must be kept from the City,
And only referred to the Privy Committee.
And they presently with an *Ex tempore* Vote,
Which they have used, so long, that they learned by rote,
They styl'd them Malignant, and to Lyes they did turn them.
Then *Corbet*, instead of the Hangman, must burn them.
And he after that an Ordinance draws,
That none should tell truth that disparag'd the Cause.
Then *Pym* like a *Pegasus* trots up and down,
And takes up an Angel to throw down a Crown.
He stand like a Creature, and makes a long Speech,
That came from his mouth, and part from his breech.
He moves for more Horse, that the Army might be
Part Mans flesh and Horse flesh, as well as he;
And hee'll be a Colonel as well as another,
But durst not ride a Horse, 'cause a Horse rid his Mother.

Friday.

Sir *Hugh Cholmley* for being no longer a Traytor,
Was accus'd of *Treason* in the highest Nature;
'Cause he (as they bad him) his Souldiers did bring,
To turn from Rebellion, and fight for the King.
They voted him out, but, nor they nor their men
Could vote him into the House agen.
Sir *Davids* Remonstrance next to them was read,
From the Cities Round-body, and *Isaac's* the head.
'Twas approv'd; but one Cause produc'd a denyal,
That all Traytors be brought to a Legal tryal.
For 'tis against Reason to vote, or to do
Against Traytors, when *They* are no other but so.
Because about nothing so long they sit still,
They hold it convenient Diurnalls to fill.
And therefore they gave their Chronographer charge
To stuff it with Orders and Letters at large.
The King by's Prerogative, nor by the Law,
Can speak nor print nothing his People to draw,
Yet *Pennyles Pamphletters* they do maintain,
Whose only Religion is Stipendary gain.
Yet *Cum Privilegio*, against King and the State.
The Treason that's taught them (like Parrats) they prate.
These Hackneys are licens't what ever they do,
As if they had Parliament priviledge too.

Thus then they consult : so zealous they are,
To settle the peace of the Kingdom by War.
But against Civil-war their hatred is such,
To prevent it they'le bring in the *Scotch* and the *Dutch*.
They had rather the Land be destroy'd in a minute,
Than abide any thing that has Loyalty in it ;
And yet their Rebellion so neatly they trim,
They fight for the King, but they mean for King *Pym*.
These all to fight for, and maintain are sent
The Laws of *England;* but *New-England* is meant.
And though such disorders are broke in of late,
They keep it the *Anagram* still of a State.
For still they are plotting such riches to bring,
To make *Charles* a rich and glorious King.
And by this Rebellion this good they will doe him,
They forfeit all their Estates unto him.
No Clergy must meddle in Spiritual affairs,
But *Layton* nere herd of it, losing his ears,
For that he might be deaf to the Prisoners cries,
To a spiritual Goalers place he must rise.
The rest have good reason for what they shall do,
For they are both Clergy and Laity too.
Or else at the best when the Question is stated,
They are but *Mechanicks* newly translated.
They may be Committees to practice their bawling,
For stealing of Horse is Spiritual Calling.
The reason why People our Martyrs ador'd,
'Cause their Ears being cut off their Fame sounds the more.

'Twas ordered the Goods of Malignants, and
    Lands,
Shall be shar'd among them, and took into their
    hands.
They have Spirits of more Malignants to come,
That every one in the House may have some
Then down to *Guild-Hall* they return their thanks,
To the Fools whom the Lottery has cheated with
    Blanks.

Saturday.

This day there came news of the taking a Ship,
(To see what strange wonders are wrought in the
    deep)
That a troop of their Horse ran into the Sea,
And pull'd out a Ship alive to the Key.
And after much prating and fighting they say
The Ropes serv'd for Traces to draw her away.
Sure these were Sea-horses, or else by their lying
They'le make them as famous for swimming as
    flying.
The rest of the day they spent to bemoan
Their Brother, the Roundhead that to *Tyburn* was
    gone.
And could not but think it a barbarous thing,
To hang him for killing a friend to the King.
He was newly baptized, and held it was good
To be washed, yet not in water, but blood.
They ordered for his honour to cut off his ears,
And make him a Martyr : but a Zealot appears,

And affirms him a Martyr, for although 'twas his
  fate
To be hang'd, yet he dy'd for the good of the State
Then all fell to plotting of matters so deep,
That the silent Speaker fell down fast asleep.
He recovers himself and rubs up his eyes,
Then motions his House that 'twas time to rise.
So home they went all, and their businesse refer'd
To the Close Committee by them to be heard ;
They took it upon them, but what they did do,
Take notice that none but themselves must know.

Postscript.

Thus far we have gone in Rythme to disclose,
What never was utter'd by any in Prose.
If any be wanting, 'twas by a mishap,
Because we forgot to weigh't by the map.
For over the Kingdom their Orders were spread,
They have made the whole Body as bad as the Head.
And now made such work that all they do,
Is but to read Letters and answers them too.
We thought to make *Finis* the end of the story,
But that we shall have more business for you:
For (as their proceedings do) so shall our *Pen*,
Run roundly from *Munday* to *Munday* agen.
And since we have begun, our Muse doth intend,
To have (like their Votes) no beginning nor end.

The holy Pedler.

From a Forraign shore
   I am come to store,
     Your *Shops* with rare devices:
No *drugs* do I bring
From the *Indian* King,
     No *Peacocks*, *Apes*, nor *Spices*.
Such Wares I do show
As in *England* do grow,
     And are for the good of the Nation,
Let no body fear
To deal in my Ware,
     For *Sacriledge* now's in fashion.

I the *Pedlar* am,
That came from *Amsterdam*
     With a pack of *new Religions*,
I did every one fit,
According to's wit,
     From the *Tub* to *Mahomets pigeons*.
Great Trading I found,
For my spiritual ground,
     Wherein every man was a Medler;
I made People decline,
The learned *Divine*,
     And then they bought *Heaven* of the *Pedler*.

First *Surplices* I took,
Next the *Common-Prayer-book*,
     And made all those Papists that us'd 'um;
Then the *Bishops* and *Deans*,
I stript of their means,
     And gave it to those that abus'd 'um.

The *Clergy-men* next,
I withdrew from their *Text*,
   And set up the gifted *Brother;*
Thus *Religion* I made,
But a matter of trade,
   And I car'd nor for one or t'other.

Then *Tythes* I fell upon,
And those I quickly won,
   'Twas prophane in the *Clergy* to take 'um.
But they serv'd for the Lay,
Till I sold them away,
   And so did Religious make 'um;
But now come away,
To the *Pedler*, I pray,
   I scorn to rob or cozen;
If Churches you lack,
Come away to my Pack,
   Here's thirteen to the dozen.

Church *Militants* they be,
For now we do see,
   They have fought so long with each other;
The Rump's-Churches threw down,
Those that stood for the Crown,
   And sold them to one another.
Then come you factious Crue,
Here's a Bargain now for you,
   With the spoyles of the Church you may revel;
Now pull down the Bells,
And then hang up your selves,
   And so *give his due to the Devil.*

The Hue and Cry after Sir John Presbyter.

With hair in Characters, and Lugs in text;
  With a splay mouth and a nose circumflext;
With a set Ruffe of Musket-bore, that wears
Like Cartrages, or linnen Bandileers,
Exhausted of their sulphurous contents,
In Pulpit fire-works, which that Bomball vents;
The *Negative* and *Covenanting* Oath,
Like two Mustachoes, issuing from his mouth;
The bush upon his chin (like a carv'd story,
In a box-knot) cut by the *Directory;*
Madams Confession hanging at his ear,
Wire-drawn through all the questions, *How* and *Where*
Each circumstance so in the hearing felt,
That when his ears are cropt he'll count them gelt;
The weeping Cassock scar'd into a Jump,
A sign that *Presbyter's* worn to the stump :
The *Presbyter* though charm'd against mischance,
With the *Divine Right* of an *Ordinance.*
  If you meet any that do thus attire 'em,
  Stop them they are the tribe of Adoniram.
What zealous frenzie did the *Senate* seize,
To tare the *Rochet* to such rags as these?
Episcopacy minc'd, reforming *Tweed*
Hath sent us *Runts,* even of her Churches breed;
Lay-interlining *Clergy,* a device
That's nick-name to the stuff call'd *Lops* and *Lice.*

The Beast at wrong-end branded, you may trace
The Devils foot-steps in his cloven face,
A face of severall parishes and sorts,
Like to a Sergeant shav'd at Innes of Courts.
What mean these Elders else, those Kirk Dragoons
Made up of *Ears* and *Ruffs* like *Ducatoons?*
That *Hicrarchy* of *Handicrafts* begun,
Those new *Exchange-men* of *Religion?*
Sure they'r the *Antick heads*, which plac'd without
The Church, do gape and disembogue a sprout:
Like them above the *Commons house* have been
So long without, now both are gotten in;
   Then, what imperious in the Bishop sounds,
The same the *Scotch* Executor rebounds.
This stating *Prelacy*, the *Classick* rout,
That spake it often, e're it spake it out;
   So by an Abbies Scelcton of late,
   I heard an Eccho supererogate
   Through imperfection, and the voice restore,
   As if she had the hiccop o're and o're.
Since they our mixt Diocesans combine
Thus to ride double in their Discipline,
That Pauls *shall to the* Consistory *call*
A Dean *and* Chapter *out of* Weavers-Hall?
Each at the Ordinance for to assist,
With the five thumbs *of his* groat-changing *fist.*
   Down Dagon Synod *with thy motley ware,*
Whilst we do swagger for the Common-Prayer;
That Dove-like Embassie, that wings our sence
To Heavens gate in shape of innocence.
Pray for the Miter'd Authors, and defie
These Demicasters *of Divinity.*
For where Sir John *with* Jack-of-all-trades *joyns,*
His Finger's thicker than the Prelates *Loyns.*

The way to wooe a Zealous Lady.

I Came unto a *Puritan* to wooe,
 And roughly did salute her with a Kiss ;
She shov'd me from her when I came unto ;
 Brother, by yea and nay I like not this :
And as I her with amorous talk saluted,
My Articles with Scripture she confuted.

She told me, that I was too much prophane,
 And not devout neither in speech nor gesture ;
And I could not one word answer again,
 Nor had not so much Grace to call her Sister ;
For ever something did offend her there,
Either my broad beard, hat, or my long hair.

My Band was broad, my 'Parrel was not plain,
 My Points and Girdle made the greatest show ;
My sword was odious, and my Belt was vain,
 My *Spanish* shooes was cut too broad at toe ;
My Stockings light, my Garters ty'd too long,
My Gloves perfum'd, and had a scent too strong.

I left my pure Mistris for a space,
 And to a snip-snap Barber streight went I ;
I cut my Hair, and did my Corps uncase
 Of 'Parrels pride that did offend the eye ;
My high-crown'd Hat, my little Beard also,
My pecked Band, my Shooes were sharp at toe.

Gone was my Sword, my Belt was laid aside,
 And I transformed both in looks and speech ;

My 'Parrel plain, my Cloak was void of Pride,
  My little Skirts, my metamorphis'd Breech,
My Stockings black, my Garters were ty'd shorter,
  My Gloves no scent; thus marcht I to her Porter.

The Porter spide me, and did lead me in,
  Where his sweet Mistris reading was a Chapter:
Peace to this house, and all that are therein,
  Which holy words with admiration wrapt her,
And ever, as I came her something nigh,
She, being divine, turn'd up the white o'th' eye.

Quoth I, dear Sister, and that lik'd her well,
  I kist her, and did passe to some delight,
She, blushing, said, that long-tail'd men would tell,
  Quoth I, I'll be as silent as the night;
And least the wicked now should have a sight
Of what we do, faith, I'll put out the light.

O do not swear, quoth she, but put it out,
  Because that I would have you save your Oath,
In truth, you shall but kisse me, without doubt;
  In troth, quoth I, here will we rest us both;
Swear you, quoth she, in troth? had you not sworn
I'd not have don't, but took it in foul scorn.

A Hue and Cry after the Reformation.

WHen Temples lye like batter'd Quarrs,
  Rich in their ruin'd Sepulchers,
When Saints forsake their painted Glasse
To meet their worship as they passe,

When Altars grow luxurious with the dye
　　Of humane bloud,
　　Is this the floud
　　Of Christianity?

When Kings are cup-boarded like cheese,
Sights to be seen for pence a piece,
When Dyadems, like Brokers tire,
Are custom'd reliques set to hire,
When Soveraignty & Scepters loose their names,
　　Stream'd into words,
　　Carv'd out by swords
　　Are these refining flames?

When Subjects and Religion stir
Like Meteors in the Metaphor,
When zealous hinting and the yawn
Excize our *Miniver* and *Lawn;*
When blue digressions fill the troubled ayr,
　　And th' Pulpit's let
　　To every Set
　　That will usurp the Chair?

Call ye me this the night's farewell,
When our noon day's as dark as Hell?
How can we lesse than term such lights
Ecclesiastick Heteroclites?
Bold sons of *Adam* when in fire you crawl,
　　Thus high to be,
　　Perch'd on the tree,
　　Remember but the fall.

Was it the glory of a King
To make him great by suffering?

Was there no way to build God's House
But rendring of it infamous?
If this be then the merry ghostly trade?
    To work in gall?
    Pray take it all
    Good brother of the blade.

Call it no more the Reformation,
According to the new translation :
Why will you wrack the common brain
With words of an unwonted strain?
As Plunder? or a phrase in senses cleft?
    When things more nigh
    May well supply
    And call it down-right theft.

Here all the *School-men* and *Divines*
Consent, and swear the naked lines
Want no expounding or contest,
Or *Bellarmine* to break a jest.
Since then the Heroes of the pen with me
    Nere scrue the sense
    With difference,
    We all agree agree.

The Times.

TO speak in wet-shod eyes, and drowned looks,
   Sad broken accents, and a vein that brooks
No spirit, life, or vigour, were to own
The crush and triumph of affliction;

And creeping with *Themistocles* to be
The pale-fac'd Pensioners of our enemy,
No 'tis the glory of the Soul to rise
By falls, and at rebound to pierce the skies.
   Like a brave *Courser* standing on the sand
Of some high-working *Fretum*, views a land
Smiling with sweets upon the distant side,
Garnish'd in all her gay embroydered pride,
Larded with Springs, and fring'd with curled Woods,
Impatient, bounces in the cap'ring flouds,
Big with a nobler fury than that stream
Of shallow violence he meets in them;
Thence arm'd with scorn and courage ploughs a way
Through the impostum'd billows of the Sea;
And makes the grumbling Surges slaves to oar
And waft him safely to the further shoar:
Where landed, in a soveraign disdain
He turns back, and surveys the foaming main,
While the subjected waters flowing reel,
Ambitious yet to wash the Victor's heel.
   In such a noble Equipage should we
Embrace th' encounter of our misery.
Not like a field of corn, that hangs the head
For every tempest, every petty dread.
Crosses were the best *Christians* arms: and we
That hope a wished *Canaan* once to see,
Must not expect a carpet-way alone
Without a red-sea of affliction.
Then cast the dice: Let's foord old *Rubicon*,
Cæsar 'tis thine, man is but once undone.
Tread softly though, least *Scyllah's* ghost awake,
And us i'th' roll of his *Proscriptions* take.

Part I. *Rump Songs.*

Rome is revived, and the *Triumvirate*
In the black *Island* are once more a State ;
The City trembles: there's no third to shield,
If once *Augustus* to *Antonius* yield,
Law shall not shelter *Cicero*, the Robe
The *Senate:* Proud successe admits no Probe
Of Justice to correct, or quare the fate
That bears down all as illegitimate ;
For whatsoere it lists to overthrow,
It either finds it, or else makes it so.
   Thus *Tyranny's* a stately *Palace*, where
Ambition sweats to climbe and nustle there ;
But when 'tis enter'd, what hopes then remain ?
There is no Salliport to come out again.
For Mischief must rowle on, and gliding grow,
Like little Rivulets that gently flow
From their first bubbling springs, but still increase
And swell their Chanel as they mend their pace ;
Till in a glorious tyde of villany
They over-run the banks, and posting fly
Like th' bellowing Waves in tumults, till they can
Display themselves in a full Ocean.
And if blind rage shall chance to miss its way,
Bring stock enough alone to make a Sea.
   Thus trebble treasons are secur'd and drown'd
By lowder cryes of deeper mouth and sound.
And high attempts swallow a puny plot,
As Cannons overwhelm the smaller shot.
Whiles the deaf senceless World inur'd a while
(Like the *Catadupi* at the fall of *Nile*)
To the fierce tumbling wonder, think it none,
Thus Custom hallows Irreligion !
And stroaks the patient beast till he admit
The now-grown-light and necessary Bit.

But whither do I ramble? Gauled times
Cannot endure a smart hand ore their crimes
Distracted age? What Dialect or fashion
Shall I assume? to passe the approbation
Of thy censorious *Synod;* which now sit
High *Areopagites* to destroy all wit?
    I cannot say, I say, that I am one
Of th' *Church* of *Ely-house*, or *Abington*,
Nor of those precious Spirits that can deal
The Pomegranates of grace at every meal.
No zealous *Hemp-dresser* yet dipp'd me in
The Laver of adoption from my sin.
But yet if inspiration or a tale
Of a long-wasted six hours length prevail
A smooth Certificate from the sister-hood,
Or to be termed holy before good,
Religious malice, or a faith 'thout works
Other than may proclaim us *Jews* or *Turks:*
If these, these hint at any thing? Then, then
Whoop! my dispairing *Hope* come back agen:
For since the inundation of grace,
All honesty's under water, or in chase.
But 'tis the old worlds dotage, thereupon
We feed on dreams, imagination,
Humours, and cross-grain'd passions which now reign
In the decaying elements of the brain.
'Tis hard to coin new fancies, when there be
So few that lanch out in discovery.
Nay Arts are so far from being cherished,
There's scarce a *Colledge* but has lost its *Head*,
And almost all its *Members:* O sad wound!
Where never an Artery could be judged sound!
To what a height is *Vice* now towred? When we
Dare not miscall it an *Obliquitie?*

So confident, and carrying such an awe,
That it subscribes it self no lesse then *Law* ?
If this be Reformation then ? The great
Account pursued with so much bloud and sweat ?
   In what black lines shall our sad story be
Deliver'd over to posterity ?
With what a dash and scar shall we be read ?
How has Dame *Nature* in us suffered ?
Who of all Centuries the first age are
That sunk the world for want of due repair ?
   When first we issued out in cryes and tears,
(Those salt presages of our future years)
Head-long we dropt into a quiet calm ;
Times crown'd with rosie Garlands, spice and balm,
Where first a glorious *Church* and mother came,
Embrac'd us in her armes, gave us a name
By which we live, and an indulgent brest,
Flowing with stream to an eternal rest.
Thus ravish'd, the poor *Soul* could not guess even,
Which was more kind to her yet, earth or heaven.
Or rather wrapped in a pious doubt
Of heaven, whether she were in or out.
   Next thé *Great Father* of our *Country* brings
His blessing too, (even the *Best* of *Kings*)
Safe and well-grounded Laws to guard our peace,
And nurse our virtues in their just increase ;
Like a pure *Spring* from whom all graces come,
Whose bounty made it double *Christendome:*
Such and so sweet were those *Halcyon* dayes,
That rose upon us in our Infant rayes ;
Such a composed *State* we breathed under,
We only heard of *Jove*, nere felt his thunder.
Terrors were then as strange, as love now grown,
Wrong and Revenge liv'd quietly at home.

The sole contention that we understood,
Was a rare strife and war in doing good.
  Now let's reflect upon our gratefulness,
How we have added, or (O !) made it less,
What are th' improvements ? what our progress, where
Those handsom acts that say that some men were ?
He that to antient wreaths can bring no more
From his own worth, dies banq'rupt on the score.
For Father's Crests are crowned in the Son,
And glory spreads by propogation.
Now virtue shield me ! where shall I begin ?
To what a labyrinth am I now slipp'd in ?
What shall we answer them ? or what deny ?
What prove ? or rather whither shall we fly ?
When the poor widdow'd *Church* shall ask us where
Are all her honours ? and that filial care
We owed so sweet a Parent as the Spouse
Of *Christ*, which here vouchsafed to own a house ?
Where are the *Boanerges ?* and those rare
Brave sons of consolation ? which did bear
The *Ark* before our *Israel*, and dispence
The heavenly *Manna* with such diligence ?
In them the prim'tive Motto's come to passe,
Aut mortui sunt, aut docent literas.
Bless'd *Virgin*, we can only say we have
Thy Prophets Tombes among us, and their grave.
And here and there a man in colours paint,
That by thy ruines grew a mighty *Saint.*
  Next *Cæsar* some accounts are due to thee,
But those in Bloud already written be ;
So loud and lasting, in such monstrous shapes,
So wide the never to be clos'd wound gapes ;
All ages yet to come with shivering, shall
Recite the fearfull pres'dent of thy fall.

Hence we confute thy tenant *Solomon*,
Vnder the Sun a new thing hath been done.
A thing before all pattern, all pretence
Of rule or copy: Such a strange offence
Of such original extract, that it bears
Date only from the *Eden* of our years.
   Laconian Agis! we have read thy fate,
The violence of the *Spartan* love and hate.
How *Pagans* trembled at the thought of thee,
And fled the horror of thy tragedie;
Thyestes cruel feast, and how the Sun
Shrunk in his golden beams that sight to shun.
The bosoms of all Kingdoms open lye,
Plain and emergent to th' inquiring eye.
But when we glance upon our native home,
As the black *Center* to whom all points come,
We rest amazed, and silently admire
How far beyond all spleen ours did aspire.
All that we dare assert, is but a cry
Of an exchanged peace for *Liberty;*
A secret term by inspiration known,
A mist that brooks no demonstration,
Unlesse we dive into our purses, where
We quickly find *Our Freedom* purely dear.
   But why exclaim you thus? may some men say,
Against the times? when equal night and day
Keep their just course? the seasons still the same?
As sweet as when from the first hand they came?
The influence of the *Stars* benigne and free,
As at first *Peep up* in their infancie?
'Tis not those standing motions that divide
The space of years, not the swift hours that glide
Those little particles of age, that come
In thronging *Items* that make up the *Sum*,

That's here intended ; But our crying crimes,
Our Monsters that abominate the times.
'Tis we that make the *Metonimie* good
By being bad, which like a troubled floud
Nothing produce but slimy mire and dirt,
And impudence that makes shame malepert.
To travel further in these wounds that lye
Rankling, though seeming closed, were to deny
Rest to an ore-watch'd world, and force fresh tears
From stench'd eyes, new alarum'd by old fears.
Which if they thus shall heal and stop, they be
The first that ere were cur'd by *Lethargie*.
    This only *Axiom* from ill *Times* increase
I gather, *There's a time to hold ones peace*.

The Commoners.

I

Come your wayes
  Bonny Boyes,
    Of the *Town*,
For now is the time or never,
  Shall your fears,
  Or your cares
    Cast you down?
  Hang your wealth,
  And your health,
    Get renown,
We all are undone for ever.
  Now the *King* and the *Crown*
  Are tumbling down,

And the *Realm* doth groan with *disasters*,
And the scum of the land,
Are the men that command,
And our *Slaves* are become our *Masters*.

2

Now our lives
Children, wives
  And Estate,
Are a prey to the lust and plunder,
  To the rage
  Of our age;
    And the fate
  Of our land
  Is at hand,
    'Tis too late
To tread these *Vsurpers* under.
 First down goes the *Crown*,
 Then follows the *Gown*,
Thus levell'd are we by the *Roundhead*,
 While *Church* and *State* must
  Feed their *Pride* and their *Lust*,
And the *Kingdom* and *King* confounded.

3

Shall we still
Suffer ill
  And be dumb?
And let every *Varlet* undo us?
  Shall we doubt
  Of each Lowt,
    That doth come,
  With a voice
  Like the noise
    Of a Drum,
And a *Sword* or a *Buff-coat* to us?

Shall we lose our estates
By *plunder* and *rates*
To bedeck those proud upstarts that *swagger*,
Rather fight for your meat,
Which these *Locusts* do eat,
Now every man's a beggar.

The Scots Curanto.

1.

COme, come away to the *English* wars,
   A fig for our Hills and Valleys,
'Twas we did begin and will lengthen their jarrs,
  We'l gain by their loss and folleys;
     Let the *Nations*
      By invasions,
  Break through our barrs,
  They can get little good by their *salleys*.

2.

Though *Irish* and *English* entred be,
  The State is become our Debtor.
Let them have our Land, if their own may be free
  And the *Scot* will at length be a getter.
     If they crave it
     Let them have it,
  What care we:
We would fain change our Land for a better.

3.
Long have we longed for the *English* Land,
　But we are hindred still by disasters,
But now is their time, when they can't withstand,
　But are their own Countries wasters.
　　　　If we venter,
　　　　We may enter
　　　By command,
And at last we shall grow to be Masters.

4.
When at first we began to rebell,
　Though they did not before regard us,
How the name of a *Scot* did the *English* quell,
　Which formerly have out-dar'd us.
　　　　For our comming
　　　　And returning,
　　　They paid us well,
And royally did reward us.

5.
The better to bring our ends about,
　We must plead for a *Reformation;*
And tickle the minds of the giddy-brain'd rout,
　With the hopes of an innovation.
　　　　They will love us
　　　　And approve us,
　　　Without doubt,
If we bring in an alteration.

6.
Down with the *Bishops* and their train,
　The *Surplice* and *Common Prayers*,

Then will we not have a King remain,
  But we'l be the *Realms* surveyers.
    So by little
    And a little
  We shall gain
All the Kingdom without gain-sayers.

7.

And when at the last we have conquer'd the *King*,
  And beaten away the *Cavaleers*,
The Parliament next must the same ditty sing,
  And thus we will set the State by the ears.
    By their jarring
    And their warring
  We will bring,
Their Estates to be *ours*, which they think to be *theirs*.

8.

And thus when among us the Kingdom is shar'd,
  And the People are all made Beggars like we;
A *Scot* will be as good as an English *Leard*,
  O! what a unity this will be.
    As we gain it
    We'l retain it
  By the sweard;
And the English shall say, *bonny blew-cap for me*.

An Answer to a Letter from Sir John
Mennis, *wherein he jeers him for
falling so quickly to the use
of the Directory.*

FRiend thou doest lash me with a story,
A long one too of Directory;
When thou alone deserves the Birch,
That brought'st the bondage on the Church.
Didst thou not treat for *Bristol* City,
And yield it up? the more's the pity.
And saw'st thou not, how right or wrong
The Common-prayer-book went along?
Did'st thou not scourse, as if enchanted
For Articles Sir *Thomas* granted?
And barter, as an Author saith,
The Articles oth' Christian Faith?
And now the Directory jostles
Christ out oth' Church and his Apostles;
And tears down the Communion rayles,
That men may take it on their tayles
Imagine, Friend, *Bochus* the King
Engraven on *Sylla's* Signet ring,
Delivering up into his hands
Fugurth, and with him, all his Lands;
Whom *Sylla* took and sent to *Rome*,
There to abide the Senates doom.
In the same posture I suppose,
John standing in's Doublet and Hose,

Delivering up amidst the throng
The Common-prayer and Wisedoms song
To hands of *Fairfax*, to be sent
A Sacrifice to the Parliament.
Thou little thought'st what Jear began,
Wrapt in that Treaty? *Busie John*
There lurk'd, the Fire that turn'd to Cinder,
The Church her Ornaments to Tinder.
There bound up in that Treaty lyes
The fate of all our Christmass-pyes;
Our Holydaies there went to wrack,
Our Wakes were laid upon their back,
Our Gossips spoons away were lurcht,
Our Feasts and Fees for Women churcht;
All this, and more ascribe we might
To thee at *Bristol*, wretched Knight.
Yet thou upbraid'st and rayld'st in rime,
On me, for that which was thy Crime.
So froward Children in the Sun,
Amidst their sports some shrew'd turn done,
The faulty Youth begins to prate,
And layes it on his harmlesse Mate.

    Dated,
From *Nympton* where the Cider smiles,
And *James* has horse as lame as *Giles*,
The fourth of *May*, and dost thou hear?
'Tis as I take the 8th. year
Since *Portugal* by Duke *Braganza*
Was cut from *Spain* without a Hand-saw.
I. S.

The Kings Disguise.

ANd why a Tenant to this vile disguise,
Which who but sees, blasphemes thee with his eyes?
My twins of light within their penthouse shrink,
And hold it their Allegiance now to wink.
Oh! for a state-distinction to arraign
Charles of High Treason 'gainst my Soveraign.
What an usurper to his Prince is wont,
Cloyster and shave him, he himself hath don't.
His muffled feature speaks him a recluse,
His ruines prove him a religious house.
The Sun hath mew'd his beams from off his lamp,
And Majesty defac'd the Royal stamp.
It's not enough thy Dignitie's in thrall,
But thou'lt transmute it in thy shape and all?
As if thy blacks were of too faint a dye,
Without the tincture of Tautology.
Flay an Ægyptian for his Cassocks skin,
Spun of his Countries darknesse, line't within
With Presbyterian budge, that drowsie trance,
The Synod-sable, foggy ignorance:
Nor bodily, nor ghostly *Negro* could
Rough-cast thy figure in a sadder mould:
This Privy-Chamber of thy shape would be
But the close-mourner of thy Royalty:
Twill break the circle of thy Jaylors spell,
A Pearle within a rugged Oyster shell.
Heaven, which the Minster of thy Person owns,
Will fine thee for Dilapidations:

Like to the martyr'd Abbeys courser doom,
Devoutly alter'd to a Pidgeon-room:
Or like the colledge by the changeling rabble,
M—— Elves, transform'd into a stable.
Or if there be a prophanation higher,
Such is the Sacriledge of thine attire,
By which th' art half depos'd: thou lookst like one
Whose looks are under sequestration.
Whose Renegado form, at the first glance,
Shews like the self-denying Ordinance,
Angel of light, and darkness too, I doubt,
Inspir'd within, and yet possess'd without:
Majestick twi-light in the state of grace,
Yet with an excommunicated face.
Charles and his Mask are of a different Mint,
A Psalm of mercy in a miscreant print
The Sun wears mid-night, Day is beetle-brow'd,
And lightning is in Keldar of a cloud.
Oh the accurst Stenography of fate!
The Princely Eagle shrunk into a Bat.
What charm, what Magick vapour can it be,
That shrinks his rayes to this Apostasie?
It is but subtile film of tiffany air,
No Cob-web vizard, such as Ladies wear,
When they are veil'd on purpose to be seen,
Doubling their lustre by their vanquish'd skreen,
Nor the false scabbard of a Princes tough
Metal, and three pild darkness, like the slough
Of an imprison'd flame: 'tis *Faux* in grain,
Dark-Lanthorn to our high Meridian.
Hell belcht the damp, the *Warwick-castle* Vote
Rang *Britains* Corfeu, so our light went out.
Thy visage is not legible, the letters,
Like a Lords name writ in phantastick fetters:

Cloaths where a Switzer might be buried quick:
Sure they would fit the Body politick.
False beard enough to fit a stages plot,
For that's the ambush of their wit, God wot.
Nay all his Properties so strange appear,
Y'are not i'th' presence, though the King be there.
A Libel is his dress, a garb uncouth,
Such as the *Hue* and *Cry* once purg'd at mouth.
Scribbling assassinate, thy lines attest
An ear-mark due, Cub of the Blatant beast,
Whose wrath before 'tis syllabled for worse,
Is Blasphemy unfledg'd, a callow curse.
The Laplanders, when they would sell a wind
Wafting to Hell, bag up thy phrase, and bind
It to the Barque, which at the Voyage-end
Shifts Poop, and breeds the Collicke in the Fiend.
But I'le not dubbe thee with a glorious scar,
Nor sink thy Skullar with a man of War.
The black mouth'd *Si-quis*, and this slandering suit,
Both do alike in picture execute.
But since we're all call'd Papists, why not date
Devotion to the rags thus consecrate?
As Temples use to have their Porches wrought
With Sphynxes, Creatures of an antick draught,
And puzling Pourtraictures, to shew that there
Riddles inhabited, the like is here.
   But pardon Sir, since I presume to be
Clerk of this Closet to your Majesty;
Methinks in this your dark mysterious dresse
I see the Gospel coucht in Parables.
At my next view my pur-blind fancy ripes,
And shews Religion in its dusky types.

Such a Text-Royal, so obscure a shade,
Was *Solomon* in proverbs all array'd.
  Come all the brats of this expounding age,
To whom the spirit is in pupillage;
You that damn more than ever *Sampson* slew,
And with his engine the same jaw-bone too:
How is't he scapes your Inquisition free,
Since bound up in the Bibles livery?
Hence Cabinet-intruders, Pick-locks hence,
You that dim jewels with your *Bristol*-sence:
And Characters, like Witches so torment,
Till they confesse a guilt, though innocent.
Keys for this Coffer you can never get,
None but St. *Peter* ope's this Cabinet.
This Cabinet, whose aspect would benight
Critick spectators with redundant light.
A Prince most seen, is least: What Scriptures call
The Revelation, is most mystical.
  Mount then thou Shadow-royal, and with hast
Advance thy morning-star, *Charles* overcast.
May thy strange journey contradictions twist,
And force fair weather from a Scotish mist;
Heavens Confessors are pos'd, those star-ey'd sages
To interpret Eclipse, thus riding stages.
Thus *Israel*-like, he travels with a cloud,
Both as a conduct to him and a shroud.
But oh! he goes to *Gibeon*, and renews
A league with mouldy bread, and clouted shooes.

The Rebell *SCOT*.

How! Providence! and yet a *Scottish* crew!
Then Madam nature wears black patches too?
What? shall our Nation be in bondage thus
Unto a Land that truckles under us?
Ring the Bells backward, I am all on fire,
Not all the Buckets in a Country Quire
Shall quench my rage. A Poet should be fear'd,
When angry, like a Comets flaming beard.
And where's the Stoick? can his wrath appease
To see his Country sick of *Pym's* disease,
By *Scotch* Invasion to be made a prey
To such *Pig-wiggin Myrmidons* as they?
But, there's charm in verse that I would not quote
The name of *Scot* without an Antidote,
Unlesse my head were red, that I might brew
Invention there that might be poyson too.
Were I a drowsie Judge, whose dismal note
Disgorgeth halters, as a Juglers throat
Doth ribbands: could I (in Sir Emp'rick's tone)
Speak Pills in phrase, and quack destruction:
Or roar like *Marshall*, that *Geneva* Bull,
Hell and Damnation a Pulpit full:
Yet to expresse a *Scot*, to play that prize,
Not all those mouth-Granadoes can suffice.
Before a *Scot* can properly be curst,
I must (like *Hocas*) swallow daggers first.
    Come keen *Iambicks* with your Badgers feet,
And Badger-like, bite till your teeth do meet.
Help ye tart *Satyrists* to imp my rage,
With all the *Scorpions* that should whip this age:

Scots are like Witches, do but whet your pen,
Scratch till the bloud come, they'l not hurt you then.
Now as the Martyrs were inforc'd to take
The shapes of Beasts, like Hypocrites at stake,
I'le bait my *Scot* so, yet not cheat your eyes;
A *Scot* within a Beast is no disguise.
   No more let *Ireland* brag, her harmless Nation
Fosters no Venom, since the *Scots* plantation:
Nor can ours feign'd antiquity maintain,
Since they came in, *England* hath Wolves again.
The *Scot* that kept the Tower, might have shown
(Within the grate of his own breast alone)
The Leopard and the Panther, and ingrost
What all those wild Collegiates had cost
The honest high-shoes in their termly fees,
First to the salvage Lawyer, next to these.
Nature her self doth *Scotch-men* Beasts confesse,
Making their Country such a wildernesse:
A Land that brings in question and suspence
Gods omni-presence, but that *Charles* came thence,
But that *Montross* and *Crawfords* loyal band
Atton'd their sins, and christen'd half the Land.
Nor is it all the Nation hath these spots;
There is a Church, as well as *Kirk* of *Scots:*
As in a picture, where the squinting paint
Shews Fiend on this side, and on that side Saint.
He that saw Hell in's melancholly dream,
And in the twi-light of his fancy's theam
Scar'd from his sins, repented in a fright,
Had he view'd *Scotland,* had turn'd Proselyte.
A Land where one may pray with curst intent,
O may they never suffer banishment!
Had *Cain* been *Scot,* God would have chang'd his *doom,*
Not forc't him wander, but confin'd him home:

Like *Jews* they spread, and as infection fly,
As if the Devil had Ubiquity.
Hence 'tis they live at Rovers, and defie
This or that place, Rags of Geography.
They'r Citizens o'th' world; they'r all in all,
Scotland's a Nation Epidemicall.
And yet they ramble not, to learn the mode
How to be drest, or how to lisp abroad;
To return knowing in the *Spanish* shrug,
Or which of the *Dutch States* a double Jug
Resembles most, in belly, or in beard;
(The Card by which the Marriners are steer'd.)
No, the *Scots-Errant* fight, and fight to eat,
Their *Ostrich-stomachs* make their *Swords* their *meat:*
Nature with *Scots*, as Tooth-drawers hath dealt,
Who use to hang their teeth upon their Belt.
Yet wonder not at this their happy choise,
The *Serpent's* fatall still to *Paradise.*
Sure *England* hath the Hemeroids, and these
On the North posture of the patient seize,
Like Leeches: thus thy Physically thirst
After our bloud, but in the cure shall burst.
Let them not think to make us run o'th' score,
To purchase villanage as once before,
When an Act pass'd to stroak them on the head,
Call them good Subjects, buy them Gingerbread;
Nor Gold, nor Acts of grace, 'tis Steel must tame
The stubborn *Scot:* a Prince that would reclaim
Rebells by yielding, doth like him, (or worse)
Who sadled his own back, to shame his horse.
   Was it for this you left your leaner soil,
Thus to lard *Israel* with *Ægypts* spoyle?
They are the Gospels Life guard: but for them
The Garrison of new *Jerusalem!*

What would the Brethren do? the Cause! the Cause!
Sack possets, and the Fundamental Laws!
Lord! what a goodly thing is want of shirts!
How a *Scotch*-stomach, and no meat, converts!
They wanted food and raiment, so they took
Religion for their Seamstresse and their Cook.
Unmask them well, their honours and estate,
As well as conscience are sophisticate.
Shrive but their titles, and their money poize,
A Laird & twenty pounds pronounc'd with noise,
When constru'd, but for a plain Yeoman go,
And a good sober two-pence, and well so.
Hence then you proud Impostors, get you gone,
You Picts in Gentry and Devotion;
You scandal to the stock of Verse, a race
Able to bring the Gibbet in disgrace.
Hyperbolus by suffering did traduce
The Ostracism, and sham'd it out of use.
The *Indian*, that Heaven did forsware,
Because he heard the *Spaniards* were there.
Had he but known what *Scots* in Hell had been,
He would, *Erasmus*-like, have hung between:
My Muse hath done. A voider for the nonce;
I wrong the Devil should I pick their bones.
That dish is his, for when the *Scots* decease,
Hell, like their Nation, feeds on Barnacles.
   A *Scot*, when from the Gallow-tree got loose,
   Drops into *Styx*, and turns a *Soland-Goose*.

The Scots Apostasie.

IS't come to this? what shall the cheeks of fame,
Stretcht with the breath of learned *Londons* name,
Be flag'd again? and that great piece of sence,
As rich in Loyalty and Eloquence,
Brought to the Test, be found a trick of State?
Like Chymists tinctures, prov'd adulterate?
The Devil sure such language did atchieve,
To cheat our un-forwarned Grandam *Eve*,
As this impostour found out, to besot
Th' experienc'd *English* to believe a *Scot*.
Who reconcil'd the Covenants doubtfull sence?
The Commons argument, or the Cities pence?
Or did you doubt persistance in one good
Would spoyle the fabrick of your Brotherhood,
Projected first in such a forge of sin,
Was fit for the grand Devils hammering?
Or was't ambition that this damned fact
Should tell the world you know the sins you act?
The infamy this super-treason brings,
Blasts more than murders of your *sixty Kings;*
A crime so black, as being advis'dly done,
Those hold with these no competition.
Kings only suffer'd then, in this doth lye
Th' Assassination of *Monarchy*.
Beyond this sin no one step can be trod,
If not t'attempt deposing of your God:
Oh were you so ingag'd, that we might see
Heavens angry lightning 'bout your ears to flee.

Till you were shrivel'd to dust, and your cold Land,
Parcht to a drought beyond the *Lybian* sand !
But 'tis reserv'd, till Heaven plague you worse :
Be Objects of an Epidemick curse.
First, may your Brethren, to whose viler ends
Your power hath bawded, cease to be your friends ;
And prompted by the dictate of their reason,
Reproach the *Traytors* though they hug the *Treason*.
And may their jealousies increase and breed,
Till they confine your steps beyond the *Tweed*.
In forrain Nations may your loath'd name be
A stigmatizing brand of infamy ;
Till forc'd by general hate, you cease to rome
The world, and for a plague to live at home :
Till you resume your poverty, and be
Reduc'd to beg where none can be so free
To grant ; and may your scabby Land be all
Translated to a general Hospitall,
Let not the Sun afford one gentle ray,
To give you comfort of a Summers day ;
But, as a guerdon for your Trayterous War,
Live cherish'd only by the Northern star.
No stranger deign to visit your rude coast,
And be to all but banisht men, as lost.
And such in heightning of the infliction due,
Let provok'd Princes send them all to you.
Your State a Chaos be, where not the Law,
But power, your lives and liberties may aw.
No Subject 'mongst you keep a quiet brest,
But each man strive through bloud to be the best ;
Till, for those miseries on us you've brought,
By your own Sword our just revenge be wrought.

To sum up all —— let your *Religion* be
As your *Allegiance*, mask'd hypocrisie:
Untill, when *Charles* shall be compos'd in dust,
Perfum'd with Epithetes of *good* and *just;*
HE sav'd, incensed Heaven may have forgot
T" afford one act of mercy to a *Scot*,
  Unlesse that *Scot* deny himself, and do
  (What's easier far) renounce his *Nation* too.

The Scots Arrears.

Four hundred thousand pounds!
  A lusty Bag indeed:
Was't ever known so vast a Sum
  Ere past the River *Tweede?*

Great pity it is, I swear,
  Whole Carts was thither sent,
Where hardly two in fifty knew,
  What *Forty shillings* meant:
But 'twas to some perceiv'd,
  Three Kingdoms were undone.
And those that sit here thought it fit,
  To settle them one by one,
Now *Ireland* hath no haste,
  So there they'le not begin;
The *Scotish* ayde must first be paid,
  For ye came freely in,
And *William Lilly* writes ——
  Who writes the truth you know;
In frosty weather they marched hither,
  Up to the chins in snow.

Free quarter at excesse,
  They do not weigh a feather,
Those Crowns for coals, brought in by shoals;
  Scarce kept their men together,
Of Plunder they esteem
  As trifles of no worth,
Of force ye dote, because recruit
  Issued no faster forth.
If once this Cash is paid,
  I hope the *Scot* be spedd,
He need not steal, but fairly deal,
  Both to be cloth'd and fedd.
Our sheep and Oxen may
  Safe in their pastures stand,
What need they filch the cow
  That's milch to sojourn in their land.

I wonder much the *Scot*
  With this defiles his hand,
Because the summ's a price of *Rome*,
  Rais'd out of the Bishops lands;
But too too well ye know
  To what intent they in come;
'Twas not their pains produc'd this gains,
  'Twas sent to pack them home:
Methinks I hear them laugh
  To see how matters proved,
And give a shout, it so fell out,
  Ye were more fear'd than loved.
If *Jockey* after this
  Reneaginge hath forgot,
From antient sires, he much retires,
  And shows himself no *Scot*.

A SONG

On the Schismatick R O T U N D O S.

ONce I a curious Eye did fix,
  To observe the tricks
Of the *Schismaticks* of the Times,
To find out which of them
   Was the merriest Theme,
And best would befit my Rimes;
Arminius I found solid,
  Socinians were not stolid,
Much Learning for Papists did stickle.
  But ah, ah, ha ha ha ha Rotundos *rot,*
 ah, ha ha ha ha Rotundos *rot,*
  'Tis you that my spleen doth tickle.

And first to tell must not be forgot,
  How I once did trot
With a great *Zealot* to a Lecture,
Where I a Tub did view,
   Hung with apron blew;
'Twas the Preachers as I conjecture,
His Use and his Doctrine too
Were of no other hue,
Though he spake in a tone most mickle:
  But ah, ha ha ha, &c.

He taught amongst other prety things
  That the Book of *Kings*
Small benefit brings to the godly,

  Beside he had some grudges
   At the Book of *Judges*,
  And talkt of *Leviticus* odly,
  Wisedome most of all
   He declares *Apocryphal*,
  Beat *Bell* and the *Dragon*, like *Michael*.
   But ah, ah, ha ha ha ha, &c.

  'Gainst Humane Learning next he envyes,
   And almost boldly say's,
  'Tis that which destroyes Inspiration,
  Let superstitious sence
   And wit be banished hence,
  With Popish Predomination
  Cut *Bishops* down in hast,
   And *Cathedrals* as fast
  As Corn that's fit for the sickle :
   But ah, ah, ha ha ha ha Rotundos *rot*,
  ah, ha ha ha ha ha Rotundos *rot*,
   'Tis you that my spleen doth tickle.

Cromwell's *Panegyrick*.

SHall Presbyterian Bells ring *Cromwels* praise,
While we stand still and do no Trophyes raise
Unto his lasting name? Then may we be
Hung like the Bells for our dependencie.
Well may his Nose, that is Dominicall,
Take pepper in't, to see no Pen at all
Stir to applaud his merits, who hath lent
Such valour, to erect a Monument

Part I. *Rump Songs.*

Of lasting praise; whose name shall never dye,
While *England* has a Church, or Monarchy.
He whom the laurell'd Army home did bring
Riding triumphant o're his conquer'd King,
He is the Generals Cypher now; and when
Hee's joyn'd to him, he makes that One a Ten.
The Kingdoms Saint; *England* no more shall stir
To cry St. *George*, but now St. *Oliver*.
Hee's the Realm Ensign; and who goes to wring
His Nose, is forc'd to cry, *God save the King*.
He that can rout an Army with his name,
And take a City, ere he views the same:
His Souldiers may want bread, but n'ere shall fear
(While hee's their General,) the want of Beer;
No Wonder they wore Bayes, his Brewing-fat
(*Helicon*-like) make Poets Laureat.
When Brains in those Castalian liquors swim,
We sing no Heathenish *Pean*, but a Hymne;
And that by th' Spirit too, for who can chuse
But sing *Hosanna* to this King of Jewes?
Tremble you *Scotish* Zealots, you that han't
Freed any Conscience from your Covenant:
That for those bal'd Appellatives of *Cause*,
Religion, and the *Fundamental Laws*,
Have pull'd the old Episcopacy down,
And as the Miter, so you'le serve the Crown.
You that have made the Cap to th' Bonnet vaile
And made the Head a Servant to the Taile.
And you curst spawne of Publicans, that sit
In every County, as a plague to it;
That with your Yeomen Sequestrating Knaves,
Have made whole Counties beggerly, and Slaves.
You Synod, that have sate so long to know
Whether we must believe in God, or no;

You that have torn the Church, and sate t' impaire
The Ten Commandements, the Creed, the Prayer;
And made your honors pull down Heavens glory,
While you set up that Calfe, your *Directory:*
We shall no wicked Jews-ear'd Elders want,
This Army's built of Churches Militant:
These are new Tribes of *Levi;* for they be
Clergy, yet of no Universitie.
Pull down your Crests, for every bird shall gather,
From your usurping back, a stollen feather.
Your great Lay Levite, whose great Margent tires
The patient Reader, while he blots whole quires,
Nay reams with Treason; and with Nonsence too,
To justifie what e're you say or do:
Whose circumcised ears are hardly grown
Ripe for another Persecution:
He must to *Scotland* for another paire;
For he will lose these, if he tarry here.
Burges that Reverend Presbydean of *Pauls*,
Must (with his Poundage) leave his Cure of Souls,
And into *Scotland* trot, that he may pick
Out of that Kirk, a nick-nam'd Bishoprick.
The Protean Hypocrites, that will ne're burn,
Must here, or else at *Tyburn* take a turn.
And *Will. the Conqueror* in a *Scotish* dance
Must lead his running Army into *France.*
Or he and's Juncto among those Crews
In *Holland* build a Synagogue of Jewes,
And spread Rebellion; Great *Alexander*
Fears not a Pillory, like this Commander.
And *Bedlam John*, that at his Clerks so raves,
Using them not like servants, but like slaves.
He that so freely rail'd against his Prince,
Call'd him *dissembling subtile Knave*, and since

Has stil'd the whole Army *Bankrupts;* said, that none
Of their Estates were equal to his own :
He that was by a strong Ambition led
To set himself upon the Cities head :
But when he has restor'd his both-side fees,
Hee'l be as poor, or they as rich as hee's.
And that still-gaping Tophet Goldsmiths Hall,
With all his Furies, shall to ruine fall.
Wee'l be no more gull'd by that Popish story,
But shall reach Heav'n without that Purgatory :
What Honour does he merit? what Renown?
By whom all these Oppression are pull'd down.
And such a Government is like to be
In Church and State, as eye did never see :
Magicians hold, hee'l set up Common-prayer ;
Looking in's face they find the Rubrick there.
His Name shall never dye by fire nor floud,
But in Church-windows stand, where Pictures stood.
And if his Soul lothing that house of clay,
Shall to another Kingdom march away,
Under some Barnes floor his bones shall lye,
Who Churches did, and Monuments defie :
Where the rude Thrasher with much knocking on,
Shall wake him at the Resurrection.
   And on his Grave since there must be no Stone,
   Shall stand this Epitaph ; *That he has none.*

15—2

The Scotch War.

WHen first the *Scottish* War began
   The *English* man, we did trepan, with Pellit and
      Pike,
The bonny blythe and cunning *Scot*
Had then a Plot, which they did not, well smell, it's
   like;
Although he could neither write, nor read,
Yet our General *Lashly* cross'd the *Tweed*
With his gay gangh of Blew-caps all,
And we marcht with our Generall;
We took *New-castle* in a trice,
But we thought it had been Paradice,
They did look all so bonny and gay,
Till we took all their Pillage away.

Then did we streight to plundering fall
Of great and small, for were all most valiant that day;
And *Jinny* in her Satten Gown the best in Town,
From Heel to Crown was gallant and gay;
Our silks and sweets made such a smother,
Next day we knew not one another:
For *Jockie* did never so shine,
And *Jinny* was never so fine;
A geud faith a gat a ged Beaver then,
But it's beat into a Blew-cap agen
By a Redcoat, that did still cry, Rag,
And a red snowt, a the Deel aw the Crag.

The *English* raised an Army streight
With mickle state, and we did wate to face them as well;

Then every valiant Musquet man put fire in pan,
And we began to lace them as well;
But before the Sparks were made a Cole,
They did every man pay for his Pole;
Then their bought Land we lent them agen,
Into *Scotland* we went with our men;
We were paid by all, both Peasant and Prince,
But I think we have soundly paid for it since,
For our Silver is wasted, Sir, all,
And our Silks hang in *Westminster* Hall.

The Godly Presbyterian, that holy man,
The War began with Bishop and King,
Where we like Waiters at a Feast
But not the least of all the guest, must dish up the thing,
We did take a Covenant to pull down
The Cross, the Crosier, and the Crown,
With the Rochet the Bishop did bear.
And the Smock that his Chaplain did wear:
But now the Covenant's gone to wrack,
They say, it looks like an old Almanack,
For *Jockie* is grown out of date,
And *Jinny* is thrown out of late.

I must confesse the holy firk did only work
Upon our Kirk for silver and meat,
Which made us come with aw our broods,
Venter our bloods for aw your goods, to pilfer & cheat;
But we see what covetousness doth bring,
For we lost our selves when we sold our King;
And alack now and welly we cry,
Our backs mow and bellies must dye;
We fought for food, and not vain-glory,
And so there's an end of a *Scottish* mans Story;

I curse all your Silver and Gold,
Aw the worst tale that ever was told.

The Power of Money.

'Tis not the silver nor gold for it self
    That makes men adore it, but 'tis for its power:
For no man does doat upon pelf because pelf,
    But all Court the Lady in hope of her dower:
The wonders that now in our dayes we behold,
Done by the irresistable power of gold,
Our Zeal, and our Love, and Allegiance do hold.

This purchaseth Kingdoms, Kings, Scepters, and Crowns;
    Wins Battels, and conquers the Conquerors bold;
Takes Bulwarks, and Castles, and Cities, and Towns,
    And our prime Laws are writ in letters of gold;
'Tis this that our Parliament calls and creates,
Turns Kings into Keepers, and Kingdomes to States,
And peopledomes these into highdomes translates.

This made our black Synod to sit still so long,
    To make themselves rich, by making us poor;
This made our bold Army so daring and strong,
    And made them turn them, like Geese, out of door;

'Twas this made our Covenant-makers to make it,
And this made our Priests for to make us to take it,
And this made both Makers and Takers forsake it.

'Twas this spawn'd the dunghill Crew of Committees and 'strators,
  Who live by picking the Crockadile Parliaments gums;
This first made, and then prospered the Rebells and Traytors,
  And made Gentry of those that were the Nations scums:
This Herald gives Armes not for merit, but store,
And gives Coats to those that did sell Coats before,
If their pockets be but lin'd well with argent and ore.

This, plots can devise, and discover what they are;
  This, makes the great Fellons the lesser condemn;
This, sets those on the Bench, that should stand at the Bar,
  Who Judge such as by right ought to Execute them;
Gives the boysterous Clown his unsufferable pride,
Makes Beggars, and Fools, and Usurpers to ride,
Whiles ruin'd Propriators run by their side.

Stamp either the Armes of the State or the King,
  St. *George* or the Breeches, *C. R.* or *O. P.*
The Cross or the Fiddle, 'tis all the same thing;
  This, still is the Queen whosoe'er the King be;
This, lines our Religion, builds Doctrine & Truth,
With Zeal and the Spirit the factious endueth,
To club with St. *Katharine*, or sweet Sister *Ruth*.

'Tis money makes Lawyers give Judgement, or plead
  On this side, or that side, on both sides, or neither;
This makes young men Clerks that can scarce write or read,
  And spawns arbitrary Orders as various as the weather;
This makes your blew Lecturers pray, preach, and prate
Without reason or sence against Church, King, or State,
To shew the thin lining of his twice-covered pate.

'Tis money makes Earls, Lords, Knights, and Esquires
  Without breeding, descent, wit, learning, or merit;
This makes Ropers, and Ale-drapers, Sheriffs of Shires,
  Whose trade is not so low, nor so base as their spirit:
This Justices makes, and wise ones we know,
Furr'd Aldermen too, and Mayors also;
This makes the old Wife trot, and makes the Mare to go.

This makes your blew aprons Right Worshipfull;
   And for this we stand bare, and before them do fall;
They leave their young heirs well fleeced with wooll,
   Whom we must call Squires, and then they pay all:
Who with beggarly souls, though their bodies be gawdy,
Court the pale Chamber-maid, and nick-name her a Lady,
And for want of good wit, they do swear and talk bawdy.

This Mariages makes, 'tis a Center of love,
   It draws on the man, and it pricks up the woman
Birth, virtue, and parts no affection can move,
   Whilst this makes a Lord stoop to the Brat of a Broom-man;
This gives virtue and beauty to the Lasses that you wooe,
Makes women of all sorts and ages to do;
'Tis the soul of the world, and the worldling too.

This procures us whores, hawks, hounds and hares;
   'Tis this keeps your Groom, and your Groom keeps your Gelding;
This built Citizens Wives, as well as wares;
   And this makes your coy Lady so coming and yielding;
This buys us good Sack, which revives like the spring,
'Tis this your Poetical fancies do bring;
And this makes you as merry as we that do sing.

Contentment.

WHat though the ill times do run crosse to our will,
    And Fortune still frown upon us,
Our hearts are our own, and shall be so still.
    A fig for the plagues they lay on us;
Let us take t'other cup, to chear our hearts up,
    And let it be purest Canary;
We'll ne'er shrink nor care, at the Crosses we bear,
    Let them plague us untill they be weary.

What though we are made both Beggars and Slaves?
    Let's endure it, and stoutly drink on't,
'Tis our comfort we suffer 'cause we won't be Knaves,
    Redemption will come e're we think on't;
We must flatter and fear, those that over us are,
    And make them believe that we love them,
When their Tyranny is past, we can serve them at last,
    As they have serv'd those have been above them.

Let the Levites go preach for the Goose or the Pig,
    To drink Wine at *Christmas* or *Easter*:
The Doctor may labour our lives to new trig,
    And make Nature fast while we feast her;
The Lawyer may bawl, out his Lungs and his Gall
    For Plaintiff, and for Defendant,
At his Book the Scholar lye, while with *Plato* he dye
    With an ugly hard word at the end on't.

Then here's to the man that delights in *sol fa*,
   For Sack is his only Rozin.;
A load of hey ho, is not worth a ha ha,
   He's a man for my money that draws in ;
Then a pin for the muck, and a pin for ill luck,
   'Tis better be blithe and frolick,
Than sigh out our breath, and invite our own death
   By the Gout, or the Stone, or the Collick.

On the Goldsmiths Committee.

COm Drawer, some wine,
  Or wee'll pull down the Sign,
   For we are all joviall Compounders :
We'll make the house ring,
With healths to our KING,
   And confusion light on his Confounders.

Since Goldsmiths Committee
Affords us no pitty,
   Our sorrows in wine we will steep 'um,
They force us to take
Two Oaths, but wee'll make
   A third, that we ne'er meant to keep 'um.

And next, who e're sees
We drink on our knees,
   To the King, may he thirst that repines :
A fig for those Traytors
That look to our waters,
   They have nothing to do with our Wines.

And next, here's a Cup
To the Queen, fill it up,
   Were it poyson we would make an end on't :
May *Charles* and she meet.
And tread under feet
   Both Presbyter and Independent.

To the Prince, and all others,
His Sisters and Brothers,
   As low in condition as high born,
We'll drink this, and pray
That shortly they may
   See all them that wrongs them at *Tyburn*.

And next, here's three bouls
To all gallant souls,
   That for the King did, and will venter ;
May they flourish when those
That are his, and their foes,
   Are hang'd and ram'd down to the Center.

And next, let a Glasse
To our undoers passe,
   Attended with two or three Curses :
May plagues sent from Hell
Stuff their bodies as well
   As the Cavaliers coyn doth their purses.

May the Cannibals of *Pym*
Eat them up limb by limb,
   Or a hot Feaver scorch 'um to embers ;
Pox keep 'um in bed
Untill they are dead,
   And repent for the losse of their Members.

And may they be found
In all to abound,
  Both with Heaven and the Countries anger,
May they never want Fractions,
Doubts, Fears, and Distractions,
  Till the Gallow-tree choaks them from danger.

The mad Zealot.

AM I mad, O noble *Festus*,
When Zeal and godly knowledge
Have put me in hope
To deal with the Pope,
As well as the best in the Colledge?
  Boldly I preach, hate a Crosse, hate a Surplice,
  Miters, Copes, and Rochets:
  Come hear me pray nine times a day,
  And fill your heads with Crochets.

In the house of pure *Emanuel*
I had my Education,
Where my friends surmise
I dazell'd mine eyes
With the light of Revelation.
  Boldly I preach, &c.

They bound me like a Bedlam,
They lasht my four poor quarters;
Whilst thus I endure,
Faith makes me sure
To be one of *Foxes* Martyrs.
  Boldly I preach, &c.

These injuries I suffer
Through Antichrists perswasions;
Take off this Chain,
Neither *Rome* nor *Spain*
Can resist my strong invasions.
    Boldly I preach, &c.

Of the beasts ten horns (God blesse us!)
I have knock'd off three already:
If they let them alone,
I'le leave him none:
But they say I am too heady.
    Boldly I preach, &c.

When I sack'd the seven-hill'd City,
I met the great red Dragon;
I kept him aloof
With the armour of proof,
Though here I have never a rag on.
    Boldly I preach, &c.

With a fiery Sword and Target
There fought I with this Monster:
But the sons of Pride
My Zeal deride,
And all my deeds misconster.
    Boldly I preach, &c.

I unhors'd the Whore of *Babel*
With the Lance of Inspirations:
I made her stink,
And spill her drink
In the cup of Abominations,
    Boldly I preach, &c.

I have seen two in a Vision,
With a flying Book between them :
I have been in despair
Five times a year,
And cur'd by reading *Greenham*,
   Boldly I preach, &c.

I observ'd in *Perkins* Tables
The black Lines of Damnation,
Those crooked veins
So stuck in my Brains,
That I fear'd my Reprobation,
   Boldly I preach, &c.

In the holy tongue of *Canaan*
I plac'd my chiefest pleasure,
Till I prickt my foot
With an *Hebrew* root,
That I bled beyond all measure.
   Boldly I preach, &c.

I appear'd before th' Archbishop,
And all the High Commission :
I gave him no Grace,
But told him to his face
That he favour'd Superstition.
   Boldly I preach, hate a Crosse, hate a Surplice,
   Miters, Copes, and Rochets :
   Come hear me pray nine times a day,
   And fill your heads with Crotchets.

Of banishing the Ladies out of Town.

1.

A Story strange I will unfold,
   Then which a sadder ne're was told,
How the Ladies were from *London* sent,
   With mickle woe and discontent.

2.

A heart of Marble would have bled,
   To see this rout of white and red,
Both *York* and *Lancaster* must fly,
   With all their painted Monarchy.

3.

Those faces which men so much prize,
   In Mrs. *Gibbes* her Liveries,
Must leave their false and borrowed hue,
   And put on grief that's only true.

4.

Those pretty patches long and round,
   Which covered all that was not sound
Must be forgotten at the Farmes,
   As useless and suspicious charmes.

5.

Now we must leave all our Designes,
   That were contriv'd within the lines;
Communication is deny'd,
   If to our Husbands we be try'd.

6.
And here's the misery alone,
   We must have nothing but our own,
Oh give us Liberty, and we
   Will never ask propriety.

7.
Alas how can a Kisse be sent,
   From Rocky *Cornwall* into *Kent* ?
Or how can *Sussex* stretch an arm
   To keep a Northern servant warm.

8.
Oh *London!* Centre of all Mirth,
   Th' Epitome of English Earth ;
All Provinces are in the streets,
   And *Warwick-shire* with *Essex* meets.

9.
Then farewell *Queen-street*, and the Fields,
   And Garden that such pleasure yields,
Oh who would such fair Lodgings change,
   To nestle in a plunder'd Grange !

10.
Farewell good places old and new,
   And *Oxford Kates* once more adieu ;
But it goes unto our very hearts,
   To leave the Cheese-cakes and the Tarts.

11.
Farewell *Bridge-foot* and *Bear* thereby,
   And those bald-pates that stand so high,

We wish it from our very Souls,
That other Heads were on those powles.

12.

But whether hands of Parliament,
Or of Husbands, we're content,
Since all alike such Traytors be,
Both against us and Monarchy.

Loyalty confin'd.

BEat on proud Billowes, *Boreas* Blow,
   Swell curled Waves, high as *Jove's* roof,
Your incivility doth shew,
That innocence is tempest proof,
   Though surely *Nereus* frown, my thoughts are calm,
   Then strike affliction, for thy wounds are balm.

That which the world miscalls a Goale,
A private Closet is to me,
Whilst a good Conscience is my Baile,
And Innocence my Liberty:
   Locks Barres and Solitude together met,
   Make me no Prisoner but an Anchorit.

I whil'st I wish'd to be retir'd
Into this private room was turn'd,
As if their wisedomes had conspir'd,
The Salamander should be burn'd.
   Or kike a Sophy yet would drown a fish,
   I am constrain'd to suffer what I wish.

The Cynick hugs his poverty,
The Pelican her wilderness,
And 'tis the *Indians* pride to be
Naked on frozen *Caucasus*.
    Contentment cannot smart, Stoicks we see
    Make torments easie to their Apathy.

These Menacles upon my Arm,
I as my Mistris's favours wear;
And for to keep my Ankles warm,
I have some Iron Shackles there.
    These walls are but my Garrison; this Cell
    Which men call Goal, doth prove my Cittadel.

So he that strook at *Jasons* life,
Thinking he had his purpose sure:
By a malicious friendly Knife,
Did only wound him to a cure.
    Malice I see wants wit, for what is meant,
    Mischief oft-times, proves favour by th' event.

I'me in this Cabinet lockt up,
Like some high-prized *Margaret*,
Or like some great Mogul or Pope,
Are cloystered up from publick sight.
    Retirement is a piece of Majesty,
    And thus proud *Sultan*, I'me as great as thee.

Here sin for want of food must starve,
Where tempting Objects are not seen;
And these strong Walls do only serve,
To keep Vice out, and keep me in.
    Malice of late's grown charitable sure,
    I'me not committed, but I'me kept secure.

Whence once my Prince affliction hath,
Prosperity doth Treason seem ;
And for to smooth so tough a Path,
I can learn Patience from him.
   Now not to suffer, shews no Loyal heart,
   When Kings wants ease, Subjects must bear a part.

Have you not seen the Nightingale,
A Pilgrim koopt into a Cage,
How doth she chant her wonted tale,
In that her narrow hermitage.
   Even then her charming melody doth prove,
   That all her Boughs are Trees, her Cage a Grove.

My soul is free as the ambient aire,
Although my baser part's immur'd,
Whilest Loyal thoughts do still repair,
T' accompany my Solitude.
   And though immur'd, yet I can chirp and sing,
   Disgrace to Rebels, glory to my King.

What though I cannot see my King,
Neither in his Person or his Coyne,
Yet contemplation is a thing,
That renders what I have not mine.
   My King from me, what Adamant can part,
   Whom I do wear engraven on my heart.

I am that Bird whom they combine,
Thus to deprive of Liberty ;
But though they do my Corps confine,
Yet maugre hate, my Soul is free.
   Although Rebellion do my Body bind,
   My King can only captivate my mind.

On the demolishing the Forts.

IS this the end of all the toil,
   And labour of the Town?
And did our Bulwarks rise so high
   Thus low to tumble down?

All things go by contraries now,
   We fight to still the Nation,
Who build Forts to pull down Popery,
   Pull down for Edification.

The Independents tenets, and
   The wayes so pleasing be.
Our City won't be bound about,
   But stands for Liberty.

The Popish doctrine shall no more
   Prevail within our Nation;
For now we see that by our works,
   There is no Justification.

What an Almighty army's this,
   How worthy of our praysing,
That with one Vote can blow down that
   All we so long were raising!

Yet let's not wonder at this Change,
   For thus 'twill be with all.
These works did lift themselves too high,
   And Pride must have a fall.

And when both Houses vote agen,
  The Cavies to be gone,
Nor dare to come within the lines
  Of Communication.

They must reserve the sense or else,
  Referr't to the Divines,
And they had need sit seven years more
  Ere they can read those lines.

They went to make a *Gotham* on't,
  For now they did begin
To build these mighty banks about,
  To keep the Cuckoes in.

Alas what need they take such pains!
  For why a Cucko here
Might find so many of his Mates,
  Hee'l sing here all the year.

Has *Isaac* our L. *Maior*, L. *Maior*,
  With Tradesmen and his Wenches,
Spent so much time, and Cakes and Beer,
  To edifie these Trenches!

All trades did shew their skill in this,
  Each Wife an Engineer;
The Mairess took the tool in hand,
  The maids the stones did bear.

These Bulwarks stood for Popery,
  And yet we never fear'd um,
And now they worship and fall down,
  Before those Calves that rear'd 'um.

But though for Superstition,
  The Crosses have been down'd,
Who'ld think these works would Popish turn,
  That ever have been round?

This spoyles our Palmistry; for when
  Wee'l read the Cities fate,
We find nor Lines nor Crosses now,
  As it hath had of late.

No wonder that the Aldermen,
  Will no more mony lend,
When they that in this seven years,
  Such learned works have pen'd.

Now to debase their lofty lines,
  In which the wits delighted,
'Tis thought they'l nere turn Poets more,
  Because their works are slighted.

These to a dolefull tune are set,
  For they that in the town.
Did every where cry Up go we,
  Now they must sing down down.

But if that *Tyburn* do remain,
  When tother slighted be,
The Cits will thither flock and sing,
  Hay, hay, then up go we.

Upon Routing the Scots Army.

A SONG.

To the Tune of *Through the Wood Lady.*

1.

Am lend, lend y'are lugs Joes, an Ise speak a Song,
   Sing heome agen Jocky, *sing heome agen* Jocky,
O hes velient Acts an hes Prowes emong,
   Sing heome agen heome agen O valent Jocky.

2.

Sirs, *Jockie's* a Man held a mickle Note,
   Sing heome agen Jocky, &c.
Tha Breech o tha Covenant stuck in hes Throte,
   Sing heome agen, heome agen, &c.

3.

For *Jockie* was riteous, whilk ye wad admire,
   Sing heome agen Jocky, &c.
A fooght for tha Kirk, bet a plunder'd tha Quire.
   Sing heome agen Jocky, &c.

4.

An *Jockie* waxt roth, and toll *Angland* a cam,
   Sing heome agen Jocky, &c.
Fro whence hee'd return, but alack a is lame,
   Sing heome agen Jocky, &c.

5.

An *Jockie* was armed fro topp toll to toe,
    Sing heome agen Jocky, *&c.*
Wi a po're o Men and th'are geod D—— I tro,
    Sing heome agen Jocky, *&c.*

6.

So valent I wis they were, an sa prat,
    Sing heome agen Jocky, *&c.*
Ne Cock nor Hen durst stand in thare gat,
    Sing heome agen Jocky, *&c.*

7.

In every strete thay ded sa flutter,
    Sing heome agen Jocky, *&c.*
Ne Child durst shaw his Bred and Butter,
    Sing heome agen, Jocky, *&c.*

8.

Whan th' *Anglish* Forces they her'd on o're night,
    Sing heome again Jocky, *&c.*
Next Morne thay harnest themsels for a fight,
    Sing heome agen, heome agen, &c.

9.

Thare D—— wes tha Mon that wad be sen stoot,
    Sing heome agen, Jocky, *&c.*
He feas't tham awhile, then turn'd Ars's about,
    Sing heome agen, heome agen, &c.

10.

Tha Men that ater this valent *Scot* went,
    Sing heome agen Jocky, *&c.*

Had ner foond him oout, bet by a strong sent,
  Sing *heome agen, heome agen O valent* Jocky.

11.

Bet se tha reward ò that Cowardly Crue,
  Sing *heome agen* Jocky, &c.
Thare Countremon *Ballatine* sent 'em to *Corfew*,
  Not home agen, home agen, O slavish Jocky.

The disloyal Timist.

1.

NOw our holy Wars are don,
  Betwixt the Father and the Son ;
And since we have by righteous fate,
Distrest a Monarch and his Mate.
And first their heirs fly into *France*
To weep out their Inheritance ;
    Let's set open all our Packs,
      Which contain ten thousand wracks ;
Cast on the shore of the red Sea
Of *Naseby*, and of *Newbery*.
If then you will come provided with Gold,
    We dwell
    Close by Hell,
    Where wee'l sell
    What you will,
    That is ill ;
For Charity waxeth cold.

2.

Hast thou done murther, or bloud spilt,
We can soon giv't another name,
That will keep thee from all blame:
But be it still provided thus,
That thou hast once been one of us;
Gold is the God that shall pardon the Guilt,
      For we have
      What shall save
      Thee from th' Grave,
      Since the Law
      We can awe;
Although a famous Prince's bloud were spilt.

3.

If a Church thou hast bereft
Of its Plate, 'tis holy-theft;
Or for Zeal-sake, if thou beest
Prompted on to take a Priest;
Gold is a sure prevailing Advocate:
      Then come
      Bring a summe,
      Law is dumb:
      And submits,
      To our wits;
For it's Policy guides a State.

A Medley.

1.

Oom for a Gamester that plays at all he sees,
Whose fickle faith is fram'd, Sir, to fit such times as these ;
One that cryes *Amen*, to ev'ry factious Prayer,
From *Hugh Peters* Pulpit, to St. *Peters* Chair :
One that can comply with Crosier and with Crown ;
    And yet can bouze
    A full carouze,
While bottles tumble down,
    Dery down.

2.

This is the way to trample without trembling.
    Since Sycophants only secure ;
Covenants and Oaths are badges of dissembling,
    'Tis the Politique pulls down the pure :
    To plunder and pray,
    To protest and betray
Are the only ready wayes to be great,
    Flattering will do the feat :
    Ne're go, ne're stir
    Have ventred farther,
Then the greatest o' th' Damme's in the Town,
    From a Copper to a Crown.

3.

I am in an excellent homor now to think well,
And I'me in another humor now to drink well ;

Fill us up a Beer-bowl boy,
That we drink it merrily;
And let none other see,
Nor cause to understand,
For if we do, 'tis ten to one we are Trepand.

4.

Come fill us up a brace of Quarts,
Whose Anagram is call'd true hearts;
If all were true as I would hav't,
And *Britain* were cured of its humor,
Then I should very well like my fate,
And drink off my Wine at a freer rate,
Without any noise or tumor;
And then I should fix my humor.

5.

But since 'tis no such matter, change your hue,
I may cog and flatter, so may you;
  Religion
  Is a wigeon,
  And reason
  Is Treason;
And he that hath a Noble heart may bid the world adieu.

6.

We must be like the *Scotish* man,
Who with intent to beat down schism,
Brought forth a Presbyterian,
A Canon and a Catechism.
If Beuk wont do't, then *Jockie* shoot,
The Kirk of *Scotland* doth command;
And what hath been, since he come in,
I am sure we ha' cause to understand.

A Medley of the Nations.

The Scot.

1.

I Am the bonny *Scot* Sir,
My name is *Mickle John;*
'Tis I was in the Plot Sir
When first the Wars began:
I left the Court one thousand
Six hundred forty one;
    But since the flight
    At *Worster* fight
We are aw undone.
I serv'd my Lord and Master
When as he liv'd at home,
Untill by sad disaster
He receiv'd his doom;
    But now we fink,
    Uds bred I think
The Deel's gat in his room,
    He ne man spares,
    But stamps and stares
At all Christendom.

2.

I have travel'd mickle grounds,
Since I came from *Worster* bounds,
I have gang'd the jolly rounds
    Of the neighbouring Nations;

And what their opinions are
Of the *Scotch* and *English* war,
In geed faith I sal declare,
 And their approbations.
　　Jockie swears
　　He has his load,
　　Bears the rod,
　　Comes from God,
　And complaints go very odd
　Since the siege at *Worster;*
　　We were wounded
　　Tag and rag,
　　Foot and leg,
　　Wemb and crag;
　Hark I hear the *Dutchman* brag,
　And begin to bluster.

The Dutch.

3.

Uds Sacrament, sal *Hoghen Moghen* States
Strike down der top sails unto puny Powers;
Ten twosand tun of Tivel Dammy Fates,
If dat der Ships and Goods prove not all ours;
Since dat bloot and wounds do delight dem,
Tararara Trumpet sounds,
Let *Van Tromp* go fort and fight dem;
All de States shall first be crown'd,
English *Skellam* fight not on goat side;
Out at last the *Flemins* bear,
Dey ha' giv'n us sush a broad side;
Dat ick sal be forc't to retreat,
See de *French man* he comes in compleat.

The French.

4.

By Gat Mounsieur 'tis much in vain
For *Dushland*, *France*, or *Spain*,
To crosse de *English* main;
De Nation now is grown so strong,
De Divla er't be long
Must learna de same tongue.
'Tis bettra den far to combine,
    To sel dem Wine,
And teasha dem to make der Laty fine;
We'll teash dem for to trip and minsh,
    To kick and winsh,
For by de Sword we never sal convince,
Since every Brewer dere can beat a Prince.

The Spaniard.

5.

What are the *English* to quarrel so prone,
Dat dey cannot now adayes let deir neighbour alone,
And sal de Grave and the Catholick King,
Before ever dus control'd wid a sword and a sling;
Sal bode de *Indias* be left unto de sway,
And purity a dose dat do plunder and pray;
E're dat we will suffer such affronts for to be,
We'll tumble dem down, as you sal sennon see:

The Welsh.

6.

Taffy was once a Cottamighty of *Wales*,
Put her Cosin *O. P.* was a Creater,
Was come in her Country Catsspluttery nailes,
Was take her welch hook and was peat her;
Was eat up her Sheese,
Her Tuck and her Geese,
Her Pick, her Capon was ty for't;
   Ap Richard, ap Owen, ap Morgon, ap Stefen,
   Ap Shenkin, ap Powel was fly for't.

The Irish.

7.

O hone, O hone, poor Teg and shone,
  O hone may howl and cry,
St. *Patrick* help dy Country men,
  Or fait and trot we dye;
De *English* steal our hoart of *Vsquebagh,*
Dey put us to de sword all in *Dewguedagh:*
Help us St. *Patrick* we ha no Saint at all but dee,
O let us cry no more, *O hone, a cram, a cree!*

The English.

8.

A Crown, a Crown, make room,
The *English* man is come,

   Whose valour
   Is taller
Than all Christendome:
The *Spanish*, *French*, and *Dutch*,
Scotch, *Welch*, and *Irish* Grutch,
   We fear not,
   We care not,
For we can deal with such.
You thought when we began in a Civil war to waste,
   Our Tillage
   Your Pillage
Should come home at last:
   For when we
   Could not agree,
You thought to share in our fall;
   But nere stir Sir,
   For first Sir
We shall noose you all.

A Medley.

1.

The English. Let the Trumpets sound,
   And the Rocks rebound,
Our English Natives comming;
  Let the Nations swarm,
  And the Princes storm;
We value not their drumming,
'Tis not *France* that looks so smug
Old fashions still renewing,
It is not the *Spanish* shrug,

Scotish cap, or *Irish* rug ;
Nor the *Dutch-mans* double jug
Can help what is ensuing,
Pray my Masters look about,
For something is a Brewing.

2.

He that is a Favorite consulting with Fortune,
If he grow not wiser, then he's quite undone;
In a rising Creature we daily see certainly,
He is a Retreater that fails to go on :
    He that in a Builder's trade
    Stops e're the Roof be made,
    By the Aire he may be betray'd
    And overthrown :
    He that hath a Race begun,
    And let's the Goale be won;
    He had better never run,
      But let 't alone.

3.

    Then plot rightly,
    March sightly,
Shew your glittering Arms brightly :
    Charge hightly,
    Fight sprightly :
Fortune gives renown.
    A right riser
    Will prize her,
She makes all the World wiser;
    Still try her,
    Wee'l gain by her
A Coffin or a Crown.

4.

If the *Dutchman* or the *Spaniard*
    Come but to oppose us,
We will thrust them out of the Main-yard,
    If they do but nose us:
Hans, *Hans*, think upon thy sins,
And then submit to *Spain* thy Master;
For though now you look like Friends,
Yet he will never trust you after;
Drink, drink, give the *Dutchman* drink
And let the tap and kan run faster;
For faith, at the last I think
A brewer will become your Master.

5.

Let not poor Teg and Shone
Vender from der Houses,
Lest dey be quite undone
In der very trowzes:
And all her Orphans bestow'd under hatches,
And made in *London* free der to cry matches;
St. *Patrick* wid his Harp do tun'd wid tru string
Is not fit to unty St. *Hewson's* shooes-strings.

6.

    Methinks I hear
    The Welch draw near,
And from each lock a louse trops;
    Ap Shon, ap LLoyd,
    Will spen'd her ploot.
For to defend her mouse-traps:
Mounted on her *Kifflebagh*
With coot store of *Koradagh*,

The Pritish war begins.
With a hook her was over come her
Pluck her to her, thrust her from her,
By cot her was preak her shins.
   Let Taffy fret,
    And Welch-hook whet,
And troop up Pettigrees;
   We only tout,
    Tey will stink us out,
Wit Leeks and toasted Sheeze.

7.

But *Jockie* now and *Jinny* comes,
Our Brethren must approve on't;
For pret a Cot dey beat der drums
Onely to break de Couvenant.
Dey bore St. *Andrew's* Crosse,
Till our Army quite did rout dem,
But when we put um to de Losse
De deal a Crosse about dem:
The King and Couvenant they crave,
Their Cause must needs be further'd;
Although so many Kings they have
Most barbarously, basely murther'd.

8.

The French. The French-man he will give consent,
Though he trickle in our veins;
   That willingly
    We may agree,
To a marriage with Grapes and Graines:
   He conquers us with kindnesse,
    And doth so far entrench,

That fair, and wise, and young, and rich
  Are finified by the *French:*
He prettifies us with Feathers and Fans,
With Petticoats, Doublets, and Hose:
    And faith they shall
    Be welcome all
If they forbear the nose.
    For love or for fear,
    Let Nations forbear;
If fortune exhibit a Crown,
    A Coward he
    Must surely be,
That will not put it on.

The Levellers Rant.

TO the *Hall*, to the *hall*,
  For justice we call,
On the *King* and his pow'rful *adherents* & *friends*
Who still have endeavour'd, but we work their ends.
'Tis we will pull *down* what e're is above us,
And make them to *fear* us, that never did *love* us,
  Wee'l *level* the *proud*, and make every degree,
  To our *Royalty* bow the *Knee*,
    'Tis no lesse then treason,
    'Gainst freedom and Reason
  For our brethren to be higher then we.

2.

  First the thing, call'd a King,
  To judgement we bring,
And the *spawn* of the *court*, that were prouder then he,
And next the two Houses united shall be,

It does to the *Romish* religion enveagle,
For the State to be two-headed, like the *spredeagle*
Wee'l purge the superfluous Members away,
They are too many Kings to sway,
    And as we all teach,
    'Tis our Liberties breach,
For the Freeborn *Saints* to obey.

3.

Not a claw, in the *Law*,
Shall keep us in aw;
Wee'l have no *cushon-cuffers* to tell us of hell,
For we are all *gifted* to do it as well,
'Tis freedom that we do hold forth to the *Nations*
To enjoy our *fellow-creatures* as at the creation.
The *Carnal* mens wives are for men of the *spirit*,
Their wealth is our own by merit,
    For we that have right,
    By the *Law* called *Might*,
Are the *Saints* that must *judge* and *inherit*.

The Safety.

Since it has been lately enacted *high Treason*,
For a man to speak *truth* of the *heads* of the *state*
Let every wise man make use of his reason,
  See and hear what he can, but take heed what he prate.
  For the proverbs do learn us,
He that stays from the battail sleeps in a whole skin,
And our words are our own, if we can keep 'um in.
What fools are we then, that to *prattle* begin,
  Of things that do not concern us?

2.

Let the three kingdoms fall to one of the *prime ones*
   My mind is a Kingdom, and shall be to me,
I could make it appear, if I had but the time once,
   I'm as happy with one, as he can be with three.
     If I could but enjoy it,
He thats mounted on high, is a mark for the *hate*,
   And the *envy* of every *pragmatical* pate,
While he that *creeps* low, lives safe in his state,
     And *greatness* do scorn to annoy it.

3.

I am never the better which side gets the battel,
   The *Tubs* or the *Crosses*, what is it to me?
They'l never increase my goods or my cattel,
   But a *beggar's* a *beggar* and so he shall be,
     Unless he turn *Traytor*,
Let *Misers* take courses to hep up their treasure,
Whose *lust* has no *limits*, whose mind has no *measure*
Let me be but quiet and take a little pleasure,
     A little contents my nature.

4.

My Petition shall be that Canary be cheaper,
   Without Patent or Custom, or cursed Excise;
That the *Wits* may have leave to drink deeper and deeper,
   And not be undone, while their heads they *baptise*,
     And in liquor do drench 'um;
If this were but granted, who would not desire,
To *dub* himself one of *Apollo's* own Quire?
We'll ring out the Bells, when our noses are on fire,
     And the quarts shall be the buckets to drench 'um.

5.
I account him no wit, that is gifted at railing,
  And *flirting* at those that above him do sit,
While they do out-wit him, with *whipping* and *goaling*,
  Then his *purse* and his *person* both pay for his wit,
    'Tis better to be drinking;
If sack were reform'd into twelve-pence a quart,
I'ld study for money to Marchandize for't,
And a friend that is true, we together will sport.
    Not a word, but we'l pay them with thinking.

The Leveller.

Nay prethee don't fly me,
  But sit thee down by me,
I cannot endure
A man that's demure,
  Go hang up your *Worships* and *Sirs;*
    Your *Congies* and *Trips*,
    With your legs and your lips,
    Your *Madams* and *Lords*,
    And such finikin words,
    With the Complements you bring,
      That do spell *NO-THING*,
  You may keep for the *Chains* and the *Furs:*
For at the beginning was no Peasant or Prince,
And 'twas policy made the distinction since.

2.
  Those Titles of Honours
  Do remain in the *Donours*,

And not in that thing,
To which they do cling,
If his soul be too narrow to wear 'um,
No delight can I see
In that word call'd degree,
Honest *Dick* sounds as well
As the name of an *ell*,
That with Titles doth swell,
And sounds like a *spell*,
To affright mortal ears that hear 'um,
He that wears a brave soul, and dares gallantly do,
May be his own Herald and Godfather too.

3.

Why should we then doat on,
One with a Fools coat on?
Whose *Coffers* are cram'd,
But yet he'l be damn'd
Ere he'l do a good act or a wise one?
What *Reason* has he
To be ruler o're me?
That's a Lord in his chest,
But in's *head* and his *breast*,
Is empty and bare,
Or but puff'd up with air,
And can neither *assist* nor *advise* one.
Honour's but *air*, and *proud flesh* but *dust* is,
'Tis we *Commons* makes *Lords*, and the *Clerk* makes the *Justice*.

4.

But since men must be
Of a different degree,
Because most do aspire,
To be greater and higher,
Then the rest of their Fellows and Brothers.

He that has such a spirit,
Let him gain it by's merit,
Spend his *brains, wealth,* or *blood*
For his *Countries* good,
And make himself fit
By his *valour* or *wit,*
For *things* above the *reach* of *all others.*
For *Honour's* a *Prize,* and who wins it may wear it,
If not 'tis a *Badge* and a *burthen* to bear it.

5.

For my part let me
Be but quiet and free,
I'le drink Sack and obey,
And let great ones sway,
And spend their whole time in thinking,
I'le ne're busie my Pate
With secrets of State,
The *News books* I'le burn all,
And with the *Diurnall*
Light *Tobacco* and admit
That they're so far fit,
As they serve *good company* and *drinking.*
All the *name* I desire is an honest *Good-Fellow,*
And that *man* has no worth that won't sometimes be mellow.

The Royalists Answer.

I Have reason to fly thee,
And not sit down by thee;
For I hate to behold,
One so sawcy and bold,

    To *deride* and contemn his Superiours,
      Our *Madams* and *Lords*,
      And such mannerly words,
      With the *gestures* that be
      Fit for every degree,
    Are things that we and you
      Both claim as our due
    From all those that are our Inferiours.
For from the beginning there were *Princes* we know,
'Twas you *Levellers* hate 'um, 'cause you can't be so.

              2.

    All Titles of Honours
    Were at first in the *Donours*.
    But being granted away
    With the Grantees stay,
Where he wear a small soul or a bigger.
    There's a necessity
    That there should be degree.
    Where 'tis due we'l afford
    A *Sir John*, and my *Lord*,
    Though *Dick*, *Tom*, and *Jack*,
    Will serve you and your Pack,
  Honest *Dick's* name enough for a Digger.
He that has a strong *Purse* can all things be or do,
He is *valiant* and *wise* and *religious* too.

              3.

    We have cause to adore,
    That man that has store,
    Though a *Bore* or a sot,
    There's something to be got;
Though he be neither *honest* nor *witty;*
    Make him high, let him rule,
    Hee'l be playing the fool,

And *transgresse*, then we'l *squeze*
Him for *fines* and for *fees*.
And so we shall gain,
By the wants of his brain,
'Tis the *Fools-cap* that maintains the *City*.
If honour be *air*, 'tis in common, and as fit,
For the *fool* & the *clown*, as for the *champion* or the *wit*.

4.

Then why mayn't we be
Of different degree?
And each man aspire
To be greater and higher
Then his *wiser* and *honester* brother,
Since *Fortune* and *Nature*
Their *favours* do scatter;
This hath *valour*, that *wit*,
T'other *wealth*, nor is't fit
That one should have all,
For then what would befall
Him that's *born* nor to *one* nor to'ther?
Though *honour* were a *prize* at first, now 'tis a *chattle*,
And as *merchantable* grown as your wares or your cattle.

5.

Yet in this we agree,
To live quiet and free,
To drink *sack* and *submit*,
And not shew our wit
By our *prating*, but *silence*, and *thinking*,
Let the politick *Jewes*
Read *Diurnals* and *Newes*,
And lard their discourse,
With a Comment that's worse,

That which pleaseth me best
Is a Song or a Jest,
And my obedience I'le shew by my *drinking*.
He that drinks well, does sleep well, he that sleeps well, doth think well.
He that thinks well, does do well, he that does well must drink well.

The Independents resolve.

COme Drawer and fill us about some Wine
    Let's merrily tipple the day's our own,
Wee'l have our delights, let the Country go pine,
    Let the King and his Kingdom groan.
The Crown is our own, and so shall continue,
    Wee'l Monarchy baffle quite,
Wee'l drink off the Kingdomes revenue,
    And sacrifice all to delight.
        'Tis Power that brings
        Us all to be Kings,
And wee'l be all crown'd by our might.

2.

A fig for divinity lectures and law,
    And all that to Loyalty do pretend,
While we by the sword keep the Kingdom in aw,
    Our Power shall never have end.
The *Church* and the *State* wee'l turn into liquor,
    And spend a whole Town in a day,
We'l melt all their *bodkins* the quicker
    Into Sack, and drink them away.

We'l keep the *demeans*
And turn *Bishops* and *Deans*,
And over the *Presbyters* sway.

3.

The nimble St. *Patrick* is sunk in his boggs,
And his Country-men sadly cry *O hone! O hone!*
St. *Andrew* and's *Kirk-men* are lost in the foggs,
Now we are the *Saints* alone.
Then on our *Superiours* and *Equalls* we trample,
And *Jockie* our stirrup shall hold,
The *City's* our *Mule* for example,
That we may in plenty be roul'd.
Each delicate dish,
Shall but *Eccho* our wish
And our *drink* shall be cordial gold.

The Lamentation.

Mourn, *London*, mourn,
Bathe thy polluted *soul* in tears;
Return, return,
Thou hast more cause for grief, then th'hadst for fears,
For the whole *Kingdom* now begins
To feel thy sorrow as they saw thy sins,
And now do no
Compassion show
Unto thy misery and woe,
But slight thy *sufferings* as thou didst theirs.

2.

Pride towring Pride,
And boyling lust, those fatal twins,
Sit side by side,
And are become *Plantations* of sins.

Hence thy *Rebellions* first did flow,
Both to the King above, and him below.
   And sordid sloth
   The Nurse of both,
Have rais'd thy crimes to such a growth,
That sorrow must conclude as sin begins.

3.

 Fire raging fire,
Shall burn thy *stately towers* down,
 Yet not expire,
Tygres and *Wolves*, or men more savage grown,
 Thy Childrens brains, and thine shall dash,
And in your *blood* their guilty tallons wash,
   Thy *Daughters* must
   Allay their lust,
 Mischiefs will be on mischief thrust,
Till thy *Cap* tumble as thou mad'st the Crown.

4.

 Cry *London* cry!
Now now petition for redresse,
 Where canst thou fly?
Thy emptied *Chests* augment thy heavinesse,
 The *Gentry* and the *Commons* loath,
Th' adored *Houses* slight thee worse than both,
   The King poor Saint
   Would help, but can't;
 To heav'n alone unfold thy *want*,
Thence came thy Plagues, thence onely Pity flow'th.

The Reformation.

TEll not me of Lords or Laws,
    Rules or *Reformation,*
All that's done's not worth two straws,
    To the welfare of the Nation.
Men in power do rant it still,
And give no *reason* but their will,
    For all their domination.
Or if they do an act that's just,
'Tis not because they would, but must,
To *Gratifie* some parties lust,
    Or merely for a fashion.

2.

Our expence of blood and purse
    Has produc'd no profit.
Men are still as bad or worse,
    And will be what e're comes of it.
We've shuffled out, and shuffled in,
The persons, but retain the sin,
    To make our game the surer,
Yet spite of all our pains and skill,
The Knaves all in the pack are still,
And ever were and ever will,
    Though something now demurer.

3.

And it cannot but be so,
    Since those toys in *fashion,*
And of Souls so base and low,
    And mere *Bigots* of the *Nation,*
Whose designs are power and wealth,
At which, by *rapines, fraud,* and *stealth,*

Audaciously they vent ye,
They lay their Consciences aside,
And turn with every *winde* and *tide*,
Puff'd on by *Ignorance* and *Pride*,
And all to look like *Gentry*.

4.

Crimes are not punish'd 'cause their *Crimes*,
But 'cause they're low and little,
Mean men for *mean faults* in these times
Make satisfaction to a tittle;
While those in *office* and in *power*,
Boldly the *underlings* devour.
Our Cobweb laws can't hold 'um.
They sell for many a *Thousand crown*,
Things which were never yet their own,
And this is *law* and *custom* grown.
'Cause those do *judge* that *sold* 'um.

5.

Brothers still with *Brothers* brawl,
And for trifles sue 'um,
For two *Pronouns* that spoyl all,
Those contentious *Meum*, *Tuum*,
The wary *Lawyer* buyes and builds,
While the *Client* sells his fields,
To sacrifice to's fury;
And when he thinks to obtain his right
He's baffled off, or beaten quite,
By th' Judges will, or Lawyers slight,
Or ignorance of the Jury.

6.

See the *Trades-man* how he thrives
With perpetual trouble,
How he *cheats*, and how he *strives*
His Estate t'enlarge and double,

Extort, oppress, grind and encroach,
To be a *Squire*, and keep a *Coach*,
  And to be one o'th' *Quorum*,
Who may with's *Brother worships* sit,
And judge without *law, fear* or *wit*
Poor petty *Thieves* that nothing get,
  And yet are brought before 'um.

7.
And his way to get all this
  Is mere *dissimulation*,
No factious Lecture does he miss,
  And *scapes no schism that's in fashion*.
But with short hair and shining shooes,
He with two Pens and's Note-book goes,
  And winks and writes at Randome ;
Thence with *short meal* and *tedious Grace*,
In a loud tone and Publick place,
Sings *Wisedoms hymnes*, that *trot* and pace,
  As if *Goliah* scan'd 'um.

8.
But when death begins his threats,
  And his *Conscience* struggles,
To call to mind his former *cheats*
  Then at heav'n he turns his juggles.
And out of all's ill-gotten store,
He gives a dribling to the poor,
  In a *Hospital* or *School-house*,
And the suborned *Priest* for's hire
Quite frees him from th' *infernal* fire,
And places him ith' *Angels* quire,
  Thus these *Jack-puddings* fool us.

9.
All he gets by's pains ith' close,
Is that he dyed worth so much,

18—2

Which he on's doubtfull seed bestows,
   That neither care nor know much,
Then *Fortunes favourite* his heir,
Bred base, and ignorant and bare,
   Is blown up like a bubble,
Who *wondring* at's own suddain rise,
By Pride, Simplicity and Vice,
Falls to's sports, *drink*, *drab* and *dice*
   And makes all fly like stubble.

10.

And the *Church* the other twin,
   Whose mad zeal enrag'd us,
Is not purify'd a pin,
   By all those broyles in which she engag'd us,
We, our Wives turn'd out of doors,
And took in *Concubines* and *Whores*,
   To make an alteration
Our *Pulpitteers* are proud and bold,
They their own *Wills* and *factions* hold,
And sell *salvation* still for *Gold*,
   And here's our *Reformation*.

11.

'Tis a madnesse then to make,
   Thriving our employment,
And *lucre* love, for *Lucres* sake,
   Since we've possession, not enjoyment.
Let the times run on their course,
For opposition makes them worse,
   We ne're shall better find 'um,
Let *Grandees* wealth and power ingrosse,
And honour too, while we sit close,
And laugh and take our plenteous dose,
   Of *sack* and never mind 'um.

CHRONOSTICON

Decollationis *CAROLI* Regis tricesimo die *Januarii*, secunda hora Pomeridiana, Anno Dom. MDCXLVIII.

Ter Deno IanI Labens ReX SoLe CaDente
CaroLVs eXVtVs SoLIo SCeptroqVe SeCVto.

CHARLES —— ah forbear, forbear ! lest Mortals prize
His Name too dearly, and Idolatrize.
His Name ! Our Losse ! Thrice cursed and forlorn
Be that Black Night which usher'd in this Morn.

CHARLES our Dread Soveraign !——hold ! lest Outlaw'd Sense
Bribe, and seduce tame Reason to dispense
With those Celestial powers ; and distrust
Heav'n can behold such Treason, and prove Just.

CHARLES our Dread Soveraign's murther'd ! tremble ! and
View what Convulsions shoulder-shake this Land,
Court, City, Country, nay three Kingdoms run
To their last stage, and Set with him their Sun.

CHARLES our Dread Soveraign's murther'd at His Gate !
Fell fiends ! dire Hydra's of a stiff-neck'd-State !

Strange Body-politick ! whose Members spread,
And Monster-like, swell bigger than their HEAD.

CHARLES of Great Britain ! He ! who was the known
King of three Realms, lyes murther'd in his own ;
He ! He ! who liv'd, and Faith's Defender stood,
Dy'd here to re-Baptize it in his bloud.

No more, no more, Fame's Trump shall Eccho all
The rest in dreadfull Thunder. Such a Fall
Great Christendom nere pattern'd ; and 'twas strange
Earth's Center reel'd not at this dismal Change.

The Blow struck Britain blinde, each well-set Limb
By dislocation was lopt off in HIM.
And though she yet lives, she lives but to condole
Three Bleeding Bodies left without a Soul.

Religion puts on Black, sad *Loyalty*
Blushes and mourns to see bright Majesty
Butcher'd by such Assassinates ; nay both
'Gainst *God*, 'gainst *Law*, *Allegiance*, and their *Oath*.

Farewell sad Isle ! Farewell ! thy fatal Glory
Is Sum'd, Cast up, and Cancell'd in this Story.

AN ELEGIE.

Upon King CHARLES *the first, murthered publickly by his Subjects.*

WEre not my *Faith* buoy'd up by sacred bloud,
It might be *drown'd* in this prodigious flood ;
Which reasons highest ground doth so exceed,
It leaves my *soul* no Anch'rage, but my *Creed;*
Where my *Faith* resting on th' *Original;*
Supports it self in this the *Copies* fall ;
So while my Faith floats on that *Bloudy wood*,
My reason's cast away in this *Red flood*,
Which ne're o'reflows us all : Those showers past
Made but Land-floods, which did some vallies wast ;
This stroak hath cut the only neck of land
Which between us, and this *Red Sea* did stand,
That covers now our world, which cursed lies
At once with two of *Ægypts* prodigies ;
O're-cast with darkness, and with bloud o're-run,
And justly, since our hearts have theirs outdone ;
Th' Inchanter led them to a lesse known ill,
To act his sin, then 'twas their *King to kill :*
Which crime hath widdowed our whole Nation,
Voided all Forms, left but Privation
In *Church* and *State;* inverting ev'ry right ;
Brought in Hells State of fire without light ;
No wonder then, if all good eyes look red,
Washing their Loyal hearts from bloud so shed ;
The which deserves each pore should turn an eye,
To weep out, even a bloudy *Agony*.

Let nought then passe for *Musick*, but sad cryes,
For *Beauty*, bloudless cheeks, and bloud-shot eyes.
All colours soil but black, all odours have
Ill scent but *Myrrh*, incens'd upon this *Grave:*
It notes a *Jew*, not to believe as much,
The cleaner made by a Religious touch
Of their *Dead Body*, whom to judge to dye,
Seems the Judaical Impiety.
To kill the *King*, the *Spirit Legion* paints
His rage with Law, the Temple and the Saints :
But the truth is, He fear'd and did repine,
To be cast out, and back into the Swine :
And the case holds, in that the Spirit bends
His malice in this Act, against his ends :
For it is like, the sooner hee'll be sent
Out of that body, He would still torment ;
Let *Christians* then use otherwise this bloud,
Detest the Act, yet turn it to their good ;
Thinking how like a *King of Death* He dies ;
We easily may the world and death despise :
Death had no sting for him, and its sharp arm,
Only of all the troop, meant him no harm,
And so he look'd upon the *Axe*, as one
Weapon yet left, to guard Him to his *Throne ;*
In His great Name then may His Subjects cry,
Death thou art swallowed up in Victory.
If this our losse a comfort can admit,
'Tis that his narrowed *Crown* is grown unfit
For his enlarged Head, since his distresse
Had greatned this, as it made that the lesse ;
His *Crown* was faln unto too low a thing
For him, who was become so great a *King ;*
So the same hands enthron'd him in that *Crown*,
They had exalted from Him, not pull'd down ;

And thus Gods truth by them hath rendred more,
Than e're mens falshood promis'd to restore;
Which, since by Death, alone he could attain,
Was yet exempt from weaknesse, and from pain;
Death was enjoyn'd by God, to touch a part,
Might make his passage quick, ne'r move his heart;
Which ev'n expiring was so far from death,
It seem'd but to command away his breath.
And thus his *Soul*, of this her triumph proud,
Broke, like a flash of lightning, through the cloud
Of flesh and bloud; and from the highest line
Of humane vertue, pass'd to be divine:
Nor is't much lesse his vertues to relate,
Than the high glories of his present state;
Since both then passe all Acts but of belief,
Silence may praise the one, the other grief.
And since, upon the Diamond, no lesse
Than Diamonds, will serve us to impresse,
I'le only wish that for his Elegie,
This our *Josias* had a *Jeremie*.

AN ELEGIE

On {
The best of Men,
The meekest of Martyrs,
CHARLES *the First, &c.*
}

Does not the Sun call in his light, and day
Like a thin exhalation melt away?
Both wrapping up their Beams in Clouds, to be
Themselves Close Mourners at the Obsequie

Of this great Monarch? does his Royal Bloud,
Which th'Earth late drunk in so profuse a floud,
Not shoot through her affrightned womb, and make
All her convulsed Arteries to shake
So long, till all those hinges that sustain,
Like Nerves, the frame of nature shrink again
Into a shuffled Chaos? Does the Sun
Not suck it from its liquid Mansion,
And Still it into vap'rous Clouds, which may
Themselves in bearded Meteors display,
Whose shaggy and dishevel'd Beams may be
The *Tapers* at this black Solemnitie?
You seed of Marble in the Womb accurst,
Rock'd by some storm, or by some Tigress nurst,
Fed by some Plague, which in blind mists was hurld,
To strew infection on the tainted World;
What fury charm'd your hands to Act a deed,
Tyrants to think on would not weep, but bleed?
And Rocks by instinct so resent this Fact,
They'ld into Springs of easie tears be slack'd.
Say sons of tumult, since you think it good,
Still to keep up the trade, and Bath in Blood
Your guilty hands, why did you then not state
Your Slaughters at some cheap and common rate?
Your gluttonous and lavish Blades might have
Devoted Myriads to one publick Grave;
And lop'd off thousands of some base allay,
Whilst the same Sexton that inter'd their clay,
In the same Urne their Names too might entomb,
But when on him you fixt your fatall Doom,
You gave a blow to Nature, since even all
The stock of man now bleeds too in his fall.
Could not Religion, which you oft have made
A specious glosse your black designs to shade,

Teach you, that we come nearest Heaven when we
Are suppled into acts of Clemency?
And copy out the Deity agen,
When we distill our mercies upon men?
But why do I deplore this ruine? He
Only shook off his fraile Humanity,
And with such calmnesse fell, he seem'd to be,
Even lesse unmov'd and unconcern'd than we;
And forc'd us from our Throes of Grief to say,
We only died, he only liv'd that Day:
So that his *Tomb* is now his *Throne* become,
T'invest him with the Crown of Martyrdome;
And death the shade of nature did not shroud
His Soul in Mists, but its clear Beams uncloud,
That who a Star in our Meridian shone,
In Heaven might shine a Constellation.

On the Death of his Royal Majestie, CHARLES *late King of* ENGLAND, *&c.*

WHat went you out to see? a dying King?
 Nay more, I fear an Angel suffering.
But what went you to see? a Prophet slain?
Nay that and more, a Martyr'd Soveraign.
Peace to that sacred dust! *Great Sir*, our fears
Have left us nothing but obedient tears
To court your hearse, and in those pious flouds
We live, the poor remainder of our goods.
Accept us in these latter Obsequies,
The unplundred riches of our hearts and eyes;

For in these faithfull streams, and emanations,
W'are Subjects still beyond all *Sequestrations*.
Here we cry more than Conquerors: malice may
Murder Estates, but hearts will still obey;
These are your glory's yet above the reach
Of such whose purple lines confusion preach.
 And now, (*Dear Sir*) vouchsafe us to admire
With envy your arrival, and that *Quire*
Of *Cherubims* and *Angels* that supply'd
Our duties at your triumphs: where you ride
With full cælestial *Joyes*, and *Ovations*,
Rich as the Conquest of three ruin'd *Nations*.
 But 'twas the heavenly plot that snatch'd you hence,
To crown your Soul with that magnificence,
And bounden rites of honour, that poor earth
Could only wish and stangle in the birth.
Such pitied emulation stop'd the blush
Of our ambitious shame, non-suited us.
For where souls act beyond mortality,
Heaven only can perform that *Jubilee*.
 We wrastle then no more, but blesse your day,
And mourn the anguish of our sad delay:
That since we cannot adde, we yet stay here
Fettered in clay: Yet longing to appear
Spectators of your blisse, that being shown
Once more, you may embrace us as your own;
Where never envy shall divide us more,
Nor City tumults, nor the worlds uproar;
But an eternal hush, a quiet peace
As without end, so still in the increase,
Shall lull humanity asleep, and bring
Us equal Subjects to the Heavenly King.

Till then I'le turn *Recusant*, and forswear
All *Calvin*, for there's *Purgatory* here.

AN EPITAPH.

STay Passenger : Behold and see
The widowed Grave of *Majestie*,
Why tremblest thou ? Here's that will make
All but our stupid souls to shake.
Here lies entomb'd the sacred dust
Of *Peace* and *Piety*, Right and Just.
The bloud (O start'st not thou to hear ?)
Of a *King*, 'twixt hope and fear
Shed and hurried hence to be
The miracle of misery.

Adde the ills that *Rome* can boast,
Shrift the world in every coast,
Mix the fire of Earth and Seas
With humane spleen and practices,
To puny the records of time,
By one grand *Gygantick* crime,
Then swell it bigger till it squeeze
The Globe to crooked hams and knees,
Here's that shall make it seem to be
But modest *Christianitie*.

The *Law-giver*, amongst his own,
Sentenc'd by a Law unknown.
Voted *Monarchy* to death
By the course *Plebeian* breath.
The *Soveraign* of all command,
Suff'ring by a *Common* hand.

A Prince, to make the odium more,
Offer'd at his very door.
The *Head* cut off, O death to see't !
In obedience to the feet.
And that by *Justice* you must know,
If you have Faith to think it so.
We'll stir no further then this Sacred Clay,
But let it slumber till the *Judgment* day :
Of all the *Kings* on Earth, 'tis not denyed,
Here lies the first that for *Religion* dyed.

The Engagement stated.

BEgon *Expositor :* the *Text* is plain,
No *Church*, no *Lord*, no *Law*, no *Soveraign :*
Away with mental reservations, and
Senses of Oaths in files out-vy the *Strand :*
Here's Hell truss'd in a thimble, in a breath,
Dares face the hazard of the second death.
The *Saints* are grown *Laconians*, and can twist
Perjury up in Pills, like *Leyden* grist :
  But hold precize *Doponents :* though the heat
Of *Zeal* in *Cataracts* digests such meat,
My cold concoction shrinks, and my advance
Drives slowly to approach your *Ordinance.*
The sign's in *Cancer*, and the *Zodiack* turns
Leonick, roul'd in curls, while *Terra* burns.
What though your fancies are sublim'd to reach
Those fatal reins ? Successe and will can teach
But rash Divinity : a sad renown,
Where one man fell to see a million drown.

When neither Arts nor Armes can serve to fight
And wrest a *Title* from its Law and Right,
Must Malice piece the *Trangum*, and make clear
The scruple? Else we will resolve to swear?
Nay out-swear all that we have sworn before,
And make good lesser crimes by acting more
And more sublime? This, this extends the Line
And shames the puny soul of *Cataline*.
On this account all those whose Fortune's crost,
And want estates, may turn *Knights* of the *Post*.
Vaulx we out-vy'd thee, since thy plot fell lame,
We found a closer *Celler* for the same,
Piling the fatal Powder in our mouths,
Which in an Oath discharg'd blew up the *House*.
Maugre *Mounteagle*, Aspes not throughly slain,
Their poyson in an age may live again.
    Good *Demas* cuff your Bear, then let us see
    The mystery of your iniquity.
May a Man course a Cur? and freely box
The Question? or the formal Paradox?
But as in Physick, so in this device
This querk of policy the point is nice.
For he that in this model means to thrive,
Must first subscribe to the Preparative;
Like Witches compact counter-march his faith
And soak up all what ere the *Spirit* saith;
Then seale and signe. *Scylla* threw three Barres
    short,
He had a Sword indeed, but no *Text* for't.
Old *Rome* lament thy infancy in sin,
We perfect what thou trembledst to begin,
Flush then to see thy self out-done. But all
The world may grieve, 'tis epidemical.

Heaven frowns indeed. But what makes Hell enraged?
Sweet *Pluto* be at Peace, we have Engaged.

On the happy Memory of Alderman Hoyle *that hang'd himself.*

ALL *hail* fair fruit ! may every Crab-tree bear
Such blossomes, and so lovely every year !
Call ye me this the slip ? marry 'tis well,
Zacheus slip'd to Heaven, the Thief to Hell :
But if the Saints thus give's the slip, 'tis need
To look about us to preserve the breed.
Th'are of the Running game, and thus to post
In nooses, blanks the reckning with their *Host.*
Here's more than *Trussum cordum* I suppose
That knit this knot : guilt seldome singly goes ?
A wounded soul close coupled with the sense
Of sin, payes home its proper recompence.
   But hark you Sir, if hast can grant the time ?
See you the danger yet what 'tis to climbe
In Kings Prerogatives ? things beyond just,
When Law seemes brib'd to doom them, must be truss'd.
But O I smell your Plot strong through your Hose,
'Twas but to cheat the Hang-man of your Cloaths.
Else your more active hands had fairly stay'd
The leasure of a Psalm : *Judas* has pray'd.

But later crimes cannot admit the pause,
They run upon effects more than the cause.
Yet let me ask one question, why alone?
One Member of a Corporation?
'Tis clear amongst Divines, Bodies and Souls
As joyntly active, so their judgement rowles
Concordant in the Sentence; why not so
In earthly Suffrings? *States* attended go.
But I perceive the Knack: Old women say
And bee't approv'd, each Dogge should have his day.
    Hence sweep the Almanack: *Lilly* make room,
And blanks enough for the new Saints to come,
All in *Red letters :* as their faults have bin
Scarlet, so limbe their *Anniverse* of sin.
And to their Childrens credits and their Wives
Be it still said, they leap fair for their lives.

The States New Coyne.

1.

Saw you the States mony new come from the Mint?
Some People do say it is wonderous fine;
And that you may read a great mystery in't,
Of mighty King *Nol*, the Lord of the Coyn.

2.

They have quite omitted his Politick head,
His worshipfull face, and his excellent Nose;
But the better to tempt the sisters to bed,
They have fixed upon it the print of his Hose.

3.
For, if they had set up his Picture there,
They needs must ha' crown'd him in *Charles* his stead;
But 'twas cunningly done, that they did forbear,
And rather set up his Ar— than his head.

4.
'Tis monstrous strange, and yet it is true,
In this Reformation we should ha' such luck,
That Crosses were alwaies disdained by you,
Who before pull'd them down, should now set them up.

5.
On this side they have circumscrib'd *God with us*,
And in this stamp and Coyn they confide;
Common-wealth on the other, by which we may guess
That *God* and the *States* were not both of a side.

6.
On this side they have Crosse and Harp,
And only a Crosse on the other set forth;
By which we may learn it falls to our part
Two Crosses to have for one fit of Mirth.

7.
A Country-man hearing this, straight way did think,
That he would procure such a piece of his own;
And knowing it like his Wifes Butter-print,
She should ha't for a Token when as he came home.

8.
Then since that this is the Parliament coyn,
Now *Lilly* by thy mysterious charms,
Or Heralds, pray tell us if these ha' not been
Carmen or Fidlers before by their Arms.

The Rebellion.

Now, thanks to the Powers below,
We have even done our do,
The Myter is down, and so is the Crown,
And with them the Corronet too :
All is now the Peoples, and then
What is theirs is ours we know ;
There is no such thing as a Bishop or K——
Or Peer, but in name or show ;
Come Clowns, and come Boys, come Hoberdehoys,
Come Females of each degree,
Stretch out your throats, bring in your Votes,
And make good the Anarchy ;
Then thus it shall be, sayes *Alse*,
Nay, thus it shall be, sayes *Amie*,
Nay, thus it shall go, sayes *Taffie*, I trow,
Nay, thus it shall go, sayes *Jemmy*.

Oh but the truth, good People all, the truth is such a thing.
For it will undo both Church and State too,
And pull out the throat of our King ;
No, nor the Spirit, nor the new Light
Can make the Point so clear,
But we must bring out the defil'd Coat,
What thing the truth is, and where,
Speak *Abraham*, speak *Hester*,
Speak *Judith*, speak *Kester*,
Speak tag and rag, short coat and long :
Truth is the spell that made us rebell,
And murder and plunder ding dong ;

Sure I have the truth, sayes *Numphs*,
Nay, I have the truth, sayes *Clem*,
Nay, I have the truth, sayes reverend *Ruth*,
Nay, I have the truth, sayes *Nem*.

Well, let the truth be whose it will,
There is something else in ours,
Yet this devotion in our Religions
May chance to abate our Powers:
Then let's agree on some new way,
It skills not much how true,
Take P—— and his club, or *Smec* and his tub
Or any Sect, old or new;
The Devil is in the pack, if choyce you can lack,
We are fourscore Religions strong,
Then take your choice, the Major voice
Shall carry't right or wrong;
Then let's have King *Charles*, sayes *George*,
Nay, wee'l have his Son, sayes *Hugh;*
Nay, then let's have none, sayes gabbering *Jone*,
Nay, wee'l be all Kings, sayes *Prue*.

Nay, but neighbours and friends, one word more,
There's something else behind,
And wise though you be, you do not well see
In which door sits the winde;
And for Religion, to speak truth,
And in both Houses sence,
The matter is all one, if any or none,
If it were not for the pretence.
Now here doth lurk the key of the work,
And how to dispose of the Crown
Dexteriously, and as it may be
For your behalf and our own;

Then wee'l be of this, sayes *Meg*,
Nay, wee'l be of this, sayes *Tib*,
Come, wee'l be of all, sayes pittifull *Paul*,
Nay, wee'l be of none, sayes *Gib*.

Oh we shall have, if we go on
In Plunder, Excise, and Blood,
But few folks, and poor, to domineer o're,
And that will not be good ;
Then let's agree on some new way,
Some new and happy course,
The Country is grown sad, the City is Horn mad,
And both the Houses are worse ;
The Synod hath writ, the Generall hath shit,
And both to like purpose, for
Religion, Laws, the Truth, and the Cause
We talk on, but nothing we do ;
Come, then let's have peace, sayes *Nel*,
No, no, but we won't sayes *Meg*,
But I say we will, sayes fiery-face *Phil*,
We will, and we won't, sayes *Hodge*.

Thus from the Rout who can expect
Ought but confusion,
Since the Unity with good Monarchy
Begin and end in one ?
If then when all is thought their own,
And lyes at their belief,
These popular pates, reap nought but debates
From these many round-headed beasts ;
Come Royalists then, do you play the men,
And Cavaliers give the word,
And now let's see what you will be,
And whether you can accord ;

A health to King *Charles*, sayes *Tom*,
Up with it, sayes *Ralph*, like a man,
God blesse him, sayes *Doll*, and raise him, sayes *Moll*,
And send him his own, sayes *Nan*.

But now for these prudent Wights,
That sit without end, and to none,
And their Committees in Towns and Cities
Fill with confusion;
For the bold Troops of Sectaries,
The *Scots* and their Partakers,
Our new British States, Col. *Burges* and his Mates,
The Covenant and its Makers:
For all these wee'l pray, and in such a way,
That if it might granted be,
Both *Jack* and *Gill*, and *Moll* and *Will*,
And all the world will agree:
Else Pox take them all, sayes *Bess*,
And a Plague too, sayes *Mary*,
The Devil, sayes *Dick*, and his Dam too, sayes *Nick*,
Amen and amen say we.

On Britannicus *his leap three Story high, nd his escape from* London.

Paul *from* Damascus in a basket slides,
 Cran'd by the faithfull *Brethren* down the sides
O' their embatel'd walls, *Britannicus*
As loath to trust the *Brethrens God with us*,

Slides too, but yet more desp'rate, and yet thrives
In his descent; needs must! the Devil drives.
Their Cause was both the same, and herein meet,
Only their fall was not with equal feet,
Which makes the Case *Iambick:* thus we see
How much News falls short of *Divinity*.
Truth was their crying crime: One takes the night,
Th' other th' advantage of the *New-sprung Light*
To mantle his escape : how different be
The Pristin and the *Modern Policy?*
Have *Ages* their *Antipodes?* Yet still
Close in the Propagation of ill?
Hence flowes this use aud doctrine from the thump
I last sustain'd (beloved) *Good wits may Jump*.

An Epigram on the People of England.

Sweating and chafing hot *Ardelio* cryes
A Boat a Boat, else farewell all the prize.
But having once set foot upon the deep
Hot-spur *Ardelio* fell fast asleep.
So we, on fire with zealous discontent,
Call'd out a *Parliament*, a *Parliament;*
Which being obtain'd at last, what did they do?
Even squeez the Wool-packs, and lye snorting too.

Another.

Ritain a lovely Orchard seem'd to be
Furnish'd with natures choise variety,
Temptations golden fruit of every sort,
Th' *Hesperian Garden* fann'd from fein'd report;
Great boyes and small together in we brake,
No matter what disdain'd *Priapus* spake:
Up, up, we lift the great boyes in the trees,
Hoping a common share to sympathize:
But they no sooner there, neglected streight
The shoulders that so rais'd them to this height;
And fell to stuffing of their own bags first,
And as their treasure grew, so did their thirst.
Whiles we in lean expectance gaping stand,
For one shake from their charitable hand.
But all in vain, the dropsie of desire
So scortch'd them, three Realms could not quench the fire.
Be wise then in your *Ale*, bold youths, for fear
The *Gardner* catch us as *Mosse* caught his *Mare*.

Upon report there should be no more *Terms* kept at Westminster.

IS't possible? will no *Terms* then prevail?
And must the *Gown* and *Bag* jog on to sale?
The *Bills* and *Answers* in our *Courts* become
Converted to the taring use of *Drum?*
And shall no more *Confederacies* pass
'Twixt *Midsomer* and dying *Michaelmas?*

Though they deprive us of Old * *Hillary*,
'Tis fit they should allow the *Trinity;*
But that's denyed too : this *Alteration*
Contracts our whole time to a long *Vacation*.
Now farewell the (¹) *Brownbowl*, and *Bonny Ale*,
The *Sanguine Herring*, and its merry tayle ;
(²) *Higgenian Quibbles*, and the *Harpean Lyre*,
Fentonian Sweetness, and the *Tow'ring Fire:*
Our (³) *Host* and *Hostess* too, they're both *Vxorums*,
As *Hermophraditus* is, in *Sex Duorums :*
Weep (⁴) *Heaven*, lament thy loss, and thou *Hell* rore,
Thy Furnace scarce will ere be heated more ;
Of *Pleasure*, *Paradise*, thou must be barren,
And *Purgatory* furnisht but with Carrion :
Th' Abomination of the (⁵) *Hole i'th' Wall*,
Now *June* is past, cry Pamphlets in the *Hall:*
And she that 's left but th' remnant of a Nose,
Who to a Chirurgion (as men do suppose)
Did pawn the other part for cure of this,
Turn *Zealot*, and be *Martyr'd* when she p——
All *Trades*, and all *Societies* lament
Your wants in us, you'le find cause to repent
The setting up your Idol Parliament :
For though on these *Terms* they'le no profit give
To Us, we'll try on other *Terms* to live.

---

* *An Attorney.*
(¹) The *Scotch* Ale house in *Harts-horne* Lane.
(²) Clerks of the Exchequer, that used to drink their Mornings Draughts there.
(³) They call'd one another so.
(⁴) To *Westminster*.] Places there where Clerks in Term time usually break their Fast.
(⁵) A Bawdy-house.

Upon the Cavaliers departing out of London.

Now fare thee well *London*,
Thou next must be undone,
   'Cause thou hast undone us before ;
This *Cause* and this *Tyrant*,
Had ne're play'd this high rant,
   Were't not for thy *argent* and *Or*.

2.

Now we must desert thee,
With the lines that begirt thee,
   And the Red-coated *Saints* domineer ;
Who with liberty fool thee,
While a Monster doth rule thee,"
   And thou feel'st what before thou didst fear.

3.

Now *Justice* and *Freedom*,
With the *Laws* that did breed 'um,
   Are sent to *Jamaica* for gold ;
And those that upheld 'um,
Have power but seldom,
   For Justice is barter'd and sold.

4.

Now the Christian Religion
Must seek a new Region,
   And the old *Saints* give way to the new ;
And we that are Loyal,
Vail to those that destroy all,
   When the Christian gives place to the Jew.

5.

But this is our glory
In this wretched story,
   Calamities fall on the best ;
And those that destroy us
Do better imploy us,
   To sing till they are supprest.

On Col. Pride.

OF *Gyants* and *Knights*, and their wonderfull *fights*
   We have stories enough in *Romances*,
But I'le tell you one new, that is *strange* and yet *true*,
   Though t'other are nothing but fancies.

2.

A *Knight* lately made, of the *Governing* trade,
   Whose name he'l not have to be known ;
Has been trucking with fame, to purchase a name,
   For 'tis said he had none of his own.

3.

He by Fortunes design, should have been a Divine,
   And a Pillar no doubt of the Church ;
Whom a *Sexton* (God wot) in the *Bellfry* begot,
   And his Mother did pig in the Porch.

4.

And next for his breeding, 'twas learned *Hog-feeding*,
   With which he so long did converse,
That his *manners* & *feature*, was so like their *nature*,
   You'ld scarce know his *sweetnesse* from theirs.

5.

But observe the device, of this *Noblemans* rise,
   How he hurried from trade to trade,
From the *grains* he'd aspire, to the *yest*, and then *higher*,
   Till at length he a *Drayman* was made.

6.

Then his *dray-horse* and *he*, in the streets we did see,
   With his *hanger*, his *sling*, and his *jacket;*
Long time he did *watch*, to meet with his *match*,
   For he'd ever a mind to the Placket.

7.

At length he did find, out a *Trull* to his mind,
   And *Vrsula* was her name;
Oh Vrsly quoth he, and oh Tom then quoth she,
   And so they began their game.

8.

But as soon as they met, O such Babes they did get,
   And Blood-royal in 'um did place,
From a *swineheard* they came, a *she-bear* was their *Dam*,
   They were suckled as *Romulus* was.

9.

At last when the Rout, with their head did fall out,
   And the Wars thereupon did fall in,
He went to the field, with a sword, but no shield,
   Strong drink was his buckler within.

10.

But when he did spy, how they dropt down and dye,
   And did hear the bullets to sing;
His armes he flung down, and run fairly to town,
   And exchang'd his sword for his sling.

11.

Yet he claimed his share, in such honours as were
   Belonging to nobler spirits;

That ventur'd their *lives*, while this *Buffon* survives
   To receive the reward of their merits.

12.
When the Wars were all done, he his fighting begun,
   And would needs shew his valour in peace,
Then his fury he flings, at poor conquer'd things,
   And frets like a *hog in his grease*.

13.
For his first feat of all, on a *Wit* he did fall,
   A *Wit* as some say, and some not,
Because he'd an art, to rhime on the quart,
   But never did care for the pot.

14.
And next on the *Cocks*, he fell like an *Ox*,
   Took them and their *Masters* together;
But the *combs* and the *spurs*, kept himself and his *Sirs*,
   Who are to have both or neither.

15.
The cause of his spight, was because they would *fight*,
   And because he durst not, he did take on;
And said they were fit, for the pot, not the spit,
   And would serve to be eaten with *Bacon*.

16.
But flesh'd with these *spoyles*, the next of his *toyles*,
   Was to fall with wild-beasts by the ears,
To the *Bearward* he goeth, and then opened his *mouth*,
   And said, *Oh! are you there with your bears*.

17.
Our stories are dull, of a *Cock* and a *Bull*,
   But such was his valour and care;
Since he bears the Bell, the tales that we tell,
   Must be of a *Cock* and a *Bear*.

18.

The crime of the *Bears*, was, they were *Cavaliers*,
  And had formerly fought for the *King;*
And pull'd by the *Burrs*, the Round-headed *Curs*,
  That they made their ears to ring.

19.

Our successor of Kings, like blind fortune flings
  Upon him both honour and store;
Who has as much right, to make *Tom* a Knight,
  As *Tom* has *desert*, and no more.

20.

But *Fortune* that Whore, still attended this *Brewer*,
  And did all his *Atchievements* reward;
And blindly did *fling*, on this lubberly *thing*,
  More *Honour*, and made him a *Lord*.

21.

Now he walks with his spurs, and a couple of curs
  At his heels, which he calls *Squires;*
So when *Honour* is *thrown*, on the head of a *Clown*,
  'Tis by *Parasites* held up, and *Lyars*.

22.

The rest of his *pranks*, will merit new *thanks*,
  With his death, if we did but know it;
But we'l leave him and it, to a time and place fit,
  And *Greg.* shall be *funeral* Poet.

Upon the General Pardon past by the RUMP, 1653.

Rejoyce, rejoyce, ye *Cavaliers*,
  For here comes that expells your fears;

A General Pardon is now past,
What was long look'd for, comes at last.

It Pardons all that are undone ;
The Pope ne're granted such a one :
So long, so large, so full, so free ;
O what a gratious State have we !

Yet do not joy too much (my friends)
First see how well this pardon ends,
For though it hath a Glorious face,
I fear there's in't but little grace.

'Tis said the Mountains once brought forth,
And what brought they? a Mouse introth ;
Our States have done the like, I doubt,
In this their Pardon now set out.

We'll look it o're then if you please,
And see wherein it brings us ease ;
And first, it Pardons words I find
Against our State, words are but wind.

Hath any pray'd for th' King of late ?
And wish'd confusion to our State ?
And call'd them Rebells ? he come in
And plead this Pardon for that sin.

Hath any call'd King *Charles* that's dead
A Martyr? He that lost his Head ?
And villains those that did the Fact ?
That man is pardoned by this Act.

Hath any said our Parliament
Is such a one as God ne're sent?
Or hath he writ, or put in Print
That he believes the Devil's in't?

Or hath he said there never were
Such *Tyrants* any where as here?
Though this offence of his be high,
He's pardon'd for his Blasphemy.

You see how large this Pardon is,
It Pardons all our *Mercuries*,
And *Poets* too, for you know they
Are poor, and have not ought to pay.

For where there's money to be got,
I find this Pardon pardons not;
Malignants that were rich before,
Shall not be pardon'd till they'r poor.

Hath any one been true to th' Crown.
And for that paid his money down;
By this new Act he shall be free,
And pardon'd for his Loyalty.

Who have their Lands confiscate quite,
For not Compounding when they might;
If that they know not how to digg,
This Pardon gives them leave to beg.

Before this Act came out in print,
We thought there had been comfort in't;
We drank some Healths to th' Higher Powers,
But now we've seen't they'd need drink ours.

For by this Act it is thought fit
That no man shall have benefit,
Unlesse he first engage to be
A Rebel to eternity.

Thus in this Pardon it is clear,
That nothing's here, and nothing's there;
I think our States do mean to choke us
With this new Act of *Hocus Pocus*.

Well, since this Act's not worth a pin,
We'll pray our States to call it in,
For most men think it ought to be
Burnt by the hand of *Gregory*.

Then to conclude, here's little joy
For those that pray *Vive le Roy:*
But since they'l not forget our Crimes,
Wee'l keep our mirth till better times.

Upon Olivers *dissolving the Parliament in* 1653.

1.

Will you hear a strange thing scarce heard of before,
   A ballad of News without any lyes,
The Parliament men are turn'd out of doors,
   And so are the Council of State likewise.

2.

Brave *Oliver* came to the House like a Spright,
   His fiery looks strook the Speaker dumb;

You must be gone hence, quoth he, by this light,
    Do you mean to sit here till Dooms-day come?

3.

With that the Speaker lookt pale for fear,
    As though he had been with the night-mare rid,
Insomuch that some did think that were there,
    That he had even done as the Alderman did.

4.

But *Oliver* though he be Doctor of Law,
    Yet he seem'd to play the Physician there;
His Physick so wrought on the Speakers maw,
    That he gave him a stool instead of a Chair.

5.

Harry Martyn wondred to see such a thing,
    Done by a Saint of such high degree;
'Twas an act he did not expect from a King,
    Much lesse from such a dry bone as he.

6.

But *Oliver* laid his hand on his sword,
    And upbraided him with his Adultery;
To which *Harry* answer'd never a word,
    Saving, humbly thanking his Majesty.

7.

Allen the Coppersmith was in great fear,
    He did as much harm since the Wars began;
A broken Citizen many a year,
    And now he is a broken Parliament-man.

8.

Bradshaw that President proud as the Pope,
    That loves upon Kings and Princes to trample;
Now the house is dissolv'd I cannot but hope,
    To see such a President made an example.

9.
And were I one of the Council of War,
   I'le tell you what my Vote should be,
Upon his own Turret at *Westminster*,
   To be hang'd up for all comers to see.

10.
My Masters I wonder you could not agree,
   You that have been long Brethren in evil;
A dissolution you might think there would be,
   When the Devil's divided against the Devil.

11.
Then room for the Speaker without his Mace,
   And room for the rest of the Rabble-rout;
My Masters methinks 'tis a pitifull case,
   Like the snuff of a Candle thus to go out.

12.
Now some like this change, and some like it not,
   Some think it was not done in due season;
Some think it was but a Jesuits plot,
   To blow up the House like a Gun-powder-treason.

13.
Some think that *Oliver* and *Charles* are agreed,
   And sure it were good policy if it were so;
Lest the *Hollander*, *French*, the *Dane*, and the *Swede*,
   Should bring him in whether he would or no.

14.
And now I would gladly conclude my Song,
   With a Prayer as Ballads are used to do,
But yet I'le forbear, for I think er't be long,
   We shall have a King and a Parliament too.

Admiral Deans *Funeral.*

1.

Nick *Culpepper*, and *William Lilly*,
Though you were pleas'd to say they were silly,
Yet something these prophesi'd true, I tell ye,
    Which no body can deny.

2.

In the month of *May*, I tell you truly,
Which neither was in *June* nor *July*,
The *Dutch* began to be unruly,
    Which no body can deny.

3.

Betwixt our *England* and their *Holland*,
Which neither was in *France* nor *Poland*,
But on the Sea, where there was no Land,
    Which no body can deny.

4.

There joyn'd the *Dutch*, and the *English* Fleet,
Our Authors opinion then they did meet,
Some saw't that never more shall see't,
    Which no body can deny.

5.

There were many mens hearts as heavy as lead,
Yet would not believe *Dick Dean* to be dead,
Till they saw his Body take leave of his head,
    Which no body can deny.

6.

Then after the sad departure of him,
There was many a man lost a Leg or a Lim,
And many were drow'd 'cause they could not swim,
    Which no body can deny.

Part I.   *Rump Songs.*   309

7.
One cryes, lend me thy hand good friend,
Although he knew it was to no end,
I think, quoth he, I am going to the Fiend,
      Which no body can deny.

8.
Some, 'twas reported, were kill'd with a Gun,
And some stood that knew not whether to run,
There was old taking leave of Father and Son,
      Which no body can deny.

9.
There's a rumour also, if we may believe,
We have many gay Widows now given to grieve,
'Cause unmannerly Husbands nere came to take leave,
      Which no body can deny.

10.
The Ditty is sad of our *Dean* to sing;
To say truth, it was a pittifull thing
To take off his head and not leave him a ring,
      Which no body can deny.

11.
From *Greenwich* toward the Bear at Bridge foot
He was wafted with wind that had water to't,
But I think they brought the Devil to boot,
      Which no body can deny.

12.
The heads on *London* Bridge upon Poles,
That once had bodies and honester souls
Than hath the Master of the Roules,
      Which no body can deny.

13.
They grieved for this great man of command,
Yet would not his head amongst theirs should stand;

He dy'd on the Water, and they on the Land,
>> *Which no body can deny.*

14.
I cannot say, they look'd wisely upon him,
Because People cursed that parcel was on him;
He has fed fish and worms, if they do not wrong him,
>> *Which no body can deny.*

15.
The Old Swan as he passed by,
Said, she would sing him a dirge, and lye down and die;
Wilt thou sing to a bit of a body, quoth I?
>> *Which no body can deny.*

16.
The Globe on the Bank, I mean on the Ferry,
Where Gentle and Simple might come and be merry,
Admired at the change from a Ship to a Wherry,
>> *Which no body can deny.*

17.
Tom Godfreys Bears began for to roare,
Hearing such moans one side of the shore,
They knew they should never see *Dean* any more,
>> *Which no body can deny.*

18.
Queen-hithe, Pauls-Wharf, and the *Fryers* also,
Where now the Players have little to do,
Let him passe without any tokens of woe,
>> *Which no body can deny.*

19.
Quoth th' Students o'th' Temple, I know not their names,
Looking out of their Chambers into the *Thames*,
The Barge fits him better than did the great *James*,
>> *Which no body can deny.*

Part I.   Rump Songs.

20.

Essex House, late called Cuckolds Hall,
The folk in the Garden staring over the wall,
Said, they knew once *Pride* would have a fall.
Which no body can deny.

21.

At *Strand* Gate, a little farther then,
Where mighty Guns numbred to sixty and ten,
Which neither hurt Children, Women nor Men,
Which no body can deny.

22.

They were shot over times one, two, three, or four,
'Tis thought one might 'heard the bounce to th' Tower,
Folk report, the din make the Buttermilk sower,
Which no body can deny.

23.

Had old Goodman *Lenthal* or *Allen* but heard 'um,
The noise worse than *Olivers* voice would have fear'd 'um,
And out of their small wits would have scar'd 'um
Which no body can deny.

24.

Sommerset House, where once did the Queen lye,
And afterwards *Ireton* in black, and not green, by,
The Canon clattered the Windows really
Which no body can deny.

25.

The *Savoys* mortified spitled Crew,
If I lye, as *Falstaffe* sayes, I am a Jew,
Gave the Hearse such a look it would make a man spew,
Which no body can deny.

26.

he House of *S*—— that Fool and Knave,

Had so much wit left lamentation to save
From accompanying a traytorly Rogue to his grave,
     Which no body can deny.

27.

The *Exchange*, and the ruines of *Durham* house eke
Wish'd such sights might be seen each day i'th' week,
A General's Carkasse without a Cheek,
     Which no body can deny.

28.

The House that lately Great *Buckinghams* was,
Which now Sir *Thomas Fairfax* has,
Wish'd it might be Sir *Thomas's* fate so to passe,
     Which no body can deny.

29.

Howards House, *Suffolks* great Duke of Yore,
Sent him one single sad wish and no more,
He might flote by *Whitehall* in purple gore,
     Which no body can deny.

30.

Something I should of *Whitehall* say,
But the Story is so sad, and so bad, by my fay,
That it turns my wits another way,
     Which no body can deny.

31.

To *Westminster*, to the Bridge of the Kings,
The water the Barge, and the Barge-men brings
The small remain of the worst of things,
     Which no body can deny.

32.

They inter'd him in triumph, like *Lewis* the eleven,
In the famous Chappel of *Henry* the seven,
But his soul is scarce gone the right way to heaven,
     Which no body can deny.

The merry Goodfellow.

WHy should we not laugh and be jolly,
    Since all the World now is grown mad?
And lull'd in a dull melancholly;
    He that wallows in store
    Is still gaping for more,
    And that makes him as poor,
As the Wretch that never any thing had.

How mad is that damn'd Money-monger?
That to purchase to him and his heirs,
Grows shriviled with thirst and hunger;
    While we that are bonny,
    Buy Sack with ready-mony,
And ne'r trouble the Scriveners, nor Lawyers.

Those guts that by scraping and toyling,
Do swell their Revenues so fast,
Get nothing by all their turmoiling,
    But are marks of each tax,
    While they load their own backs
    With the heavier packs,
And lye down gall'd and weary at last.

While we that do traffick in tipple,
Can baffle the Gown and the Sword,
Whose jaws are so hungry and gripple;
    We ne'r trouble our heads
    With Indentures or Deeds,
And our Wills are compos'd in a word.

Our mony shall never indite us,
Nor drag us to Goldsmiths Hall,
No Pyrats nor wracks can affright us;
    We, that have no Estates,
    Fear no plunder nor rates,
    We can sleep with open gates,
He that lyes on the ground cannot fall.

We laugh at those Fools whose endeavours
Do but fit them for Prisons and Fines,
When we that spend all are the savers;
    For if Thieves do break in,
    They go out empty agin,
Nay, the Plunderers lose their designs.

Then let us not think on to morrow,
But tipple and laugh while we may,
To wash from our hearts all sorrow;
    Those Cormorants which
    Are troubled with an itch,
    To be mighty and rich,
Do but toyl for the wealth which they borrow.

The Maior of the Town with his Ruff on,
What a pox is he better than we?
He must vail to the man with the Buff on;
    Though he Custard may eat,
    And such lubbardly meat,
Yet our Sack makes us merrier than he.

The Rebells Reign.

NOw we are met in a knot, let's take t'other pot,
    And chirp o're a cup of Nectar;
Let's think on a charm, to keep us from harm,
    From the Fiend and the new Protector.

Heretofore at a brunt, a Cross would have don't,
    But now they have taken courses,
With their Laws and their theft, there's not a Cross left
    In the Church nor the Farmers Purses.

They're with you to bring, for stuffing at a King,
    For now you must make no dainty,
To have your Nose ground, on a stone turned round
    By *Noll*, and one and twenty.

But our Rights are kept for us, in *Oliver's* store-house,
    'Twere as good they were set in the Stocks:
They were just in the pickle, in the thirtieth Article,
    Like *Jack* in a Juglers box.

We are loath for to look, for the Saints in a book,
    But would not a man be vext,
To see them so rough with their blades and their bluff,
    But not a word on't in the Text.

We have been twelve years together by the ears
    To prepare for a spiritual raign:
Men were never so spic'd, with the Scepter of Christ
    In the hands of a Saint in grain.

'Twas brewed in their Hives by Citizens wives,
  Who ventured their husbands far,
With *Robin* the fool, there was ne're such a tool
  To lead in the womens War.

He was ill at Command, but worse at a stand,
  So they sought out another more able:
Then *Fair.* undertakes, but *Nol* keeps the stakes,
  And sends away *Fax* with a bauble.

Will, Conqueror the second, without his host reckon'd,
  And so did *B*—— billet his Mate;
They made a great noise, 'mongst women and boys,
  But now they are both out of date.

Cowardly *W*—— had but a foul Fortune,
  And wanted a knife to scrape it,
When his Oriphice ran, there was no mortal man,
  But *omnibus hor is sapit*.

Bradshaw, the Knave, sent the King to his grave,
  And on the Bloud Royal did trample,
For which the next *Lent*, he was made President,
  And ere long may be made an example.

Dorislaus did steer, to *Hans mine heer*,
  And *Askew* to *Don* at *Madril*,
Ere a man could have scratcht, they were both dispatcht,
  Yet there they lye Leger still.

Martin and *St. Johns*, and more with a Vengeance,
  Had each a finger i'th' pye:
Some for the Money, and some for the Conny,
  And some for they knew not why.

Part I. *Rump Songs.*

The Parliament sate as snug as a Cat,
   And were playing for mine and yours:
Sweep-stakes was their Game, till *Oliver* came,
   And turn'd it to Knave out of doors.

Then a new one was cast, and made up in hast,
   But alas they could do no more
Than empty our purse, and empty us worse
   Than e're we were married before.

But in a good hour, they gave up their power
   To one that was wiser than they;
By common consent, 'twas the first Parliament
   That ever was *felo de se*.

After all this Jeer, we are never the near,
   There sits one at the Helm commanding;
One that doth us nick, with a trick for our trick,
   And the stone in our foot notwithstanding.

He'll not relax, one groat of the Tax,
   Though it come to more then he need,
He may keep it in store, till his need be more;
   'Tis an Article of our new Creed.

So well he hath wrought, that now he hath brought
   The Realm to the manner he it meant;
The fishes, and the foul, and the Devil and all,
   And the monthly pay his high rent.

All this we must bear, but 'twould make a man swear
   When they call us a Reformed Nation:
It can never sink into my head for to think
   That this is a Reformation.

'Tis the man in the Moon, or the Devil as soon,
   Our Laws are asleep upon shelves :
Our Charter and Freedom, we may bid God speed um,
   'Tis well we can beg for our selves.

Since *Nol* hath bereft us, and nothing hath left us,
   Not a Horse or a Oxe to plough land,
Let *Oliver* passe, come fill up my Glasse,
   And here's a good health to *Rowland*.

The Resolve.

1.

THere's no man so worthy of Envy as he,
      Drinks Sack, and is free,
Can draw his mind to his present Condition,
      And at that ebbe, can
      Shew himself a better man,
Then his Enemy at his full tide of Ambition;
Has a breast so well Man'd, he fears not the thunder
      Of those Bastards of fame,
      That have got a Name
         By Rapine and Plunder;
      But bravely despiseth,
      The *Mock-Sun* that riseth :
He that's quiet within, what need he to care,
Though not worth a groat, h'as the whole world to spare.

2.

He's arm'd 'gainst the Chances and Changes of State,
      And still meets his Fate,

With a Conquering Cup of the stoutest Canary,
    Drinks healths to the best,
    And he Wrastles with the rest,
Yet never is foyl'd, 'less his liquor miscarry;
His thoughts are more soft then the bed that he lies on;
    Who puts his cares to flight,
    A Prince is o're Night,
        And next Morn doth rise one;
    Let th' Fates do what they will,
    He's the self-same Man still:
Scepters have Palsies, and Crowns too are shaking,
Who soundly doth sleep, need not keep others waking.

          3.

Then give us the *Sack*, let the *Hen-hearted Cit*,
    Drink *Whey*, and submit,
  His *Cucumber* Courage does ne're well till beaten;
    He, *Camel*-like, kneels,
    And his Burthen ne're feels,
Till his back become gall'd, and his carcasse near eaten;
'Has a spirit so poor, that ev'ry Fool rides him;
    He's soul-lesse, alone;
    At best, but a Drone,
        And no Man abides him;
    He's a compact of Clay,
    That will yield any way:
Tis Sack and good Company sets the Soul free,
Like the Musick of that there's no Harmonie.

Upon Cromwell's *pulling out the Long Parliament.* 1 6 5 3.

The Alligory.

1.

AS *Plutarch* doth write, (a Man of known Credit)
  A *Serpent* there was had a Mutinous *Tayle*,
Rebell'd 'gainst the *Head*, that so oft had fed it,
  And would not permit it to lead, or prevaile:
Is't not fit that by turns we Leaders should be
Quoth the *Tayle?* follow me, as I've follow'd thee.

2.

Now, the *Body*, being grown too strong for the *Head*,
  Quoth the *Head*, if it must be, then let it be so;
For quietnesse sake I yield to be lead,
  But fear that from hence some mischief will grow;
A thing so un-naturall never was read,
As the *Head* to turn *Tayle*, and the *Tayle* to turn *Head*.

3.

A Monster like this, but of stranger Conditions,
  Engender'd there was in the year *thirty nine;*
Rebell'd 'gainst the *Head*, but with fawning *Petitions*,
  To have him his Pow'r and his Right to resign;
This Monster (the truth on't to speak) was begot
By a Mongrell *Parson*, and that Hagg the *Scot*.

4.

So large and so mighty this *Tayle* grew in length,
 That where e're it came, it swept all before it ;
There was no resisting so pow'rfull a strength,
 The *Head* at the last was forc't to implore it :
All our Castles and Towns this *Tayle* did subdue,
A sad tale to tell, but believe me 'tis true.

5.

Above seven years Conflict this *Head* did endure,
 With that Monsterous *Tayle*, and the Spawn it begot :
During which time no Man's life was secure,
 Our Goods and our Cattle all went to the Pot :
At last came a Champion with an Iron flayle,
And ended the strife 'twixt the *Head*, and the *Tayle:*

6.

The *Head* being departed, the *Body* began
 To consult with the *Tayle* what was best to do ;
St. *George* (quoth the *Body*) 'tis said was a Man,
 But what can this thing be is called St. *O.*
Why he (quoth the *Tayle*) was one of our Rout,
And 'tis wonderous strange he should turn *Tayle* about.

7.

While thus they did argue in rusht our St. *O.*
 With Courage more keen then the Sword that he wore ;
Quoth he, ye are vile things, not fit here to grow,
 Such Fiends ne're was known in this place heretofore.
The wealth and the fat of the Country doth feed you,
And now I do guesse it is high time to bleed you.

8.

Some say that this *Tayle* wore the mark of a *P*,
   O, is a Letter in rank known before it;
How e're 't makes no matter, 'tis all one to me,
   Save this, that I'm sure the *O* had the more wit;
There's no Man so blind, but may easily see
He hath added unto his small *O*, a tall *P*.

9.

My Story now ended come *viva* St. *George*,
   That old true-blew Lad, and Hospitable-Saint,
Bring a Butt of good Sack to fill up my Gorge,
   At this tale of *Head* and *Tayle* I almost faint;
Howe're let it pass, if you studdy upon't,
I hope you will neither make *Head* or *Tayle* on't.

The Advice.

1.

NE're trouble thy self at the Times nor their turnings,
   Afflictions run circular, and wheele about,
Away with these Murmurings, and these Heartburnings,
   With the Juyce of the Grape wee'l quench the Fire out,
Ne're chain, nor imprison thy Soul up in sorrow,
What fails us to day, may befriend us to morrow,
Wee'l scorn our Content from others to borrow.

2.

Though Fortune hath left us wee'le strive to regain her,
  And court her with Cupps till her Favourite come,
Then with a Courage untam'd wee'le maintain her,
  And silence the noyse of the Enemies Drum,
Wee'le link her unto the Man most deserving,
Shall keep her at work, as well as from starving,
She shall not hereafter be at her own Carving.

3.

I hold him a Novice in Humane affairs,
  Thinks whirlings in State a wonderous thing,
To daub up old Ruines with dirty repairs,
  And instead of a Scepter to set up a Sling.
Such Atomes of Greatnesse are but Fortune's laughter,
She fattens them up 'till they're fitted for slaughter,
Then leaves them at *Tiburn* to Tittar and Tauter.

Sharers in the Government.

A MEDLEY.

To 8. several Tunes.

SOme say the World is but a Cheat,
  Troth we see't
  For the feet

Still rebell against the Head,
When Antipodian Rulers sway,
    Who'le obey?
    Thus some say,
Shall we not his own steps tread?
Pray were we not in the late Quarrel,
And pickl'd up in the same Barrel?
    Then why that? or why this?
    Our hearts are as great as his.

Here is One that claims a share
In the Scepter, and the Chaire,*
Though he cryes Religion down,
Hee's Ambitious for a Crown;
Fain hee'd have his Head to shine
Where his Father hangs his Signe,
So he should, had I the Power
In the twinkling of an how're
I, of his disease would cure him.

What think you of the Man of War,†
Whose Muzle is the Sea-mans Star?
Hee's Arm'd within, and Wall'd without
To give the Rout, if that we dare;
But faith the *Dutch* will hem him in,
And make him either sink or swim;
This is the News brought Mr. P——
To which he lent scarce half an Eare.

There is one, and a sly one,
In *Scotland*, lurks to quarter with the Lyon,
He is your comeing Man sir,
Will lead the Van sir,
Upon the least Commotion; ‡

---

* *Harrison.*   † *Blake.*   ‡ *Pick out the meaning if you can.*

He wears a Coat, with double-colours faced,
On one side whereof the States is gravely placed,
But on the other the Cavies rudely raced;
Hold Ambodexter whither wilt thou go?

    Then comes a stout Heart,
      A Man very pert,*
Reaking with Revenge, for Disgrace;
      He swore he was true
    To give the Devil his due,
And as firm as the Nose on his Face.

    Another puts in
    To be a States Pin,†
Good reason it should be so,
    He can Circumvent
    A Parliament;
Then why not Our *Oliver* O?

Some talk this, and some talk that,
Some talk of New wars, and some they know not what,
But well fare the Cavalier, for at a bare word,
Hee's scarce left either Tongue or Sword.

Then Turbulent-spirited *Jack*‡ bring up the Reere,
For thou hast a Spleene farr keener than any one here;
Thou spurn'st at Authoritie, art Ambition's Minion,
And boyl'st like thy Soap to advance a New-fangled
    Opinion;

    * *Lambert.*   † *Ludlow.*   ‡ *John Lilborn.*

Promotion's thy drift, to rule doth make thy Wits roame,
But a Gibbet 'tis thought will stand betwixt thee and home.

Upon Cromwell's *refusing the Kingly Power.*

1.

How poor is his Spirit? how lost is his Name,
Deceiveth Opinion, and Curtailes his Fame?
When as his Designs come near to their height,
'Twixt *shall I* and *shall I*, suspect their own weight,
He has traffiqu'd for Honour, but lost the whole Freight:
He that's stout in the Front, not so in the Rear,
Doth forfeit his Fame, and is Cow'd out by Fear.

2.

A small part of Honor to him doth belong,
Consults not the Glory, but faints in the throng;
   That dares not embrace what his own Soul doth Vote,
   But yields up Our Liberties to a Red-coat;
   Sure Midsommer's near, and some Men doth dote:
I like the bold Romanes, (whose Fame ever rings)
That kept in Subjection such pittifull things.

3.

He that will be Bug-bear'd, is turn'd again Child,
A Reed than a Scepter is fitter to weild:

Examine the Story, no Story you'l find,
Saving the Story, *that Kat will to kind*,
The World is deluded, the Common-wealth blind ;
These false stamps of Honour prove but Copper-Mettle,
And Fame sounds as loud from a Tinkers old Kettle.

4.

He that past has the Pikes, and found Canon-free,
Which shews that noe Curse from his Parents could be,
    Had a Soul so devout, it made Killing a Trade ;
    And now to retreat at the sent of a Blade
Doth show of what Mold our *Knight-Errant* was made ;
He that flagges in his Flight, when's Ambition sores high,
Doth stabb his own Merit, & gives Fame the lye.

5.

Then *Cicero*-like, yea Gown-men drench Cares,
O're-whelm'd with your Own, and your Countries Affairs ;
    And Pulpit-men too be as Airy as Wee ;
    Do you but preach Sack up, we'l ne'r disagree,
That Common-wealth's best that is the most free :
Then fret not, nor care not, when the Sack's in our Crown,
We can fancy a King up, or fancy Him down.

The Encounter.
A SONG.

1.

Hang the Presbyters Gill,
Bring a Pinte of Sack *Will*,
More Orthodox of the two;
Though a slender dispute
Will strike the Elfe mute,
Hees one of the honester Crue.

2.

In a Pinte there's small heart,
Sirrah, bring us a Quart,
There's substance and vigor met,
'Twill hold us in Play,
Some part of the day,
But we'll suck him before Sun-set.

3.

The dareing old Pottle
Does now bid us Battle;
Let's try what his strength can do;
Keep your Ranks and your Files:
And for all his Wiles,
Wee'l tumble him down Staires too.

4.

The Stout-breasted Lumberd,
His Brains ne'r encumber'd
With drinking of Gallons three;
Tricongius was named,
And by *Cæsar* famed,
Who dubbed him Knight Cap-a-pe.

5.
If then Honour be in't,
Why a pox should we stint
Our selves of the fullness it bears?
  H' has lesse wit than an Ape
  In the blood of the Grape,
Will not plunge himself o're head and ears.

6.
Then summon the Gallon,
A stout Foe, and a tall One,
And likely to hold us to't;
  Keep Coyn in your Purse,
  The Word is disburse,
I'le warrant he falls at your foot.

7.
See, the bold Foe appears,
May he fall that him fears;
Keep you but close Order, and then
  We will give him the Rout,
  Be he never so stout,
And prepare for his Rallying agen.

8.
Wee'l dreyn the whole Cellar,
Pipes, Butts, and the Dweller,
If the Wine does flow no faster;
  Will, when thou dost slack us,
  By Warrant from *Bacchus*,
Wee'l Cane thy Tun-belly'd Master.

The Good Old Cause.

NOw *Lambert's* sunk, and valiant *M*——
   Does ape his General *Cromwell*,
And *Arthur's* Court, 'cause time is short,
   Does rage like Devils from Hell;
Let's mark the fate and course of State,
   Who rises when t'other is sinking,
And beleive when this is past
   'Twill be our turn at last
To bring the Good Old Cause by drinking.

First, red nos'd *Nol* he swallowed all,
   His colour shew'd he lov'd it:
But *Dick* his Son, as he were none,
   Gav't off, and hath reprov'd it;
But that his foes made bridge of's nose,
   And cry'd him down for a Protector,
Proving him to be a fool, that would undertake to rule,
   And not drink and fight like *Hector*.

The Grecian Lad, he drank like mad,
   Minding no work above it;
And *Sans question* kill'd *Ephestion*,
   Because he'd not approve it;
He got command, where God had land,
   And like a *Maudlin* Yonker,
When he tippled all and wept, he laid him down to sleep,
   Having no more Worlds to conquer.

Rump-Parliament would needs invent
   An Oath of Abjuration,
But Obedience and Allegiance are now come into fashion:
   Then here's a boul, with a heart and soul
To *Charles*, and let all men say Amen to't,
   Though they brought the Father down
From a triple Kingdom Crown,
   Wee'l drink the Son up agen to't.

The Protecting Brewer.

A Brewer may be a Burgess grave,
   And carry the matter so fine and so brave,
That he the better may play the Knave,
                  Which no body can deny.

A Brewer may be a Parliament-man,
For there the Knavery first began,
And brew most cunning Plots he can,
                  Which no body, &c.

A Brewer may put on a *Nabal* face,
And march to the Wars with such a grace,
That he may get a Captains place,
                  Which no body, &c.

A Brewer may speak so wonderous well,
That he may raise strange things to tell,
And so to be made a Collonel,
                  Which no body, &c.

A Brewer may make his foes to flee,
And raise his Fortunes, so that he
Lieutenant-General may be,
      Which no body, &c.

A Brewer he may be all in all,
And raise his Powers both great and small,
That he may be a Lord General,
      Which no body, &c.

A Brewer may be like a Fox in a Cub,
And teach a Lecture out of a Tub,
And give the wicked world a rub,
      Which no body, &c.

A Brewer by's Excize and Rate,
Will promise his Army he knows what,
And set it upon the Colledge-gate,
      Which no body, &c.

Methinks I hear one say to me,
Pray why may not a Brewer be,
Lord-Chancellor o'th' University,
      Which no body, &c.

A Brewer may be as bold as *Hector*,
When as he has drunk off his cup of *Nectar*,
And a Brewer may be a Lord Protector.
      Which no body, &c.

Now here remans the strangest thing,
How this Brewer about his Liquor did bring,
To be an Emperour, or a King,
      Which no body, &c.

Part I.   *Rump Songs.*   333

A Brewer may do what he will,
And rob the Church and State, to sell
His soul unto the devil of hell,
    Which no body can deny.

The Power of the Sword.

LAY by your Pleading, Law lyes a bleeding,
 Burn all your Studies down, and throw away your Reading;
Small power the Word has, and can afford us
Not half so many Priviledges as the Sword has:
It fosters your Masters, it plasters Disasters,
And makes your Servants, quickly greater than their Masters;
It venters, it enters, it circles, it centers,
And makes a Prentice free in spight of his Indentures.

This takes off tall things, and sets up small things,
This masters Money, though Money masters all things;
'Tis not in season, to talk of Reason,
Or call it Legal, when the Sword will have it Treason;
It conquers the Crown too, the Furres and the Gown too,
This set up a Presbyter, and this pull'd him down too;
This subtil Deceiver, turn'd Bonnet to Beaver,
Down drops a Bishop, and up starts a Weaver.

This fits a Lay-man to preach and pray man,
'Tis this can make a Lord of him that was a Dray-
  man ;
Forth from the dull pit, of Follies full pit,
This brought an Hebrew Iron-monger to the Pul-
  pit ;
Such pittifull things be, more happier than Kings
  be,
This got the Herauldry of *Thimblebee* and *Slingsbee;*
No Gospel can guide it, no Law can decide it,
In Church or State, untill the Sword hath sanctify'd
  it.

Down goes the Law-tricks, for from that Matrix
Sprung holy *Hewson's* power, and tumbled down St.
  Patricks;
The Sword prevails so highly in *Wales* too,
Shinkin ap Powel cryes, and swears Cuts-pluttera-nails
  too;
In *Scotland* this Waster, did make such disaster,
They sent their Money back for which they sold their
  Master ;
It batter'd so their *Dunkirke*, and did so the *Don*
  firke,
That he is fled, and swears, the Devil is in *Dun-
  kirke.*

He that can tower o'er him that is lower,
Would be but thought a Fool to put away his
  Power ;
Take Books and rent 'um, who would invent 'um,
When as the Sword replyes, *Negatur argumentum?*

Your grand Colledge Butlers, must stoop to your Sutlers,
There's not a Library living like the Cutlers;
The bloud that is spilt, Sir, hath gain'd all the gilt, Sir,
Thus have you seen me run the Sword up to the hilt, Sir.

Cromwell's *Coronation*.

O*Liver, Oliver*, take up thy Crown,
For now thou hast made three Kingdoms thine own;
Call thee a Conclave of thy own creation,
 To ride us to ruine, who dare thee oppose:
Whilst we thy good people are at thy Devotion,
 To fall down and worship thy terrible Nose.

To thee and thy Mermydons, *Oliver*, we,
Do tender our homage as fits thy degree,
We'll pay the Excise and Taxes, God blesse us,
 With fear and contrition, as penitents should,
Whilst you, great Sir, vouchsafe to oppresse us,
 Not daring so much as in private to scold.

We bow down, as cow'd down, to thee and thy Sword,
For now thou hast made thy self *Englands* sole Lord,
By Mandate of Scripture, and Heavenly warrant,
 The Oath of Allegiance, and Covenant too;

To *Charles* and his Kingdoms thou art Heir apparent,
And born to rule over the *Turk* and the *Jew*.

Then *Oliver*, *Oliver*, get up and ride,
Whilst Lords, Knights, and Gentry do run by thy side;
The Maulsters and Brewers account it their glory,
  Great God of the Grain-tub's compared to thee:
All Rebells of old are lost in their story,
  Till thou plod'st along to the *Padington*-tree.

The *BREWER*.

To the Tune of the *Black-smith*.

THere many a Clinching Verse is made
  In honour of the *Black-smiths* trade,
But more of the *Brewer* may be said,
      Which no body can deny.

I need not much of this repeat,
The *Black-smith* cannot be compleat,
Unlesse the *Brewer* do give him a heat,
      Which no body can deny.

When *Smug* unto the forge doth come,
Unlesse the *Brewer* doth liquor him home,
He'll never strike thy pot and my pot *Tom*.
      Which no body can deny.

Part I.   *Rump Songs.*

Of all professions in the town
The *Brewers* trade hath gain'd renown,
His liquor reacheth up to the Crown,
    Which no body can deny.

Many new Lords from him there did spring,
Of all the trades he still was their King,
For the *Brewer* had the world in a sling,
    Which no body can deny.

He scorneth all Laws and Martial stops,
But whips an Army as round as tops,
And cuts off his foes as thick as hops,
    Which no body can deny.

He dives for Riches down to the bottom,
And cryes, my Masters, when he had got um,
Let every tub stand upon his own bottom,
    Which no body can deny.

In War-like acts he scorns to stoop,
For when his Army begins to droop,
He draws them up us round as a hoop,
    Which no body can deny.

The Jewish *Scots* that scorns to eat
The flesh of Swine, and *Brewers* beat,
'Twas the sight of this hogs-head made 'um retreat,
    Which no body can deny.

Poor *Jockie* and his basket hilt
Was beaten, and much blood was spilt,
And their bodies like barrels did run atilt,
    Which no body can deny.

Though *Jemy* gave the first assault,
The *Brewer* at last made them to halt,
And left them what the Cat left in the Mault.
                Which no body can deny.

They cry'd that Antichrist came to settle
Religion in a Cooler and a Kettle,
For his Nose and Copper were both of one mettle,
                Which no body can deny.

Some Christian King began to quake,
And said, with the *Brewer* no quarrels we'll make,
We'll let him alone, as he Brews let him Bake,
                Which no body can deny.

He hath a strong and very stout heart,
And thought to be made an Emperor for't,
But the Devil put a spoke in his Cart,
                Which no body can deny.

If any intended to do him disgrace,
His fury would take off his head in the place,
He alway did carry his Furnesse in his face,
                Which no body can deny.

But yet by the way you must understand,
He kept his foes so under command,
That *Pride* could never get the upper hand,
                Which no body can deny.

He was a stout *Brewer*, of whom we may brag,
But now he is hurried away with a hag;
He brew'd in a bottle, and bak'd in a bag,
                Which no body can deny.

And now may all stout Souldiers say,
Farewell the glory of the day,
For the *Brewer* himself is turn'd to clay,
                Which no body can deny.

Thus fell the brave *Brewer*, the bold son of slaughter,
We need not to fear what shall follow after,
For he dealt all his life time in fire and water,
                Which no body can deny.

And if his Successor had had but his might,
We had not been in a pittifull plight,
But he was found many grains too light,
                Which no body can deny.

Let's leave off singing and drink off our Bub,
Wee'll call for a Reckoning, and every man Club,
For I think I have told you a *Tale of a Tub.*
                Which no body can deny.

In imitation of Come my Daphne, *a Dialogue between* Pluto *and* Oliver.

Pluto. Come Imp Royal, come away,
      Into black night we will turn bright day.
Oliver. 'Tis *Pluto* calls, what would my Syre?
Pluto. Come, follow me to the Stygian fire,
      Where *Ireton* doth wait
      To welcome thee in state.
Oliver. Were I in bed with *Lamberts* wife,
      I'de quit those joyes for such a life.

Pluto. My Princely *Nol* make hast,
　　For thee we keep a Fast.
Oliver. In these dismal shades will I
　　Unto thee unfold my Villany.
Pluto. In my bosome I'll thee lay,
　　For thy sake wee'l all keep holyday.

Chorus. We'll rage and roar, and fry in flames,
　　And *Charles* himself shall see
　　How damn'dly we agree,
　　Yet scorn to change our Chains
　　For his eternal diety.

A Quarrel betwixt Tower-hill *and* Tyburn.

I'LE tell you a Story that never was told,
　　A tale that hath both head and heel,
And though by no Recorder inroll'd,
　　I know you will find it as true as steel.

When General *Monck* was come to the Town,
　　A little time after the Rump had the rout,
When Loyalty rose, and Rebellion fell down,
　　They say, that *Tower-hill* and *Tyburne* fell out.

Quoth terrible *Tyburne* to lofty *Tower-hill*,
　　Thy longed-for daies are come at last,
And now thou wilt dayly thy belly fulfill
　　With King-killers bloud whilst I must fast.

The High Court of Justice will come to the Bar,
   There to be cooked and dressed for thee,
Whilst I, that live out of Town so far,
   Must only be fed by Fellony.

If *Treason* be counted the foulest fact,
   And dying be a *Traytor's* due,
Then why should you all the glory exact?
   You know, they are fitter for me than you.

To speak the plain truth, I have groan'd for them long,
   For when they had routed the Royal Root,
And done the Kingdom so much wrong,
   I knew at the last they would come to't.

When *Titchburne* sate upon the Bench,
   Twirling his Chain in high degree,
With a Beardless Chin, like a withered Wench,
   Thought I, the Bar is fitter for thee.

But then, with stately composed face,
   Tower-hill to *Tyburne* made reply,
Do not complain, in such a Case
   Thou shalt have thy share as well as I.

There are a sort of Mongrils, which
   My Lordly Scaffold will disgrace:
I know *Hugh Peters* his fingers itch
   To make a Pulpit of the place.

But take him *Tyburn*, he is thine own,
   Divide his quarters with thy knife,
Who did pollute with flesh and bone
   The quarters of the Butchers wife.

The next among these Petticoat-Peers
  Is *Harry Martin*, take him thither,
But he hath been addle so many years,
  That I fear he will hardly hang together.

There's *Hacker*, zealous *Tom Harrison* too,
  That boldly defends the bloudy deed,
He practizeth what the Jesuites do,
  To murder his King, as a part of his Creed.

There's single-eyed *Hewson* the Cobler of Fate,
  Translated into Buff and Feather,
But bootless are all his seams of State
  When the soul is unript from the upper-leather.

Is this prophane mechanical Brood
  For me, that have been dignify'd
With loyal *Laud* and *Straffords* blood,
  And holy *Hewet*, who lately dy'd?

Do thou contrive with deadly *Dun*
  To send them to the River of *Stix*,
'Tis pitty, since those Saints are gone,
  That Martyrs and Murtherers bloud should mix.

Then do not fear me that I will
  Deprive thee of that fatal Day;
'Tis fit those that their King did kill
  Sould hang up in the Kings high-way.

My Priviledge, though I know it is large,
  Into thy hand I'le freely give it,
For there is *Cook* that read the Kings Charge,
  Is only fit for the Devils tribute.

Then taunting *Tyburn*, in great scorn,
   Did make *Tower-hill* this rude reply:
So much rank bloud my stomack will turn,
   And thou shalt be sick as well as I.

These Traytors made those Martyrs bleed
   Upon the Block, that thou dost bear,
And there it is fit they should dye for the deed;
   But *Tower-hill* cryed, they shall not come there.

With that grim *Tyburn* began to fret,
   And *Tower-hill* did look very grim:
And sure as a Club they both would have met,
   But that the City did step between.

The Bloody Bed-roll, or *Treason displayed in its Colours.*

Triumphing News for Cavaliers,
The Rump smells strong, cast out by th' Peers.

OLd OLIVER's gone to the Dogs,
   Oh! No I do mistake,
      Hee's gone in a Wherry
      Over the Ferry,
Is call'd the *Stygian* Lake.
But *Cerberus* that Great Porter
Did read him such a Lecture,
      That made him to roar
      When he came a-shoar

For being *Lord Protector*.
News, news, news,
Brave Cavaliers *be merry,*
Chear up your sad souls
With Bacchus *Bowls,*
Of Claret, White, and Sherry.

Where is that Cursed Crew
Were of the last Kings Jury,
 By thy damned soul
 Go fetch them *Nol*
Quoth *Pluto* in his fury.
Where is old *Joan* thy wife?
Her Highness I would see,
 Come let her in
 She shall be my Queen,
For a Cuckold thou shalt be.
News, news, &c.

Make room for a *Ramping Lady,*
One of the Devils race,
 This ugly Witch,
 And nasty Bitch
Spat in the King's sweet face.
I'le make her a Lady of Honour,
Quoth *Pluto* let her in,
 And open the door;
 For this old Whore
Shall wait upon my Queen.
News, news, &c.

Here comes Sir H E N R Y M A R T Y N
As good as ever pist,

This wenching beast
Had Whores at least
A thousand on his list :
This made the Devils laugh,
So good a friend to see,
    At *Pluto's* Court
    There's better sport,
Come thou shalt dwell with me.
   News, news, &c.

Bid *Caron* bring his Boat,
Here comes a man of fame,
    Who hath waited here
    Above a year,
JACK BRADSHAW is his name,
O ho quoth *Pluto* then,
As loud as he could yawl,
    By *Oliver's* Nose
    I did suppose
Thou hadst been at *White-hall.*
   News, news, &c.

Thou'rt welcome to my Court,
Here on my Scroul I find,
    I have in store
    A thousand more
As Arrant Rogues behind.
Why art thou sad quoth *Pluto ?*
My Servants must appear,
    Then do not grudge
    I'le made thee Judge
Of all my Subjects here.
   News, news, &c.

Here comes a friend of mine,
Make room for the Lord LISLE,
  His guests at last
  Did come so fast
That made old *Pluto* smile.
Thou must along with me,
Now 'tis too late to rue it,
  Thy damned Soul
  Is on my Scroul,
Remember Doctor *Hewet*.
  News, news, &c.

What is the Cause Sir ARTHUR
Your Pulses go so quick?
  'Tis Bishops Lands
  That's in your hands
Which makes them beat so thick.
Thy Oath of Abjuration
Was far a worser thing,
  For the Devil and thou
  Did study how
We should abjure our K I N G.
  News, news, &c.

Next comes Sir HENRY MILDMAY
As good as ever twang'd,
  What Laws had we
  When he scap'd free
And honest men were hang'd?
Perhaps the KING's good grace
May pardon what is past,
  But that's all one
  At *Pluto's* Throne
Thou must appear at last,
  News, news, &c.

Shall *Traytors* be conceal'd?
Oh! no Sir HENRY VANE,
   'Tis a pittifull thing
   For our good K I N G
When Traytors are in grain.
If thou wilt take the pains,
Then pray thee go and look,
   For I am told
   Thou art enrol'd
In *Pluto's* bloody Book.
  News, news, &c.

Here comes the *Learned* SPEAKER,
Whose baggs of Gold do rust,
   Who would not hear
   A *Cavalier*
Though his Cause were nere so just.
Corruption bears the sway
Where Justice is deny'd,
   The Devil take him,
   And Mr. P Y M,
And likewise Collonel P R I D E,
  News, news, &c.

Make room for one-ey'd HEWSON,
A *Lord* of such account,
   'Twas a pretty Jest
   That such a Beast
Should to such honour mount.
When *Coblers* were in fashion,
And *Nigherds* in such grace;
   'Twas sport to see
   How PRIDE and he

Did justle for the Place.
News, news, &c.

What dreadfull shew is this?
'Tis PRIDEAUX or his Ghost,
   He makes such hast,
   And comes so fast,
I think He's riding Post.
A *Lawyer* if thou art,
Amongst the damned souls,
   At *Pluto's* Barre,
   'Tis better farre
Then pleading at the Roles.
News, news, &c.

Oh welcome Dr. P E T E R S,
And Cornet J O Y C E also,
   One of these twain
   Was worse than *Cain*
That gave the deadly blow:
One of these *Cursed Rogues*
Was he that did the feat,
   But some men say
   'Twas that Lord G R A Y
That made the work compleat.
News, news, &c.

A Boat for this Old *Doctor*
To cross the River *Styx,*
   For *Pluto* he
   Desired to see
Some of his Antick tricks;
My *Chaplain* thou shalt be,
What more can be desired?

Oh! quoth he
   That cannot be,
My Lease is not expir'd.
News, news, &c.

Oh! my *Rump*, my *Rump*, my *Rump*,
My *Rump* smells wonderous strong,
   The blisters rise
   About my Thighs
With voting here so long,
My *Rump* is grown so sore,
I can no longer sit,
   Hold up thy Bum,
   The Devil is come
With a Plaister to cure it.
News, news, &c.

When *Pluto* keeps his feasts,
The Rogues must all appear,
   And Mr. SCOT
   I had forgot,
Must tast of this good Chear.
Find out the Man, quoth *Pluto*,
That is the greater sinner,
   If COOK be he
   Then COOK shall be
The *Cook* to *Cook* my dinner,
News, news, &c.

God blesse the *KINGS* good grace,
And keep him from his foes,
   I wish the rather
   Because his *Father*
Had too too many of those.

350   *Rump Songs.*   Part I.

God blesse the *Duke of YORK*,
His Sister, and Another,
   Accurst be those
   That do oppose
The sending for their Mother.
  News, news, news,
  Brave Cavaliers be merry,
  Chear up your sad souls
  With Bacchus Bowls,
  Of Claret, White, and Sherry.

The four Legg'd Elder; or a Relation of a Horrible Dog and an Elders Maid.

To the Tune of *The Ladies fall;* Or *Gather your Rose Buds*, and 50 other Tunes.

1.

ALL *Christians* and *Lay-Elders* too,
  For shame amend your Lives,
I'll tell you of a Dog-trick now,
  Which much concerns your wives.
An *Elder's* Maid near *Temple-bar*
  (Ah what a Quean was she!)
Did take an ugly Mastiff Cur
  Where Christians use to be.
Help House of Commons, House of Peers!
  Oh now or never help!
Th' Assembly having sate four years
  Have now brought forth a whelp!

2.
One Evening late she stept aside,
    Pretending to fetch Eggs,
And there she made her self a Bride
    To one that had four leggs :
Her Master hears a Rumblement,
    And wonder'd she did tarry,
Not dreaming (without his consent)
    His Dog would ever marry.
Help House of Commons, &c.

3.
He went to peep, but was afraid,
    And hastily did run
To fetch a Staff to help his Maid,
    Not knowing what was done;
He took his *Ruling Elder's* Cane,
    And cry'd out, *Help, help here!*
For *Swash* our Mastiff and poor *Jane*
    Are now, *fight Dog, fight Bear.*
Oh House of Commons, &c.

4.
But when he came he was full sorry,
    For he perceiv'd their strife,
That according to the *Directory*
    These two were Dog and Wife:
Ah (then he said) thou cruel Quean,
    Why hast thou me beguil'd?
I wonder'd *Swash* was grown so lean,
    Poor Dog he's almost spoyl'd.
Oh House of Commons, &c.

5.
I thought thou hadst no carnal sense
    But what's in other Lasses,

And could have quench'd thy Cupiscence
　According to the *Classis;*
But all the Parish see it plain,
　Since thou art in this pickle,
Thou art an *Independent* Quean,
　And lov'st a *Conventicle.*
Oh House of Commons, &c.

6.

Alas now each *Malignant* Rogue
　Will all the world perswade
That she that's Spouse unto a Dog,
　May be an *Elder's* Maid;
They'll jeer us if abroad we stir,
　Good Master *Elder* stay,
Sir, of what *Classis* is your Cur;
　And then what can we say?
Oh House of Commons, &c.

7.

They'll many graceless Ballads sing
　Of a *Presbyterian,*
That a *Lay-Elder* is a thing
　Made up half-Dog half-Man:
Out, out, (said he, and smote her down)
　Was Mankind grown so scant?
There's scarce another Dog in town
　Had took the *Covenant.*
Oh House of Commons, &c.

8.

Then *Swash* began to look full grim,
　And *Jane* did thus reply,
Sir, you thought nought too good for him,
　And fed your Dog too high:
Tis true, he took me in the lurch,
　And leapt into my arm,

But (as I hope to come to Church)
I did your Dog no harm.
Oh House of Commons, &c.

9.

Then she was brought to *Newgate* Gaol,
And there was naked stript,
They whipt her till the Cord did fail,
As Dogs use to be whipt:
Poor City Maids shed many a tear
When she was lash'd and bang'd,
And had she been a *Cavalier*,
Surely she had been hang'd.
Oh House of Commons, &c.

10.

Her's was but *Fornication* found,
For which she felt the lash,
But his was *Buggery* presum'd,
Therefore they hanged *Swash*.
What will become of *Bishops* then,
Or *Independency*,
For now we find both Dogs and Men
Stand for *Presbytery*.
Oh House of Commons, &c.

11.

She might have took a *Sow-gelder*,
With *Synod-men* good store,
But she would have a *Lay-Elder*
With two legs, and two more.
Go tell the *Assembly* of *Divines*,
Tell *Adoniram Blew*,
Tell *Burges*, *Marshall*, *Case*, and *Vines*,
Tell *Now-and-Anon-too*.
Oh House of Commons, &c.

12.

Some said she was a *Scotish* Girl,
  Or else (at least) a Witch;
But she was born in *Colchester*,
  Was ever such a Bitch!
Take heed all Christian Virgins now,
  The *Dog-star* now prevails;
Ladies beware your Monkeys too,
  For Monkeys have long tails.
Oh House of Commons, &c.

13.

Blesse *King* and *Queen*, and send us peace,
  As we had seven years since,
For we remember no *Dog-dayes*
  While we enjoy'd our Prince:
Bless sweet Prince *Charles*, two Dukes, three Girls,
  O save His *Majesty!*
Grant that his *Commons*, *Lords*, and *Earls*,
  May lead such lives as He.
Oh House of Commons, House of Peers!
  Oh now or never help!
Th' Assembly having sate four years,
  Have now brought forth a whelp!

News from Colchester.

Or, A Proper new Ballad of certain Carnal passages betwixt a *Quaker* and a *Colt*, at *Horsley* near *Colchester* in *Essex*. To the Tune of *Tom of Bedlam*.

I.

ALL in the Land of *Essex*,
  Near *Colchester* the Zealous,

Part I. *Rump Songs.*

On the side of a bank,
Was play'd such a Prank,
As would make a Stone-horse jealous.

2.

Help *Woodcock*, *Fox*, and *Nailor*,
For Brother *Green's* a Stallion,
  Now alas what hope,
  Of converting the Pope,
When a Quaker turns *Italian!*

3.

Even to our whole profession
A scandall 'twill be counted,
  When 'tis talkt with disdain
  Among the Profane,
How Brother *Green* was mounted.

4.

And in the Good time of Christians,
Which though our Saints have damn'd all,
  Yet when did they hear
  That a damn'd Cavalier
Ere play'd such a Christmas gamball?

5.

Had thy flesh, O *Green*, been pamper'd
With any Cates unhallow'd,
  Hast thou sweetned thy Gums
  With Pottage of Plums,
Or prophane minc'd Pie hadst swallow'd.

6.

Roll'd up in wanton Swine's-flesh,
The Fiend might have crept into thee,
  Then fulnesse of gut
  Might have made thee rut,
And the Devil have so rid through thee.

7.
But alas, he had been feasted
With a Spiritual Collation,
   By our frugal Mayor,
   Who can dine on a Prayer,
And sup on an Exhortation.

8.
'Twas meer impulse of Spirit,
Though he us'd the weapon carnal,
   Filly Foal, quoth he,
   My Bride thou shalt be :
And how this is lawfull, learn all.

9.
For if no respect of Persons
Be due 'mongst the sons of *Adam*,
   In a large extent,
   Thereby may be meant
That a *Mare's* as good as a *Madam*.

10.
Then without more Ceremony,
Not bonnet vail'd, nor Kist her,
   But took her by force,
   For better for worse,
And us'd her like a Sister.

11.
Now when in such a Saddle
A Saint will needs be riding,
   Though we dare not say
   'Tis a falling away,
May there not be some back-sliding ?

12.
No surely, quoth *James Nailor*,
'Twas but an insurrection

Of the Carnal part,
For a Quaker in heart
Can never lose perfection.

13.
For (as our Masters teach us)
The intent being well directed,
Though the Devil trapan
The Adamical man,
The Saint stands un-infected.

14.
But alas a Pagan Jury
Ne're judges what's intended,
Then say what we can,
Brother *Green's* out-ward man
I fear will be suspended.

15.
And our Adopted Sister
Will find no better quarter,
But when him we inroul
For a Saint, Filly Foal
Shall passe her self for a Martyr.

16.
Rome that Spiritual *Sodome*,
No longer is thy debter,
O *Colchester*, now
Who's *Sodome* but thou,
Even according to the Letter?

The Four-legg'd Quaker.
To the Tune of *The Four-legg'd Elder.*

1.

ALL that have two or but one ear,
  (I dare not tell ye half)
You of an *Essex* Colt shall hear
  Will shame their very *Calf.*
In *Horsley* Fields near *Colchester*
  A *Quaker* would turn Trooper;
He caught a Foal and mounted her
  (O base!) below the Crupper.
    Help Lords, and Commons, once more help,
      O send us Knives and Daggers!
    For if the Quakers be not gelt
      Your Troops will have the Staggers.

2.

Ralph Green (it was this Varlet's name)
  Of *Colchester* you'll swear,
For thence the *Four-legg'd Elder* came,
  Was ever such a Pair!
But though 'twas foul 'tween *Swash* and *Jane,*
  Yet this is ten times worse;
For then a Dog did play the Man,
  But Man now play'd the Horse.
    Help, &c.

3.

The Owner of the Colt was nigh,
  (Observing their Embrace)
And drawing nearer did espy
  The *Quaker's* sorrel Face:

My Foal is ravish'd (then he cryes,
  And fiercely at him ran)
Thou Rogue, I'll have thee haltered twice,
  As Horse and eke as Man!
    Help, &c.

4.
Ah Devil, do'st thou tremble? now
  'Tis sore against thy will;
For Mares and preaching Ladies know
  Thou hast a Colts tooth still:
But mine's not guilty of this Fact,
  She was by thee compelled;
Poor thing, whom no man ever backt
  Thou wickedly hast Bellied.
    Help, &c.

5.
O friend (said *Green*, with sighs and groans)
  Let this thy wrath appease!
(And gave him then eight new Half-crowns
  To make him hold his peace.)
The man reply'd, though I for this
  Conceal thy Hugger Mugger,
Do'st think it lawfull for a Piece
  A filly Foal to Bugger?
    Help, &c.

6.
The Master saw his Colt defil'd,
  Which vext his Soul with doubt;
For if his Filly prov'd with Childe
  He knew all would come out:
Then he afresh began to rave,
  (For all his Money taking)
Neighbours, said he, I took this Knave
  Ith' very act of *Quaking*.
    Help, &c.

7.

Then to the Pinfold (Gaol I mean)
    They dragg'd him by the Mane,
They call'd him Beast, and call'd her Quean,
    As if she had been *Jane*.
O stone him (all the Women cry'd)
    Nay geld him (which is worse)
Who scorn'd us all, and took a Bride
    That's Daughter to a Horse!
      Help, &c.

8.

The Colt was silent all this while,
    And therefore 'twas no Rape,
The Virgin foal he did beguile,
    And so intends to scape:
For though he caught her in a Ditch
    Where she could not revolt,
Yet he had no *Scott'sh spurr* nor Switch
    To ride the willing Colt.
      Help, &c.

9.

O *Essex, Essex, England's* pride,
    Go burn this long-tail'd Quean,
For though the *Thames* runs by thy side,
    It cannot wash thee clean!
'Tis not thy Bleating Sonn's complaints,
    Hold forth such wanton courses,
Thy Oysters hint the very Saint
    To horn the very Horses.
      Help, &c.

10.

Though they salute not in the Street
    (Because they are our Masters)
'Tis now reveal'd why *Quakers* meet
    In Meadows, Woods, and Pastures.

But Hors-men, Mare-men, all and some
 Who Man and Beast perplex,
Not only from *East-Horsley* come,
 But from *West-Middle-Sex.*
  Help, &c.

11.

This was not GREEN the *Feltmaker*,
 Nor Willow GREEN the *Baker*,
Nor GEORGE the Sea-GREEN *Mariner*,
 But RALPH the Grasse-GREEN *Quaker*,
Had GREEN the Sow-gelder but known,
 And done his Office duly,
Though RALPH was GREEN when he came on,
 He had come off most blewly.
  Help, &c.

12.

Alas you know by Man's flesh came
 The *Foul-disease* to *Naples*,
And now we fear the very same
 Is broke into our Stables;
For Death hath stoln so many Steeds
 From Prince and Peer, and Carrier,
That this new Murrain rather needs
 A **FARRAR* than a Farrier.
  Help, &c.

13.

Nay if this GREEN within the walls
 Of *Colchester* left forces,
Those Cavaliers were Caniballs,
 Eating his Humane Horses!
But some make Man their *second course*,
 (In cool Blood will not spare)

* *Physician to the Earl of* Pembrook, *who is no Quaker nor Quacker.*

Who butcher Men and favour Horse
  Will couple with a Mare.
    Help, &c.

14.

This *Centaur*, unquoth *Other* thing,
  Will make a dreadfull Breach :
Yet though an Ass may *speak* or **sing*,
  O let not Horses *preach!*
But *bridle* such wilde Colts who can
  When they'll obey no Summons,
For things begot 'tween Mare & Man
  Are neither Lords nor Commons.
    Help, &c.

15.

O *Elders, Independants* too,
  Though all your Power's combin'd
Quakers will grow too strong for you
  Now Horse and Man are joyn'd :
While *Cavaliers*, poor foolish Rogues,
  Know only Maids Affairs,
She-Presbyters can deal with Dogs,
  And *Quaking-men* with Mares.
    Help, &c.

16.

Now as when *Milan* Town was rear'd,
  A Monstrous Sow untam'd,
With Back *half Hair half Wool* appear'd,
  'Twas *Mediolanum* nam'd :
So *Colchester* must have recourse
  To some such four-legg'd Sister,
For sure as *Horsley* came from Horse,
  From Colt 'twas call'd *Col-chester*.
    Help, Lords and Commons, &c.

* *A new Sect of young Men and Women, who pray, eat and sing* ex tempore.

A JOLT on Michaelmas day 1654.

To the Tune of

To himself that hath fool'd
More than Mahomet *could, &c.*

1.

IT fell on a day,
When good People say
   St. *Michael* beat the Dragon,
My Lord the *Protector*
Did drive (like a *Hector*)
   A Coach instead of a * Wagon.

2.

Because he did hear
The Charateer
   Did antiently wear a Crown,
Up went the Horse-heels,
Round round went the Wheeles,
   'Till his *Highnesse* came head-long down.

3.

He reign'd them so hard,
They look'd back and were scar'd
   To see him so red and so grim
Away then they fled,
And though he us'd to lead,
   This *new-modell'd* Horse would lead him.

* *Londinium petere solebat gestatorio, seu vehiculo communi.*

4.

But O how they snuff
When his Pistol flew off,
  For which all the Saints suspect him,
Doth Providence attend him,
Thirty thousand defend him,
  Yet a poor Pocket-pistol protect him;

5.

How many a Hurl
Had poor Mr. *_Thurl_——
  —_Lo!_ He in the Coach did prank it:
He thought he had sate
Chief Secretary of State,
  But was toss'd like a Dog in a Blanket.

6.

Nay had they run faster
Hee'd follow his Master
  Through all the Sceans of this Mad-show:
A Brewer, a Collonel,
A Preacher, a General,
  A Protector, a King——then comes _Bradshaw_.

7.

They slander my _Lord_
With a bug-bear Word,
  That he did like _Phaeton_ drive;
But his _Highness_ try'd
Six Horses to guide,
  And _Phaeton_ had now _five_.

---

* Vocem τῷ THURLO rithmicè respondentem nostrates desiderant: nomen itaque (ipsius homulli instar crucis) hanc τμῆσιν patitur; nostroque vel versiculo, ac ipso curru, huc illuc impellitur.

Part I. *Rump Songs.*

8.
Mad *Phaeton* hurl'd
Fire all o're the World,
   Then dead in a River was found:
But my Lord had no ayme
To set all in a flame,
   And never was born to be drown'd.

9.
'Twas *Nero* did strive
Such Charets to drive,
   And publickly shew'd his Work;
But when my Lord sticks
Up his Bills to shew tricks,
   Hee'l undo th'other *dauncing Turk.*

10.
But if you look high,
There's some reason why
   These Jades did so fling and skip,
For though we afford
Him the *power of the Sword,*
   He had no command of the *Whip.*

11.
Enthron'd in his Chair
(What a pox did He there?)
   He took such Protectorly courses,
He seem'd Horse and Mule,
But 'tis easier to rule
   Three Kingdoms, than six Horses.

12.
Not a day nor an hour
But we felt his Power,
   And now he would shew us his Art:

His first Reproach
Is a fall from a Coach,
    And his last will be from a Cart.

The House out of Doors.

April 20. 1653.

To the Tune of *Cook Laurell.*

1.

YOu saw *Eleven Members* turn'd out of Doors,
    And 200. more were driven from home,
And then their own *Lords* were voted down stairs,
    (When some of them crept into the *Lower room :*)
We purg'd and we purg'd, but all would not do't,
    (The Body had got such a damnable Paunch)
'Till *OLIVER* fell upon *Branch and Root,*
    Then down with it, down with it, down *Root and Branch.*
        With a hey down, down a down down,
            Sing ho down down to make up the Ditty,
        With a hey down down a down down,
            The Parliament's broke as well as the City.

2.

These Remnant *Members* began to say
    Their *General* was fit to be had in suspition ;
And offered to Vote his Commission away.
    As if (forsooth) they had given him his Commission :
He did (yet did not) make use of his Sword,
On Men that could vote, and vote, but no more

He shew'd them his Hilt, and spake but a word,
  And that word blew the whole House out of door.
    With a hey down, &c.
    The Parliament's broke as well as the City.

3.

This day was *Strafford* all-to-be-Traytor'd,
  Because (they say) *He had an Intent*
(As this day *Nol* the *Members* scatter'd*)
  By an Army to force the Parliament.
At which old *VANE* now rants and raves,
  For *Strafford's* bloud is not yet grown cold)
And yet we must say while we speak of Knaves,
  The *Old* is the *Young*, and the *Young* is the *Old*.
    With a hey down, &c.
    The Parliament's broke as well as the City.

4.

Sir *MILDMAY* then with his hand on his groin,
  (As for a *Knave of the Diamonds*) stood :
He eat the Kings Bread, & drank the Kings Wine,
  So long till at last he drank of his Bloud.
So did *CORNELIVS HOLLAND* too,
  Whose share i'th' *Revenue* doth fill three Pages,
But now when the *House* is broke up (you know)
  'Tis fit *Houshold Servants* be paid their Wages.
    With a hey down, &c.
    The Parliament's broke as well as the City.

5.

The Judge of *Morocco* (*Treason HILL*)
  Devour'd at a Morsell all *Taunton Dean*,
He keeps five Chambers i'th' *Temple*, but will
  (Now th' *House* is pull'd down) be a *Hillock* again.
And the Devil too for his *BOND* doth call,

    * *April* 20. 1641, 1653.

Though *Dennis* from Chamber to Chamber did hop,
He sate *Lord President* at *Whitehall*,
But now must go home to sit in his shop.
   With a hey, &c.
      The Parliament's broke as well as the City.

6.

Now Alderman *Fustian* cocks not his Beaver,'
Who chang'd his Name from *Perry* to *PVRY*,
A Dean and a Bishop made out of a Weaver,
   That had been refus'd to be of a Jury:
He vow'd to *leave not a Gentleman*,
   Though every House were big as Rome:
In all bloody Votes he highest ran;
   But now may run down to his *Bottom* and *Loom.*
      With a hey, &c.
         The Parliament's broke as well as the City.

7.

Now look to your Wives, for I am inform'd
   That carnal *SCOT* is again broke loose;
But the *House* that shelter'd his Lust is Reform'd
   As he did the Hall of *Lambeth-house;*
(For he knew the *High Commission* sate there)
   Both *King* and *Cromwell* he openly curs'd,
But *Oliver* now will pay his Arrear,
   For of all kind of *Scots* the *English* is worst.
      With a hey down, down a down down,
         Sing ho down down to make up the Ditty,
      With a hey down down a down down,
         The Parliament's broke as well as the City.

The *RUMP*.

December 26. 1659.

To the Tune of *The Blacksmith*.

Now Master & Prentice for Rimes must pump
On *Hab*,* *Noll, Arthur*, and *Lawson Vantrump*,
A *Long Parliament* of a *Short Rump*.
                  Which no body can deny.

For Wits and No-Wits now have an Itch
To prepare some damnable tearing Switch
For them whose very Face is a Breech.
                  Which, &c.

Twelve years they sate above *Kings* and *Queens*,
Full twelve, and then had enter'd their *teens*
When *Oliver* came to out-sin their Sins.
                  Which, &c.

And yet after all his signal *Septembers*,
Both he and his Babe, and his *Other-House* Members
Saw *Rump* was but asleep in its Embers.
                  Which, &c.

For up it rose, then out 'twas blown,
For *Lambert* and *Rump* like my Lady and *Joan*,
Blew in and out till *Rump* blew out *John*.
                  Which, &c.

* *St. John's.*

And then it swell'd with such monstrous growth
That by and by it broke out in the South,
From whence it was called PORTS-MOUTH.
Which, &c.

From thence to *London* it rode tan-tivy,
(Though *London* then wore *Holly* and *Ivy*)
And sate at *Whitehall* in a *Council-Privy*.
Which, &c.

Then suddenly *Fleetwood* fell from Grace,
And now cryes *Heaven hath spit in his face*,
Though he *smelt* it came from *another place*.
Which, &c.

Janizary *Desbrow* then look'd pale,
For, said he, if this *Rump* prevail,
'Twill blow me back to my old Plough-tayl,
Which, &c.

But when he felt his own Regiment kick,
Oh, quoth he, this was my own Trick
'Gainst my Brother *Nol* and my Nephew *Dick*.
Which, &c.

Now whom the Devil doth *Rump* represent?
'Twas This that Sir *Thomas Jermyn* meant
When he call'd it a *Whipping Parliament*.
Which, &c.

We're stript of all shelter from the *long Robe*,
As rich and warm as the Devil left *Job*,
For Satan *Rump* sits Lord of the Globe.
Which, &c.

Part I. *Rump Songs.*

And yet when all is examin'd and ponder'd,
You'll find three Kingdoms enslav'd & plunder'd,
For saying *Fourty* is lesse than *Four hundred.*
                                    Which, &c.

And now behold the Sign is *in Clune,*
But if *Monck* be honest or wise, then soon he
Makes *Rump* but the *Italian's Domo Communi.*
                                    Which, &c.

Heaven bless the *King,* with his two brave *Brothers,*
From *Rumps* and *Lords* of the *House* call'd *Others,*
And hang these *Rumping* Sons of their Mothers.
                                    Which, &c.

And that He may blesse both Us and our Heirs,
Let all the Members of Commons and Peers,
Turn honest as He that wants his Ears.
                            Which no body can deny.

Sir Eglamor *and the Dragon :*

Or a Relation how Generall George Monck *slew a most Cruell Dragon* Febr. 11. 1659.

To the Tune of Sir Eglamor.

1.

Generall *George* that Valiant wight,
He took his Sword and he would go fight,
And as he rode through *London* Town,
Men, Women, Posts, and Gates, fell down.

2.

But turning about towards *Westminster*,
He saw it must come to *Fight Dog, Fight Bear*,
For there an old Dragon sate in its Den,
Had devour'd (God knows how many) brave Men.

3.

This Dragon it was and a monstrous Beast,
With fourty or fifty heads at least,
And still as this Dragon drank down Blood,
Those heads would wag and cry *good—good—good!*

4.

No *Hidra* nor *Leviathan*,
For every Head look'd like a man,
And yet they all grew *Hidra*-wise,
For cut off one and another would rise.

5.

Besides it had most Devilish claws,
Call'd *Committees* of the *Good Old Cause;*
But Devil and his Dam had no such Paunch
As this which swallow'd *Root and Branch.*

6.

It swallow'd Churches, Pallaces,
Forrests, Islands, Lands, and Seas,
Cathedrall Choires it made but a Sallad,
And left not a man to sing a Ballad.

7.

But that which made this Dragon prevaile,
Was a damnable Sting stuck in his *Tayle*,
This *Tayle* 'gainst Christendom made Wars,
And swept down all St. *Georges Stars.*

8.

Then *Ægypts* Plagues we understood,
Darknesse, Rivers turn'd to *Blood,*

Part I.   *Rump Songs.*   373

Upstart *Vermin* thick as wooll,
And *Frogs* and *Locusts* Pulpits full.

9.

Yet that which most did Plague these Isles,
Three Kingdoms lay so sick of th' Piles,
For every man in dolefull dump
Was tortur'd with a *Bloody Rump*.

10.

But as in its Den this Dragon did sit,
𝕲𝖊𝖔𝖗𝖌𝖊 gave it many a gay good hit,
Though then he had no Sword nor Sythe on,
But fought as *Phœbus* slew old *Python*.

11.

For 𝕲𝖊𝖔𝖗𝖌𝖊 shot at him a flaming Letter,
(Which some then thought might have been better)
He wipe'd the *Rump* away with a Paper,
And out it flew like a stinking Vapour.

12.

Now *London* had her own desire,
For every Street was pav'd with fire,
All Men and Bells with many a thump,
Cry'd *Rump-Rump-Rump-Rump-Rump-Rump-R.*

13.

Six thousand fifty Bone-fires then,
(By twenty more then th' Army had Men)
O monstrous *Rump*, that thus requires
(Though but half broyl'd) six thousand Fires!

14.

This very day that *Rump* was burn'd,
Old *Magna Charta* was confirm'd;
This day they Voted that monstrous thing,*
That no Addresses be made to the King.

* *Febr.* 11. 1647.

15.

Now God bless 𝕮𝖍𝖆𝖗𝖑𝖊𝖘, & 𝖄𝖔𝖗𝖐, & 𝕲𝖑𝖔𝖚𝖈𝖊𝖘𝖙𝖊𝖗,
From many or from one Impostor,
May *Kings*, and *Peers*, and *Commons* joyn
To save us both from 𝕽𝖚𝖒𝖕 and 𝕷𝖔𝖞𝖓.

The Cities Feast to the Lord Protector.

To the Tune of Cook Laurell.

SIR Mayor invites his Highnesse his guest,
And bids him to *Grocers-Hall* to dinner,
There never was Saint at so great a Feast
Provided him at the Charge of a Sinner.
    With a ran tan the Devil is dead.

And what was the day do you think, without jesting,
Of all the year it was *Ash-wednesday*,
This pious Reformer set apart for his Feasting,
When all good Christians should Fast and Pray.
    With a ran tan the Devil is dead.

The Souldiers in clusters throng'd for place,
To see this Monster of their own making,
And said it was a Protectors grace,
But that it wanted not much of *A King*.
    With a ran tan the Devil is dead.

The *Bucks* of the City in herds were met,
And were paled in with a very good sence,
But what their *Does* did, I cannot tell yet,
Of that ye may hear three quarters hence.
    With a ran tan the Devil is dead.

Part I. *Rump Songs.*

With that the Recorder marcht up to the Hall
With a dish of Divinity drest for his pallate,
And laid before him a shoulder of *Saul,*
With a savory *simily* by for a salate.
            With a ran tan the Devil is dead.

His Highnesse commanded to lay it by,
'Twas fit for his people he'd make it known,
And they should have it, good reason why,
For they wanted more shoulders than their own.
            With a ran tan the Devil is dead.

A dish of Delinquents heads in a Charger
Was sent as a present from *Goldsmiths* Hall,
He wisht his stomack ten times larger,
Yet made a long neck and poach'd them all.
            With a ran tan the Divil is dead.

A Prelate was next, and to him he buckles,
With a Bishoprick truss'd before and behinde,
His Highness was in with him up to the knuckles,
And to his own kitchin the skuers assign'd.
            With a ran tan the Divel is dead.

His Highness then call'd for a boule of Canary,
And drank so deep that it made him reel,
He toss'd it to *Lambert,* and *Lambert* to *Harry,*
And *Harry* to the *Mayor,* and the *Mayor* to *Steel.*
            With a ran tan the Devil is dead.

When Dinner was ended, away to the banquet,
Where snatching of Sugar-plums one from another,
Hal fill'd up his pockets, and said God be thanked,
And carried them home to his Lady Mother.
            With a ran tan the Devil is dead.

Then his *Highness* commanded the *Mayor* to kneel,
The *Beast* of the *City* was soon on his knees,
He made him a Knight with iron and steel,
And bid him rise up, and pay him his fees.
    With a ran tan the Devil is dead.

Up rose my *Lords* worship and made him a leg,
With that the *Knight-maker* did give him the Sword ;
His *Highnesse* did spice him without a nutmeg,
When he made a bad *Knight* of a pittifull *Lord*.
    With a ran tan the Devil is dead.

When he left the City he broke a jest,
His words were pithy, and I'le repeat them,
Farewell (quoth his Highness) *thou spur-gall'd Beast,*
Fools make the Feasts, and wise men eat them.
    With a ran tan the Devil is dead.

FINIS.

www.ingramcontent.com/pod-product-compliance
Lightning Source LLC
Chambersburg PA
CBHW030346230426
43664CB00007BB/554